SO FRUITFUL A FISH

Biology and Resource Management in the Tropics Series

Michael J. Balick, Anthony B. Anderson, and Kent H. Redford, Editors

Biology and Resource Management in the Tropics Series

Edited by Michael J. Balick, Anthony B. Anderson, and Kent H. Redford

Alternatives to Deforestation: Steps Toward Sustainable Use of the Amazon Rain Forest, edited by Anthony B. Anderson

Useful Palms of the World: A Synoptic Bibliography, compiled and edited by Michael J. Balick and Hans T. Beck

The Subsidy from Nature: Palm Forests, Peasantry, and Development on an Amazon Frontier, by Anthony B. Anderson, Peter H. May, and Michael J. Balick

Contested Frontiers in Amazonia, by Marianne Schmink and Charles H. Wood

Conservation of Neotropical Forests: Working from Traditional Resource Use, edited by Kent H. Redford and Christine Padoch

The African Leopard: Ecology and Behavior of a Solitary Felid, by Theodore N. Bailey

Footprints of the Forest: Ka'apor Ethnobotany—the Historical Ecology of Plant Utilization by an Amazonian People, by William Balée

Medicinal Resources of the Tropical Forest: Biodiversity and Its Importance to Human Health, edited by Michael J. Balick, Elaine Elisabetsky, and Sarah A. Laird

The Catfish Connection: Ecology, Migration, and Conservation of Amazon Predators, Ronaldo Barthem and Michael Goulding

SO FRUITFUL A FISH

Ecology, Conservation, and Aquaculture of the Amazon's Tambaqui

Carlos Araujo-Lima

and

Michael Goulding

Columbia University Press

New York

Columbia University Press

Publishers Since 1893

New York   Chichester, West Sussex

Copyright © 1997 Columbia University Press

All rights reserved

Library of Congress Cataloging-in-Publication Data

Araujo-Lima, Carlos.

   So fruitful a fish : ecology, conservation, and aquaculture of the Amazon's tambaqui / Carlos Araujo-Lima and Michael Goulding.

      p. cm. — (Biology and resource management in the tropics series)

   Includes bibliographical references (p. 157) and index.

   ISBN 0–231–10830–3 (alk. paper)

   1. Tambaqui—Amazon River Region.   I. Goulding, Michael.

II. Title. III. Series.

QL638.C5A73 1997

597'.48—dc21   96–45658

                                                                      CIP

Casebound editions of Columbia University Press books
are printed on permanent and durable acid-free paper.

Printed in the United States of America

c 10 9 8 7 6 5 4 3 2 1

CONTENTS

Preface   IX

Acknowledgments   XI

1   PROMISE FROM THE RAINFOREST   1

    Tambaqui: A Flagship Fish   4
    Ecology, Conservation, and Aquaculture   6

2   CLASSIFICATION AND GENERAL DESCRIPTION   7

    Taxonomic Classification   9
    Higher Classification   12
    Ontogeny, Shape, and Color Patterns   13
    Size   15
    Mouth, Dentition, and Gill Rakers   15
    Air Bladder, Intestines, and Pyloric Caeca   17
    Tambaqui as a Food and Market Fish   18

3   DISTRIBUTION   21

    Tambaqui as a Place Name   23
    Extant Distribution   23
    River Type and Distribution   25
    Seasonal Flooding   27
    Floodplain Lakes, Floating Meadows, and Flooded Forests   30
    Air and Water Temperature   32
    Dissolved Oxygen   34
    Current Speed   35

4   MIGRATION AND REPRODUCTION   37

        Recruitment from the Rio Amazonas (Brazil)   38
        Size at First Spawning and Sex Ratio   40
        Spawning Season and Sites   41
        Fecundity and Egg Size   43
        Reproductive Investments   44
        Downstream Displacement of Newborn   44
        Observations in the Orinoco System   47

5   NURSERY HABITATS   49

        Food for Larvae   49
        Food for Juveniles   51
        Tambaqui and Zooplankton   54
        Wild Rice   57

6   FRUITS AND SEEDS   59

        Fruit- and Seed-Eating by Tambaqui   60
        Sensory Location of Fruits and Seeds   65
        Fruit and Seed Diversity in Tambaqui Diets   67
        Visual Essay on Fruits and Seeds Eaten by Tambaqui   68

7   NUTRITION   79

        Food Assimilation and Body Composition   82
        Carbon Isotopic Composition of Tambaqui   83

8   AGE, GROWTH, METABOLISM, AND BIOMASS   87

        Environmental Influence on Growth Rates   89
        Respiration   92
        Metabolism   93
        Daily Ration and an Approximate Energy Budget   94
        Biomass   96

9   TAMBAQUI FISHERIES   97

        Technology of Tambaqui Fishing   102
        Estimates of Annual Tambaqui Catches   105
        Tambaqui Prices   109

10 INDUCED SPAWNING AND FRY CULTURE   113

        Inducing Spawning in Captivity   114
        Brood-Stock Management   116

Egg Incubation   117
Care of Larvae   118
Pond Treatment, Zooplankton Production, and Predation   120
Larval Feeding in Captivity   121

11   DISEASE AND PARASITES   123

Bacteria   124
Fungi   125
Protozoans   125
Trematodes (Flatworms)   126
Acanthocephalan Worms   127
Nematodes   127
Copepod and Branchiuran Crustaceans   127

12   INTENSIVE FISH FARMING   131

Traditional Food Sources   131
Alternative Food Sources   133
Fish Orchards   135
Monoculture in Ponds   136
Monoculture in Cages   138
Polyculture   138
Mortality and Production   139
Hybrids   141
Costs   142

13   EXTENSIVE FISH FARMING   145

Hatcheries   145
Reality of Increasing Floodplain Production   146
Economic and Cultural Considerations   149

14   CONCLUSION   151

Evolutionary Ecology   151
Tambaqui for Fish Culture   153
Habitat Protection   154
Genetic Considerations   155
Minimum Area for Wild Populations   155

References   157
Index   185

South America has the most diverse freshwater fish fauna on earth. A large—if not the largest—part of this incredible diversity has evolved with the rainforest. The Amazon Basin alone probably has at least 2,500 fish species, or about three times the total for all of North America. The vast floodplains along South American rivers and streams provided an unmatched opportunity for the evolution of fruit- and seed-eating fishes. More than two hundred fish species in South America feed on fruit material that falls seasonally into the water. These might be referred to as "orchard fishes." None is more ecologically spectacular, more economically important, larger in size, or better tasting than the tambaqui (pronounced 'tom-bah-key). The tambaqui and other "orchard" species offer great opportunities for tapping rainforest energy for human food, not only through the management of wild stocks and the forests they depend on, but also through the development of fish culture.

This book presents a holistic view of the tambaqui, explaining how an understanding of its merits can promote the conservation of the floodplains and the development of fish farming in the Amazon. To help the reader understand the process through which an Amazonian rainforest species has become known, a historical component has been added to many of our discussions. The light of history also illuminates the human influence on one of the most incredible and interesting animals found in the Amazonian rainforest. The optimism of our conclusions is aimed at stimulating the scientific and economic quest for other plants and animals that undoubtedly offer similar promise—and a better economic and ecological future for the Amazon.

Although jargon-free, this work is in scientific format. Wherever scientific concepts or evidence might not be obvious, we attempt to explain them. Most of the quantitative data appear in graphs. When we use scientific names, as we must in many cases because no vernacular alternatives exist, we usually also present illustrations of the organisms discussed.

ACKNOWLEDGMENTS

We are especially indebted to the Rainforest Alliance, the National Institute of Amazonian Research (INPA), the W. Alton Jones Foundation, and the Tinker Foundation for making this project possible. For additional financial and personal support we thank Judy Sulzberger and Joel Edelstein. The Amazon Rivers Program of the Rainforest Alliance initiated the project, and Daniel R. Katz, executive director, has provided much time and advice to make the work possible. José Seixas Lourenço, former director of INPA and now Secretary of the Amazon for Brazil, lent his full support to the project. Pete Myers, executive director of the W. Alton Jones Foundation, and Renate Rennie, executive director of the Tinker Foundation, have lent their professional support to a greater understanding of Amazon fish resources. Thomas Lovejoy, of the Smithsonian Institution, and the late Guilherme de La Penha, former director of the Goeldi Museum, have strongly supported conservation research on Amazonian fishes, including the present project, and we are grateful to them. Karin Kreider, Helene Weitzner, and former board member Leonard Schwartz of the Rainforest Alliance provided their professional and personal skills to administrative aspects of the project.

For help in supplying data and literature we thank Efrem Ferreira, Vernon Thatcher, Barbara Robertson, José Celso de Oliveira Malta, Angela M. B. Varella, Rogério Gribel, Rodrigo Roubach, and Raimundo Sotero da Silva of INPA; Michel Jégú of the Institut Français des Recherches pour le Développement en Coopération (ORSTOM); Ronaldo Barthem, Vitória Isaac, and Raimundo Aragão Serrão of the Museu Goeldi; Peter Bayley (Oregon State Unviersity); Mírian Leal Carvalho of the Ministry of the Environment (MMA); Christopher Kohler of Southern Illinois University; Antonio Machado-Allison of Central University of Venezuela; John Lundberg of the University of Arizona; Heraldo Britski, José F. Lima, and Naércio Menezes of the Zoology Museum at the University of São Paulo; Luis Campos Baca of the Universidad Nacional de La Amazonia Peruana

(UNAP); Waldener Garutti of the Universidade Estadual Paulista (UNESP); Leo Nico of the National Biological Service; John Hemming (Royal Geographical Society); Jeff Moats of Kapok International; Mauro Ruffino of the Iara Project; Richard Vari of the Smithsonian Institution; Harriet Kline of Montclair University; Leonard Lovshin of Auburn University; Odilon J. Araujo of the Companhia de Desenvolvimento do Vale do São Francisco (CODEVASF); and Fonchii Chang of the Universidad Nacional Mayor de San Marcos (UNMSM). The Max Planck and ORSTOM laboratories based at INPA in Manaus also supplied data. For help in sampling and laboratory work we thank Rosseval Galdino Leite and José Wagner V. Silva of INPA. Jorge Palheta and Antonio Carlos Martins prepared the artwork.

We thank Rosemary Lowe-McConnell, Stanley H. Weitzman, Vernon Thatcher, and Leo Nico for reviewing all or part of the manuscript and for making useful suggestions.

SO FRUITFUL A FISH

CHAPTER ONE

PROMISE FROM THE RAINFOREST

Tropical rainforests present one of the greatest challenges on earth for conservationists and developers alike (figure 1.1). Tropical countries have been severely
criticized for not controlling deforestation, but pressure has also been exerted on
North American and European states and nongovernmental organizations
(NGOs) to help come up with solutions.

We believe that science and business will have to be at the leading edge of any
major programs to transform the economy of the Amazon in ways that would be
ecologically positive. Too little research has been invested in realistic alternatives
to livestock ranching, the major driving force behind deforestation in the Amazon
(Smith et al. 1995; Goulding et al. 1996). Yet there are alternatives, and the amazing
rainforest fish called tambaqui is one of them.

As of 1996, no economically valuable rainforest product was being exploited in
the Amazon Basin on what might be called a long-term, sustainable basis. All the
rainforest products heavily exploited, such as timber and fisheries, were not being
replenished by planting or controlled production systems. Little is yet known
about the biology of the native plants and animals that might be brought into large-
scale production for cash economies. Agricultural research institutes in South
America concentrate mostly on introduced plant and animal species for which
considerable information and strong markets are already available. In the Amazon
region, mining operations have generated large amounts of capital since the early
1980s, but almost none of the revenues from this billion-dollar activity have been
used to improve local food production. No plant- or animal-production system
comes even close in total revenues to the mining sector. Yet the mining sector has
done little to alleviate poverty, and mining has caused considerable environmental damage, especially the mining of gold.

Although the Amazon Basin is mostly covered with trees, relatively few species
are logged on a large scale for export. Timber exports have increased in the last

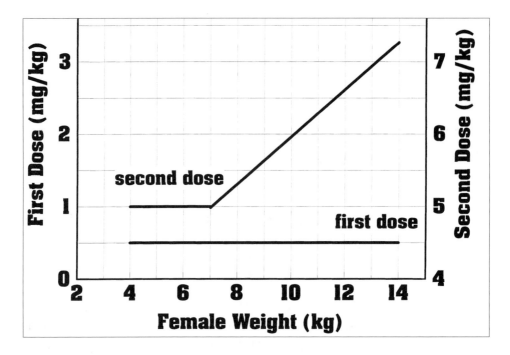

FIGURE 1.1

The floodplain rainforest in its natural state.

decade, and it has already become clear that the most precious species, such as the mahoganies, will ultimately not be sustainable. Most of the floodplain areas have already been logged, though large-scale operations continue in the estuary and upper Amazon River regions (Anderson 1990; Ayres 1994). The agricultural sector in the Amazon has expanded greatly along the thousands of kilometers of new highways and roads, but the region is still a net importer of foodstuffs, and the average annual income for farmers is less than $1,500. The principal limiting factor to agricultural expansion—and thus to average incomes—in the Amazon Basin is poor soil. No significant agricultural technologies are appearing on the horizon to suggest that the Amazon will become a breadbasket or large-scale cattle-ranch economy. Increased agricultural attention is now being given to some Amazonian floodplain areas, such as along the Rio Solimões-Amazonas (Amazon River) in Brazil, because of their richer soils. The resulting programs, however, have not been sufficiently weighed against their effects on the local fisheries (Goulding 1993; Goulding et al. 1996).

Beginning in the 1970s, government tax breaks provided one of the principal incentives for agricultural investment in the Amazon Basin (Hecht and Cockburn 1990). Most investment was allocated to converting rainforest into cattle pasture for animal-protein production. Poor soils, disease, and other problems have prevented cattle ranching from becoming the booming business for which government officials and entrepreneurs had hoped. Productivity is low, hence prices are high. Environmentalists also continue to criticize large-scale deforestation for cat-

FIGURE 1.2

Livestock ranching threatens the floodplain ecosystems on which Amazonian fish depend.

tle ranching. Government tax breaks for cattle ranching in the Amazon were with-drawn in the 1980s, but livestock ranching continues to attract capital investment because of cheap land and labor and the historical prestige associated with it. Also, most people like meat and will pay a relatively high price for it. Pasture develop-ment is by far the most serious ecological problem in the Amazon, though logging operations often get more attention (figure 1.2).

Fishing and hunting have traditionally been the two principal ways of procur-ing animal protein in the Amazon Basin. Both are still widely practiced and impor-tant. Hunting is now mostly a subsistence activity for rural communities. The main food animals hunted are medium to large mammals, reptiles, and birds (Robinson and Redford 1991). The Amazon rainforest does not produce large herds of mam-mals, and productivity is too low for significant commercial harvests. Experiments with capybara farming have shown that these farms are unable to compete with cattle ranches. Turtles are the reptile most sought as food, though their exploitation is technically illegal. Turtles command a high price in urban Amazonian markets, though little has yet been done to raise large numbers of them in captivity. Populations of most species have been greatly depleted, and commercial produc-tion from farming is insignificant. Large birds are heavily hunted for subsistence and sport, and such hunting has led to greatly reduced numbers, especially along the rivers.

Fishing is by far the most important source of animal-protein procurement in the Amazon Basin and also the main generator of cash for peasants along the rivers. Manaus has a fishing fleet of at least eight hundred boats. Many of the larger vessels travel more than a thousand kilometers to fishing sites in the tributaries. Fish has traditionally been relatively cheap in Manaus and other Amazonian cities; however, increases in fish prices have accompanied the explosive growth of Manaus in the last two decades. The preferred species have become rarer and more difficult to capture. Some first-class fish species are now more expensive than beef. During the four or five months of the high-water season each year, the fish supply does not meet the demand, and meat and chicken become more important. An export market has opened for Amazon fish, and this offers great opportunities for the development of aquaculture.

Within the last decade scientists, entrepreneurs, and conservationists have begun to look intensively for rainforest products that might be harvested on a much larger scale. Scientists and conservationists in general would prefer to find alternatives to destructive cattle ranching. To date, however, no rainforest products have been found that would significantly stimulate Amazonian economies. Fish is the most promising resource for greatly increasing animal-protein production in the Amazon Basin with a minimum of environmental degradation. Fisheries data show that the total wild harvest of the Amazon will not exceed about 200,000 tons per year (Bayley and Petrere Jr 1989). The potential, then, does not lie in greater exploitation of wild stocks, but rather in their careful management alongside the development of fish culture.

The Amazon Basin is the largest river system in the world. Its plentiful water supplies and cheap labor appear to make it a haven for aquaculture. Aquaculture is growing rapidly in Asia, Oceania, and some parts of Africa. Asia alone is reported to be harvesting nearly 10 million tons of inland fish annually, most of which is produced on farms (FAO 1992; Groombridge 1992). The Amazon, with its rich hydrological and fish resources, is potentially a major player in the aquaculture business. The Amazon has great fish-production potential and probably has a disproportionate share of the best tasting species in the world. This book is about one of the most promising species.

TAMBAQUI: A FLAGSHIP FISH

Historically, Amazonian fish have been known more for their reputed ferocity than economic value. The most infamous group was the piranhas because of travelers' tales about their aggressiveness. The most famous food fish in the Amazon since at least mid-nineteenth century has been the giant pirarucu (*Arapaima gigas*). It was mostly salted and dried and served as a substitute for the cod that was traditional in Portuguese cuisine. The pirarucu will undoubtedly receive more attention in the future, but at present too little is known about its biology to assess its full potential.

As urban centers began to grow in the 1960s and 1970s, especially Manaus, tambaqui replaced pirarucu in the local cuisine. Gill-net technology led to a rapid

FIGURE 1.3
Tambaqui feeding in the flooded forest.

expansion of tambaqui fisheries, and by the mid-1970s this species alone accounted for more than 40% of all fish consumed in Manaus (Petrere Jr 1978). Probably in no other region in the world could low-income urban people afford to buy a first-class fish species at a relatively low price compared with its price on the international market.

The tambaqui was the first Amazonian fish species to which a relatively large number of researchers were attracted (figure 1.3). Field ecologists, fisheries biologists, physiologists, and aquaculturalists understood its importance in the local fisheries and recognized its potential for aquaculture (Saint-Paul 1984a, 1990, 1991a, 1991b). Most fish farming of tambaqui has taken place outside of the Amazon Basin. Because of its fruit- and seed-eating habits, however, the tambaqui has become an ichthyological symbol of the rainforest and of the need to protect floodplain habitats (Goulding 1989, 1993). Fish culturalists in the United States, southern Brazil, Colombia, Thailand, Panamá, China, and other countries imported the tambaqui and began to experiment with it in tanks and ponds. Considerable experimentation took place in Venezuela as well, where the species is also found naturally. By the late 1980s the tambaqui was being bred in captivity in many countries, and fry were available for sale.

Although the tambaqui continues to be one of the most important food species exploited in the Amazon, young instead of adult fish now make up most of the commercial catch—a reversal in the maturity of the catch of a decade ago. Almost no serious attempt to prevent the overexploitation of young populations has taken place. Adult fish are much rarer than a decade ago and command high prices. For example, in 1995 a 20-kg tambaqui in the Manaus market was selling for the equivalent of $100.

The tambaqui has become the flagship fish of the Amazon because it embodies most of the problems that need to be resolved to manage the fisheries while developing aquaculture. It is not the only Amazon fish that deserves special attention, but it will be the first species about which enough is known to both manage wild stocks and develop large-scale aquaculture. The fish's unique and highly regarded fruity flavor is now recognized in international cuisine. For the species to find a niche in the international market, a large and continuous supply will have to be available. More tonnage of this one species alone could be sold on the international market than the total annual catch of all wild stocks taken in the Amazon Basin. For this to happen, however, fish culture in the Amazon must come of age. As will be discussed later, this is beginning to happen, and our hope is that this book will further catalyze this development. We present the tambaqui as the first rainforest animal with the potential to outproduce cattle ranching.

ECOLOGY, CONSERVATION, AND AQUACULTURE

A study of the tambaqui provides an excellent opportunity to approach ecology, conservation, and aquaculture holistically. Aquacultural experiments in the Amazon and elsewhere have usually been launched with inadequate ecological knowledge of the species when placed in ponds and tanks. Parasitism is often a problem because fry are placed in contaminated water or are poorly handled. Failure to account for the distribution of wild populations and the genetic diversity of a species within an area can also limit yields. Most of the tambaqui now being artificially bred for fry are derived from a limited original gene pool that consisted of no more than two dozen individuals. In the future fish farmers must incorporate greater genetic diversity into the reproducers. In addition, the diet of captive Amazonian fish may confuse neophyte fish farmers. As discussed in later chapters, young and adult tambaqui feed heavily on fruits and seeds. The concept of fish orchards may seem strange, but the tambaqui grows rapidly when given its natural diet. Some experiments have already taken place, but almost no attention has been given to the botanical side of fish-fruit production (for fruit-feeding experiments, see Saint-Paul et al. 1981; Campos Baca and Padilla 1985; Roubach 1992). Field studies point to plant species that could be domesticated for fruit production.

Young tambaqui are now being heavily exploited along most of the Amazon River. It may turn out to be difficult to prevent overexploitation. An alternative would be to restock nursery regions by artificially reproducing tambaqui and then releasing them in the wild. A combination of ecological and aquacultural knowledge could produce a better fisheries management plan than policing efforts alone and might also produce a lot more fish.

CHAPTER TWO

CLASSIFICATION AND GENERAL DESCRIPTION

Within its area of distribution (see next section), the species known scientifically as *Colossoma macropomum* is referred to by three principal names. The name *tambaqui* is used over the largest area and almost exclusively in Brazil, though it is derived from an indigenous Tupi word (*tãba'ki*) and not Portuguese (Cunha 1987). The Portuguese evidently adopted the corrupted Tupi word from lingua geral, a type of lingua franca that the Jesuits used to communicate with various Amazonian Indian tribes.

None of the first European chroniclers to travel down the Amazon, such as Gaspar de Carvajal of the Orellana Expedition in the sixteenth century or Samuel Fritz in the eighteenth century, mentions the word *tambaqui* (Medina and Heaton 1934; Fritz 1922). The first explicit reference to it appears to be by the German Jesuit João Filippe Betendorf in his *Chronicles of the Mission of the Jesuit Fathers in the State of Maranhão*, which was originally published in 1699 (Betendorf 1901).

The earliest known published illustrations of the tambaqui were by an unnamed artist working for the Portuguese naturalist Alexandre Rodrigues Ferreira (figure 2.1). Although completed in the late eighteenth century, these watercolors were not published until just recently and can be found in a box-set of paintings in what has been collated as the *Philosophical Voyage Through the Captaincies of Grão Pará, Rio Negro, Mato Grosso and Cuiabá (Viagem Filosófica pelas Capitanias do Grão Pará, Rio Negro, Mato Grosso e Cuiabá)* (Ferreira 1972). Ferreira made the first natural-history inventory of the Amazon for the Portuguese crown. He traveled widely in the Amazon between 1783 and 1792. Two different color plates of the tambaqui accompany his natural-history notes. Only one of these is labeled *tambaqui*, and it is such a poor artistic rendition that it is not positively iden-tifiable as the right fish. It was probably painted from memory rather than direct observation, but it could also be a mistake. The other plate is labeled *curupeté* and is of a young adult tambaqui. Interestingly, the highly praised Brazilian dictionary

FIGURE 2.1

The first known illustration of the tambaqui.

(From Ferreira 1972.)

Novo Dicionário da Língua Portuguesa, states that *curupeté* is a synonym of tambaqui in the Brazilian Amazon (Buarque de Holanda Ferreira 1975). Indians along parts of the lower Amazon may have used *curupeté* instead of tambaqui. There are no longer any intact Indian tribes along the Brazilian part of the lower Amazon River, and today *curupeté* is used only in headwater areas for some other species related to the tambaqui. These are areas where the tambaqui is not found.

As discussed below, tambaqui undergo considerable morphological change as they grow. In Brazil very young tambaqui (to about 30 cm in length) are called bocó, a Portuguese name for infants. Bocó is not used in the Amazon to describe other species of young fish. Medium-sized tambaqui (25–40 cm in length) are usually called ruelo.

In Bolivia, Peru, and Ecuador the tambaqui is sometimes grouped by fishermen with the pacu lineage of fishes. In both Spanish and Portuguese, *pacu* is derived from the Tupi word *pa'ku.* In Brazil most fishes related to but smaller than the tambaqui are called pacu, and this appears to have been the usage among the Indians. Peruvians normally use the common name gamitana for the species (Ortega and Vari 1986). In Colombia and Venezuela the tambaqui is called cachama (Machado-Allison 1987; Taphorn 1992). Colombians prefer to add a color adjective: thus, their tambaqui is cachama negra, in contrast to the cachama blanca (*Piaractus brachypomus*), a close relative. Several names have also been invented for cultivated hybrids of tambaqui and its relatives.

Pacu is also commonly used in English for the tambaqui. In the United States, fish farmers in Florida are selling tambaqui fry under the label black pacu. Fry are often quite dark and resemble, in shape, many of the silver dollars or pacus of the aquarium trade. Aquarists have also referred to very young tambaqui as red-finned pacu (e.g., Axelrod and Vorderwinkler 1957; Axelrod et al. 1979).

TAXONOMIC CLASSIFICATION

Scientifically, the tambaqui is classified as *Colossoma macropomum* (Cuvier 1818). As with many if not most Amazonian fish species, the classification of the tambaqui has been confusing. Only recently was a consensus reached concerning the various Latin synonyms used for the species and closely related fish (Britski 1977, 1992; Machado-Allison 1982; Gery 1986). Altogether about a dozen scientific names have been used since the species was first described in the early nineteenth century (table 2.1).

The Alexandre Rodrigues Ferreira excursion collected the type specimen, or the individual fish that was the basis of the first scientific description. No exact date or place information accompanied the specimen that was sent back to Lisbon. The capture location was listed only as "Brazil." By tracing Ferreira's travels in the Amazon, and comparing these with what we now know to be the distribution of the tambaqui, the capture date had to have been either between November 1784 and February 1785 or in the September–November period of 1788. The evidence favors the earlier date because that is when the Ferreira expedition made most of

TABLE 2.1

Scientific Names (Synonymy) Used for the Tambaqui Since It Was First Described in 1818

Genus	Species	Described	Date	Listed Type Locality
Myletes	*macropomus*	Cuvier	1818	rivers from Brazil
Myletes	*bidens*	Castelnau	1855	?
Salmo	*tambaqui*	Natterer	1860	?
Myletes	*oculus*	Cope	1871	Rio Ampiyaco, Peru
Myletes	*nigripinnis*	Cope	1878	Nauta, Peru
Colossoma	*oculus*	Eigenmann and Kennedy	1903	Rio Ampiyaco, Peru
Waiteina	*nigripinnis*	Fowler	1906	Nauta, Peru
Piaractus	*macropomus*	Eigenmann	1910	?
Piaractus	*nigripinnis*	Eigenmann	1915	?
Piaractus	*nigripinnis*	Eigenmann and Allen	1924	?
Colossoma	*macropomum*	Norman	1928	Amazonas, Brazil
Colossoma	*nigripinnis*	Norman	1928	Amazonas, Brazil
Mellonina	*tambaqui*	Campos	1946	?

FIGURE 2.2
Baron George von Cuvier, the first scientist to describe the tambaqui.

its fish collections and when the two watercolor paintings of the young tambaqui were made. Neither of the paintings is of the type specimen, since it was an adult. The capture site could have been anywhere between about Santarém and Manaus in the middle Amazon region. The second period of the Ferreira expedition mentioned above included a fast trip down the Rio Negro and then a trip to the Rio Madeira. We know that Ferreira collected relatively few fish specimens in the Rio Madeira; thus we doubt that the original tambaqui specimen came from that river or from the later trip.

The zoological specimens captured during the 1784–1785 period were taken to Barcelos, 300 km up the Rio Negro. At the time, Barcelos was the capital of the Captaincy of São José do Rio Negro; and Manaus, then called Barra, was a village of secondary importance. In August 1785 a large collection of zoological and

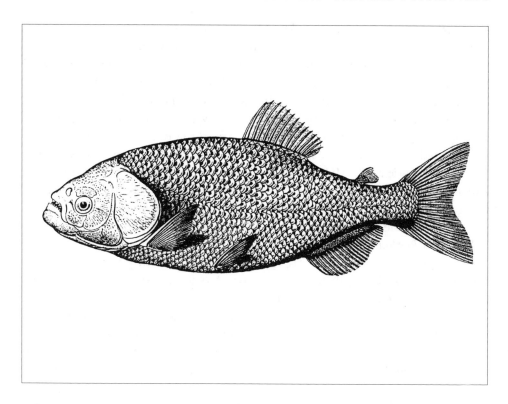

FIGURE 2.3
Cuvier's drawing of the tambaqui type specimen.
(Based on Cuvier 1818.)

anthropological specimens was sent from Barcelos to Lisbon, and the tambaqui
specimen was most likely part of this scientific treasure. This material was sent to
the Ajuda Natural History Museum (Museu de História Natural de Ajuda), which
was then part of the gardens of the Royal Palace in Lisbon. Due to illness and other
problems, Alexandre Rodrigues Ferreira was never able to complete a study of his
Amazonian collections (Carvalho 1983).

   As part of a forced "agreement" after the Napoleonic invasion of Portugal in
1811, France was able to remove scientific specimens from the Lisbon Museum
(Simon 1983; Daget and Saldanha 1989; Bauchot et al. 1990). The French zoologist
Auguste Saint-Hilaire chose the tambaqui, among other specimens, to take back to
the famous Jardin des Plantes in Paris. The tambaqui and some others ended up in
the laboratory of the famous paleontologist and comparative anatomist Baron
George von Cuvier of the Musée d'Histoire Naturelle in Paris.

   Cuvier was the greatest paleontologist of his day, but he also worked exten-
sively describing extant animals (figure 2.2). His ability to rearticulate ancient
beasts from their fossil bones brought him the title "Magician of the Charnel
House" and great admiration even among the general public. He was not only a
great scientist; he also served in various high posts in government. The tambaqui
was thus scientifically christened in 1818 by one of the most famous people in

Europe (figure 2.3). Cuvier, whose knowledge of bone structures was quite impressive, must have been in awe of the tambaqui's massive dentition, though he also had specimens of three other South American species with similar teeth. Although describing the unusual teeth, he did not speculate about their possible use.

Among the Lisbon collection taken to Paris was another fish greatly resembling the tambaqui, and Cuvier named it *Myletes brachypomus*. Since the tambaqui was also placed in the genus *Myletes,* Cuvier clearly recognized that the two species were related. In the same genus, however, he also included a fish from Egypt, from which the generic name *Myletes* was derived, and two smaller pacus from South America. We now know that the fish Cuvier had from Egypt is not directly related to any of the pacus. The specific names *macropomus* and *brachypomus* used by Cuvier refer to the cheeks, or opercula. Thus *macropomus* means large operculum in Latin; *brachypomus* means wide operculum.

Cuvier was fortunate in having specimens of both of the large species mentioned above. His descriptions, however, were too general and thus caused much confusion for the next 160 years as to the proper identity of these fishes. Most of the confusion was due to the great morphological changes that both large species undergo during development. Later researchers described juveniles as species distinct from those already described by Cuvier. Finally, Eigenmann and Kennedy (1903) discovered that Cuvier's generic name, *Myletes,* had been used for an African fish previous to the original description of *macropomus* and *brachypomus*. Thus they substituted *Colossoma* and included only the tambaqui. The Latin generic name *Colossoma* means "body without horns," an allusion to the fact that the tambaqui does not have a pre-dorsal fin spine, as do most other members of the pacu subfamily. Eigenmann (1903) placed *brachypomus* in the genus *Piaractus,* though this designation was ignored until Britski (1977, 1992) and Machado-Allison (1982b) showed conclusively that it was correct. A recent study correlating conclusions from RNA analysis, parasitology, and cytogenetics suggests that the genera *Colossoma, Piaractus,* and *Mylossoma* form a "primitive" branch within the tambaqui's subfamily (Orti et al. 1996).

HIGHER CLASSIFICATION

The tambaqui belongs to the family Characidae and subfamily Serrasalminae. The pacus and piranhas comprise the subfamily Serrasalminae. The pacus, to which the tambaqui is related, have often been placed in their own subfamily Myleinae (Eigenmann 1915; Campos 1944; Gery 1977). The pacus and piranhas have also been assigned their own family, Serrasalmidae (Gery 1977). Most taxonomists, however, believe that pacus belong within the family Characidae. The Characidae is the most diverse family of freshwater fishes in South America, and little is yet known about the relationships among the hundreds of species (Weitzman and Weitzman 1982; Bohlke et al. 1978; Vari and Weitzman 1990). The Serrasalminae family includes at least ten genera (Machado-Allison 1982b). Occasionally, U.S.

newspapers report that giant piranhas in excess of ten pounds have been captured in rivers, lakes, and canals. These reputed giants are usually small tambaqui that were introduced by the aquarium trade or fish farmers (Brittan and Grossman 1978; Howells et al. 1991).

At present there is no evolutionary evidence that suggests to which specific groups, within the family Characidae, pacus and piranhas might be related. Some of the deep-bodied tetras, such as those of the loosely defined genus *Moenkhausia* of aquarium fame, look superficially similar, but they are probably not directly related. There are no small pacus or piranhas—under 40 mm in adult length—and too little is known about tetras to speculate whether the former groups might have evolved from diminutive relatives. Africa is the only other continent that has characins (fishes of the order Characiformes, to which the tambaqui belongs), but none of Africa's extant groups is directly related to any of the pacus or piranhas.

ONTOGENY, SHAPE, AND COLOR PATTERNS

As mentioned earlier in reference to taxonomic problems, the tambaqui undergoes great shape and color changes during its development from juvenile to adult. Larvae are spindle shaped (fusiform) for the first few weeks. Juveniles are rhomboidal in shape but gradually become more elongate (figure 2.4). Young tambaqui resemble adult pacus (e.g., the genera *Mylossoma* and *Metynnis*) in general shape. Within the subfamily Serrasalminae, the tambaqui is morphologically one of the most aberrant species because of the elongation of adults. None of the other pacus becomes elongate as adults, and only one group of piranhas does.

Young tambaqui are characterized by a distinct dark spot near midbody and below the dorsal fin. This gradually disappears when the fish reach about 75 mm in length. Also present are numerous round and oval markings, which can become almost bandlike before disappearing when the fish reach about 100 mm in length. Within the subfamily Serrasalminae, the dark ocellus is also found in the genera *Piaractus* (pirapitinga) and *Mylossoma* (pacus). The presence of an ocellus, in addition to other shared characteristics, suggests that the three genera had a common ancestry (Machado-Allison 1982a).

Juveniles of the above three genera are also found in the same floodplain nursery habitats in the Central Amazon. The principal nursery habitat for young with mottled bodies is floating meadows. It is reasonable to believe that spotting contributes to disruptive coloration and provides greater protection from predators, though there is no quantitative proof for this hypothesis. Most nursery habitats on the Amazon floodplain have muddy water. Furthermore, young tambaqui live below floating meadows. In these habitats there is little light, and the use of vision among predators would seem to be limited.

By the time tambaqui reach about 30 cm in length, they lose their paculike rhomboidal shape and become more elongate. By this stage they have also developed the distinct countershading they will retain through adulthood. Tambaqui change

FIGURE 2.4

Ontogeny of young tambaqui. Top: 6 mm; middle: 13 mm; bottom: 43 mm.

color with water type. In black-water rivers, such as the Rio Negro and Rio Tefé of the middle Amazon region, the fish can become very dark, and countershading is minimal. In relatively clear waters, such as the right-bank tributaries of the Rio Madeira, tambaqui are olive green dorsally and dark green to black ventrally. In muddy waters, such as the Amazon River and Rio Madeira, they become more yellowish and much lighter in color. Personal observations of fish kept in large tanks indicate that they can change color within a day or two. The color of large tambaqui seen in markets is a good indication of the type of water in which the fish were captured.

SIZE

Tambaqui can reach over one meter in total length and 30 kg in weight, though no specimen this large has been preserved in a museum (figure 2.5). The largest individuals seen by scientists are from the Rio Mamoré and Rio Beni in the upper Rio Madeira drainage and from the western Amazon in Peru. These regions were barely exploited for tambaqui until the mid-1970s. It is unclear whether populations in the upper Rio Madeira drainage and Peru had a larger average size than fish in the central Amazon. Individuals larger than 85 cm and 20 kg were commonly captured in the central Amazon until the late 1970s, but they are only rarely seen in markets today. Most of the large individuals arriving in the Manaus market are reported to come from the middle Rio Purus or Rio Juruá.

Characins are the most diverse group of fishes in South America, and the tambaqui is the largest species of this order. The tambaqui is the second largest scaled and strictly freshwater fish in South America. Of the scaled fishes, only the giant pirarucu (*Arapaima gigas* [Arapaimidae]) exceeds it in length and weight. Headwater species of pirapucu (*Boungerella* [Ctenolouciidae]) and traíras (*Hoplias* [Erythrinidae]), other Amazonian characin groups, might also reach a meter in length, but no measurements are yet available. Some of the headwater traíras weigh more than 20 kg, but the tambaqui is heavier. There are seven species of Amazonian catfishes that attain greater lengths than the tambaqui, and all belong to the family Pimelodidae.

MOUTH, DENTITION, AND GILL RAKERS

Compared to most other Amazonian fish species, tambaqui have very fleshy lips. The lips are covered with numerous small protuberances (papillae). Young fish (to about 15 cm) also have barbel-like appendages on the lips, which they use to direct water and zooplankton into the mouth. Irish (1986) has also suggested that the fleshy lower lip acts as a passive holding device to prevent seed loss during mastication. Larval tambaqui have conical teeth, but these soon give way to sharp molarlike elements. There are two rows of teeth in each jaw (figure 2.6). The sec-

FIGURE 2.5
A large tambaqui captured in the channel of the upper Rio Madeira.

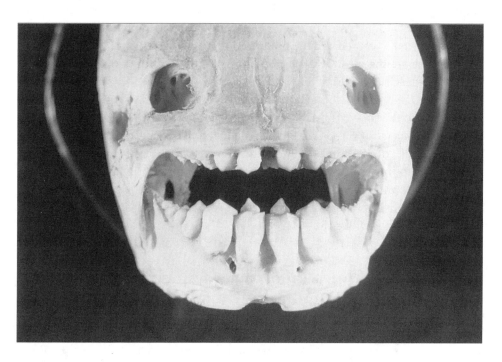

FIGURE 2.6
Dentition of the tambaqui.

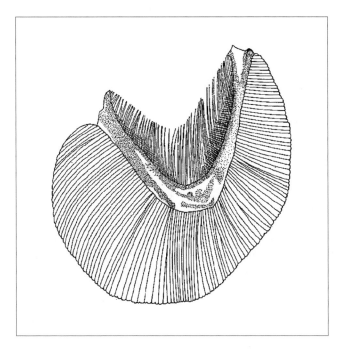

FIGURE 2.7
Gill rakers of adult
tambaqui.

ond row in the lower jaw consists of only a single pair of teeth, and these give the impression of being supports for the front series. By preadult size, tambaqui have massive jaws and dentition. Despite crushing hard nuts, the teeth are almost always in nearly perfect condition because additional teeth lie below the apparent members and periodically replace them.

Compared to other species of the pacu and piranha subfamily, the tambaqui has aberrant gill rakers. The number of gill rakers increases as the fish grows. The highly developed gill-raker structures are associated with filtering zooplankton (figure 2.7).

AIR BLADDER, INTESTINES, AND PYLORIC CAECA

Little is yet known about the relationship between internal anatomical features and the ecology of South American fishes, yet it is worth pointing out some peculiarities of the tambaqui. Like other species of the subfamily Serrasalminae, the tambaqui's air bladder is divided into two chambers (figure 2.8). Unlike the other pacu species, but similar to some of the piranhas, the tambaqui has a much larger anterior than posterior chamber. This might be related to the greater amount of time that the tambaqui spends near the surface for feeding on zooplankton when young and for fruit- and seed-feeding during its young to adult stages. The enlarged anterior air bladder might help the fish stabilize when it feeds in the diagonal position it assumes near the surface.

Adult tambaqui can have as many as seventy-five pyloric caeca, or appendages attached to the stomach that supply enzymes for digestion (Torrealba 1982; Honda

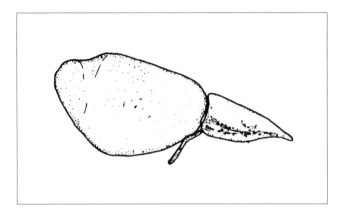

FIGURE 2.8
Air bladder of tambaqui.
Based on Machado-
Allison, 1982b.

1974). This large number of caeca probably help with the digestion of vegetable matter. The intestinal length in adult tambaqui averages about 5.0–5.5 times body length. This ratio is similar to that of many detritus-feeding fishes and vegetarian animals (figure 2.9).

TAMBAQUI AS A FOOD AND MARKET FISH

The tambaqui is considered a medium to large food fish. In the Amazon region, the large juvenile and adult tambaqui are generally classified as either the first or second most delicious fish species. The marketable portion of tambaqui raised in fish culture, after the head, viscera, fins, and scales have been removed, is about 59–65% of live weight (Freitas and Gurgel 1985; Lovshin forthcoming). In South America the percentage is even higher because the head is seldom removed, as the muscle internal to the facial bones is considered delicious. All characin fishes, including the tambaqui, have intramuscular bones in the dorsal part of the body above and to the side of the vertebral column. These bones have not presented a problem to Amazonian consumers. The international market will probably demand that these intramuscular bones be removed before filets can be sold at higher prices.

In South America the tambaqui is considered best when roasted on charcoal. It is also served in fish soup and sauces and occasionally fried. The most expensive part of the tambaqui is the rib cage. The ribs are separated by meat and fat; thus the flesh remains quite moist after roasting. Tambaqui have twelve ribs on either side. Approximately 25% of a 5–10-kg fish is made up of ribs and associated flesh. The restaurant community has already recognized that tambaqui ribs would find a ready high-end market (Moats personal communication). A 2-kg fish is probably the minimum size from which satisfactory ribs could be extracted for the international market. A 2-kg tambaqui would produce enough ribs for two 230-g servings, including the bones.

Tambaqui meat is quite lean. The fat content of the muscles of wild tambaqui is

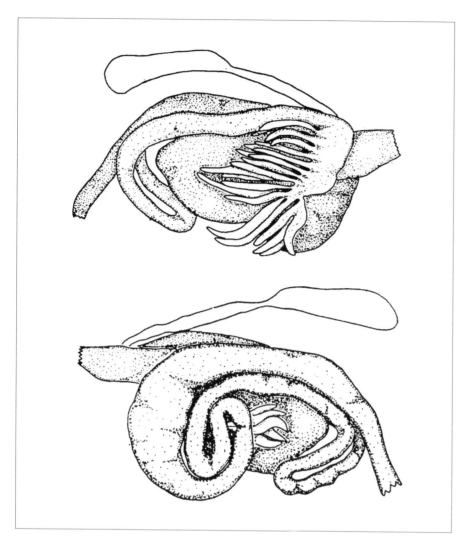

FIGURE 2.9

Above: right view of tambaqui's digestive system; below: left view. The fingerlike
appendages are pyloric caeca.

(Based on Machado-Allison 1982a.)

less than 1.5% (Junk 1985a) but increases in cultured fish to 2–6% (Freitas and
Gurgel 1985; Maia 1992). The fat content in cultured tambaqui can be reduced by
dietary management, a practice already common in aquaculture (Landau 1992).
Saturated fat comprises 40% and 25% of total fat in cultivated and wild fish, respectively (Maia 1992).

CHAPTER THREE

DISTRIBUTION

The tambaqui is widely distributed in northern South America and belongs to a diverse group of fishes. Although characins, the main group of fishes to which the tambaqui is related, are found in both Africa and South America, no species or genera are shared. The subfamily Serrasalminae, to which the tambaqui belongs, is found only in South America. Fossilized characin teeth somewhat resembling those of the tambaqui have been found in African Miocene/Pliocene deposits (circa 26 million years ago) in the Lake Edward and Lake Albert rifts (Greenwood and Howes 1975). There are no extant African characins with teeth similar to those of the tambaqui or any of the pacus and piranhas (Gery 1977).

The most tantalizing evidence for a long and conservative evolution of the tambaqui comes from fossils discovered in the La Venta fauna deposits of Miocene age of the upper Magdalena River Valley in Colombia (Lundberg et al. 1986). The Magdalena drains the northern Andean area between the Cordillera Oriental, where Bogotá is located, and the Cordillera Central to the west (figure 3.1). Before the major rise of the Andes, which began in the Miocene, the Magdalena Valley was probably broader and lower. Today the Magdalena fauna contains only about 150 fish species, and none of these is shared with the Amazon or Orinoco systems.

The *Colossoma* fossil evidence suggests that the tambaqui has remained morphologically conservative for at least 15 million years (figure 3.2). It has probably remained ecologically conservative as well in the sense of depending on fruits and seeds in its diet. The unusual teeth are used for chewing plant material. Geological events after the rise of the Andes may have led to the disappearance of or great reductions in floodplains and riparian forests along the Magdalena, hence the extinction of *Colossoma* from that river system. The Rio Magdalena does not have any extant pacu or piranha species; thus, no other members of the subfamily Serrasalminae survived in that river system, if they were ever in fact present there (Miles 1971; Dahl 1971).

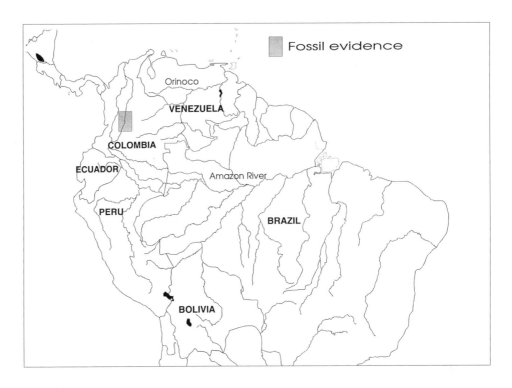

FIGURE 3.1
Site of tambaqui fossil evidence.

FIGURE 3.2
Fifteen-million-year-old tambaqui fossil teeth from the Rio Magdalena basin in Colombia.
(Photographs courtesy of Antonio Machado-Allison and John Lundberg)

There is no fossil evidence of tambaqui south of the Amazon Basin. The pacu-caranha (*Piaractus mesopotamicus*), the only other species closely related to the tambaqui, is found in the Paraná-Paraguay system but not in the Amazon Basin. Fish culturalists have hybridized the tambaqui and pacu-caranha although they are classified in different genera. The tambaqui and the pirapitinga (*Piaractus brachypomus*) also occasionally hybridize in the wild in the Amazon. The Goeldi Museum in Belém, Brazil, has a large specimen of one of these hybrids collected in the Rio Juruá by Ronaldo Barthem. We can conclude, then, that the tambaqui or a close relative has been widespread in South America for many millions of years.

TAMBAQUI AS A PLACE NAME

Places named after an animal or plant can often indicate the presence of that species. When used as a place name in Brazil, *tambaqui* usually refers to a stream, floodplain lake, or arm of a river channel. The place name occurs most often in the Brazilian state of Amazonas, followed by Pará, with at least one occurrence in the state of Amapá (Vanzolini and Papavero 1968; DNAEE 1982). In general, the distribution of the place names agrees with what is known about the distribution of the species (see below). The great *Diccionário Geográphico do Brazil* of Alfredo Moreira Pinto (1894) lists *tambaqui* as a name for seven locations. The most curious is a small channel, called a *furo* in Portuguese, in the Amazon estuary near Breves. As discussed below, the tambaqui is thought to be rare in this region. The name may have been given because of the surprise of finding this species in the Breves area, rather than as an indication of its abundance there.

EXTANT DISTRIBUTION

The tambaqui is found naturally only in the Amazon and Orinoco Basins (figure 3.3). In terms of political geography, the species inhabits Brazil, Venezuela, Colombia, Peru, and Bolivia. The cachama, as it is called in Venezuela, is known in the Orinoco system from the tributaries Apure, Caroní, Guanare, Meta, and the main river. It has not been reported in the southern drainage of the Orinoco, which is the area just north of the Rio Negro Basin in the Amazon. A popular book by Finkers (1986) on the Yanomami Indians of the upper Orinoco, however, shows a large cachama in the possession of a native fisherman. The cachama is a common food fish throughout most of the Orinoco region where it is found, and in the upper part of the drainage it is often the most important species (Machado-Allison 1987; Novoa 1989; Taphorn 1992). A popular book by Roman (1983) shows fishermen catching a school of adult cachamas in the Rio Orinoco.

The tambaqui's widest distribution is found in the Amazon Basin. The area included within the periphery of its distribution embraces about 2 million square kilometers. As with many Amazon food-fish species, there is a central population

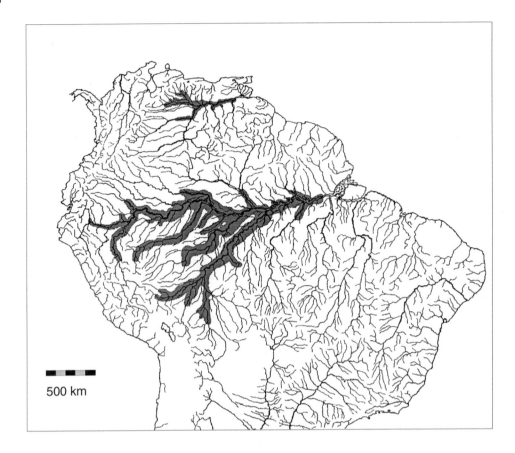

FIGURE 3.3

Natural distribution of the tambaqui.

(*Sources*: Barthem 1984; Bayley, 1983; Cala 1977; Cope 1871; Ferreira 1992; Gerra et al. 1981; Goulding and Carvalho 1982; Junk et al. 1983; Lauzanne et al. 1991; Machado-Allison 1982; Machado-Allison et al. 1993; Mansutti 1988; Merona 1988; NEODAT; Ortega and Chang 1992; Petrere Jr 1986; Santos 1991; Santos and Carvalho 1982; Soares et al. 1986; Winemiller 1990.)

of relatively high density, as indicated by fisheries, experimental fishing, and local knowledge. There are also peripheral wanderers that are occasionally captured far outside the core area. To the east, the tambaqui is only rarely captured in the Rio Xingu (lower mouth-bay only), in the Rio Tocantins, on the island of Marajó (Lago do Ariri), and in the Rio Araguari of the state of Amapá. There are no commercial fisheries for it in the eastern region, undoubtedly because of low population densities. Novoa (1982) reports that the species is found in the freshwater part of the Orinoco estuary.

Tambaqui become common in the floodplain lakes of the Amazon River west of the Rio Xingu and remain so to the Rio Marañon and Rio Ucayali in Peru. The Rio Curuá-Una, just downriver from Santarém, appears to be the first southern tributary in the eastern region in which tambaqui were abundant enough to be exploited commercially. Farther upstream, the Rio Trombetas is the first northern tributary in the eastern part of the basin to sustain a tambaqui fishery.

The tambaqui is found throughout most of the southern drainage of the central Amazon and in all river types. The species is more widely distributed in the Rio Madeira than in any other tributary in the Amazon Basin. Only in the Rio Madeira is the tambaqui found above major cataracts, and this is in the Rio Mamoré, Rio Guaporé, and Rio Beni. Most of this area lies in Bolivia. The tambaqui's distribution in the northern part of the central Amazon drainage is much more restricted, especially in the Rio Negro, where it is only rarely encountered above the mouth of the Rio Branco, 250 km upstream.

The western limits are close to the pre-Andean foothills, though the tambaqui appears to be only rarely encountered in this region (personal communication from ichthyologist Donald Stewart who has explored the Peruvian and Ecuadorean regions; also see Ibarra and Stewart 1989).

RIVER TYPE AND DISTRIBUTION

Both Alfred Russel Wallace (1853) and Richard Spruce (1908) commented on the distribution of the tambaqui in their travel accounts. Wallace mentioned being served tambaqui by the local residents while exploring floodplain lakes in the lower Rio Solimões (Amazon River). Subsequently, he explored the Rio Negro and noted how different its fish fauna was compared with that of the Amazon River. Wallace, always on the lookout for curious facts concerning the distribution of animals, was alerted when he found the tambaqui absent from the upper Rio Negro but present in the muddy waters on the Venezuelan side of the Casiquiare. Wallace concluded that the tambaqui was a white-water—by which he meant muddy-water—fish.

Spruce was in northern South America between 1849 and 1864 and spent much of his time in the Amazon and in the Orinoco region. After Spruce's return to England, one of the papers he wrote was called "Notes on Some Insect and Other Migrations Observed in Equatorial America," and he published it in the *Journal of the Linnaen Society* (Spruce 1867 and 1908). In this paper the great botanist also discussed what he had perceived of the distribution of fishes. Spruce noted that fish were most abundant in muddy rivers. He suggested that this was due to the presence of aquatic plants. He concluded that, with the exception of the pirarucu, all of the large fish of the Amazon were found in the Orinoco. These species, as he mentioned, included the tambaqui.

One of the concluding chapters in Wallace's *Travels on the Amazon and Rio Negro* is titled "The Physical Geography and Geology of the Amazon Valley." In that chapter he outlined the three major river types found in the Amazon, as a precursor to his discussions of the distribution of plants and animals. He called these white-water, black-water, and clear-water (or blue-water) rivers. Although most limnologists (scientists studying various aspects of aquatic biology and chemistry) working in the Amazon still use Wallace's threefold limnological classification to some extent, many now question its usefulness because there are transitional types of rivers that cannot easily be pigeonholed (see Sioli 1984 for traditional views; see

FIGURE 3.4

The meeting of the Amazon and Rio Tapajós (a clear-water river) illustrates the great contrast in river types found in the Amazon Basin.

Furch 1984 for modern views). When only the large rivers are considered, however, the classification still makes sense, even from a chemical point of view.

Based on modern studies, the following generalizations can be made about the three main river types. The term *white water* can be confusing in English because in most countries it refers to torrential streams and rivers. It is not used in this sense in the Amazon. *Água branca* (Portuguese) or *água blanca* (Spanish) refers to muddy water in the Amazon. These rivers are more café-au-lait or yellowish-olive in color than white. The main point is that they are heavily laden with silt and hence muddy. All large muddy rivers in the Amazon have headwaters in the Andes. Heavy erosion in the Andes supplies the sediments found in these rivers. The principal muddy rivers are the Amazon, Rio Madeira, Rio Purus, and Rio Juruá. There are no muddy tributaries east of the Rio Madeira. All muddy rivers have high sediment loads, nearly neutral pH, and relatively high electrical conductivities compared with those of the other two water types. In the Amazon Basin, electrical conductivity is a good general indication of the amount of minerals and nutrients found in the water.

Clear-water rivers, as the adjective suggests, have light sediment loads (figure 3.4). None of the large rivers of the Amazon could be classified as crystalline. At best they have only 3–4 meters of transparency. The largest clear-water rivers drain the Brazilian Shield and are found in the eastern Amazon region. From east to west these are the Rio Tocantins (not a tributary of the Amazon River, but connected to it via the estuary), Rio Xingu, and Rio Tapajós. Several of the right-bank tributaries of the Rio Madeira also have relatively clear waters. The pH of these rivers ranges from about 4.7 to 5.5, and the electrical conductivity rarely exceeds 6.0. Clear-water rivers have relatively poor nutrient levels because of the ancient and highly weathered geological regions they drain.

Black-water rivers transport minimum sediment loads but are stained dark by organic compounds originating in plant communities growing on extremely sandy soils. Visibility is usually limited to less than a meter. All of the large black-water rivers are found in the central Amazon region, though some of these have headwaters on the Guiana Shield. By far the largest black-water river in the Amazon, and in the world, is the Rio Negro. The pH of black-water rivers is generally below 4.2. Chemically, they can be considered "slightly contaminated distilled water." This means that these waters are extremely poor in nutrients.

Muddy water is the principal determinant of the tambaqui's distribution. The muddy Amazon River and Rio Madeira are the main axes of the far-flung distribution of the species. Much of the Orinoco is also a muddy river, though too little information has been published to determine the tambaqui's exact distribution in that system. We can conclude, then, that the tambaqui depends on muddy water, or some ecological component associated with it, for its survival.

The tambaqui has not penetrated the clear-water rivers of the Brazilian Shield to any great extent but is found in the lower reaches of most of them. The presence of insurmountable cataracts in the lower reaches of all of these tributaries may to some extent limit its distribution in these rivers. Surveys above the cataracts of all black-water and clear-water tributaries have not found tambaqui (Ferreira 1984, 1992; Ferreira et al. 1988; Goulding personal observation). The tambaqui, however, is known to be able to pass through some cataracts, such as the Cachoeira do Teotônio of the upper Rio Madeira.

Black-water rivers are numerous in the central and western Amazon Basin. Only the Rio Negro and some of its tributaries reach lengths in excess of 500 km. The tambaqui is, or was, common in all of the large black-water tributaries of the central Amazon Basin. In the Rio Negro, however, the tambaqui is found only below the Rio Branco and hence is absent from the middle and upper black-water tributaries, such as the Rio Marié, Rio Urubaxi, and Rio Cuiuni, all of which are greater than 500 km in length. We can conclude, then, that black-water chemistry in itself does not limit the distribution of the tambaqui in the Amazon Basin. In black-water rivers the tambaqui is rarely found more than 200–300 km from a muddy river.

SEASONAL FLOODING

Large rivers with extensive floodplains characterize the hydrographic region occupied by the tambaqui (figure 3.5). River-level fluctuation, which varies, depending on the exact site and year, between about 5 and 13 m (figure 3.6), causes great seasonal change in the environment. River-level fluctuation in the central Amazon averages 8–10 m.

FIGURE 3.5
Aerial view of extensive floodplain area and deforestation along the Amazon River.

The Amazon River functions as a type of natural dam; the result is longer periods of flooding along the main trunk and the lower courses of its tributaries than
might be expected (Meade et al. 1991). This extended inundation is due to the temporal differences in rainfall, hence river discharge, between the southern and northern tributaries. The north-south latitudinal spread—about 15°C—of the Amazon
Basin is sufficient to separate the main rainy seasons in the drainage areas on either
side of the main river by several months. If only the southern tributaries controlled
the level of the Amazon River, the peak of the annual floods would be in April or
May. The northern tributaries flood about two to three months later in the year than
their southern counterparts. The northern waters are thus added to the already
swollen Amazon River, and the main trunk remains in flood until July or August,
though peak levels are reached around the end of June near Manaus in 80% of the
years since 1903. The lower reaches of the southern tributaries are dammed back
during this period and remain in flood. Likewise, the lower reaches of the northern
tributaries begin to rise in December and January, when their waters are dammed
back by the rising Amazon River. At this time the middle and upper reaches of the
northern tributaries are in their low-water period. This extended flooding effect
includes the main river and 200–300 km of the lower reaches of its tributaries. This
region is heavily inundated for about six to eight months each year, compared with
five to six months for the middle and upper tributary areas of the central Amazon.
    In the Amazon Basin the tambaqui is not found in any significant numbers—
meaning that it is not common enough to be fished commercially—in areas where

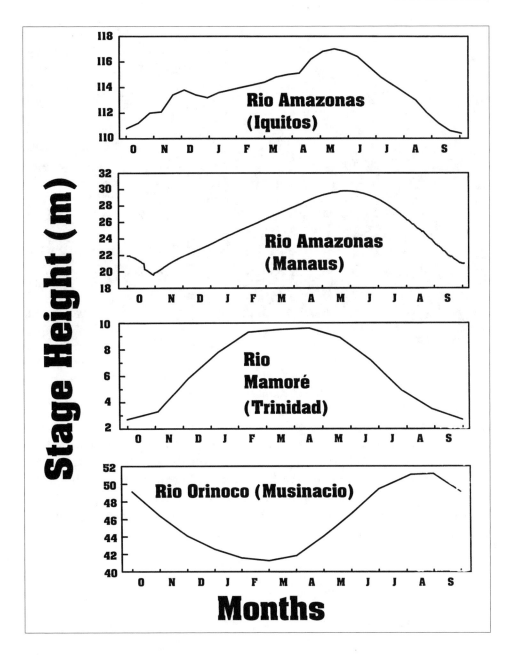

FIGURE 3.6
Monthly average river-level fluctuations in the Amazon and Orinoco Basins.

river-level fluctuation is less than about 5 m. This appears to be the minimum fluctuation required for the development of seasonal floods of at least five months duration. The estuarine area of the Amazon River has vast floodplain areas that are inundated twice daily with fresh water to depths of 3–4 m. Significantly, the tambaqui has not colonized tidal floodplains, although most of these areas are inundated with fresh water. As mentioned earlier, however, the

FIGURE 3.7
A flooded forest of the Amazon River floodplain.

species is reported in the Orinoco estuary. The largest flooded forests in the Orinoco region are evidently found in the estuary, whereas in the Amazon they are well developed along most of the inland rivers (Worbes et al. 1992; Novoa 1989). Given the long and conservative history of the tambaqui as revealed by fossil evidence (see above), the present distribution pattern of the species in the Amazon Basin was possibly established even before major changes in the drainage patterns began to occur after the rise of the Andes in the late Miocene some 12 million years ago.

FLOODPLAIN LAKES, FLOATING MEADOWS, AND FLOODED FORESTS

Floodplains account for the largest habitat area of the river systems where the tambaqui is found in the Amazon and Orinoco Basins. In the central Amazon and lower Rio Ucayali, for example, floodplains comprise more than 75% of the total areas occupied by rivers. Of the total river area, lakes account for about 9% and river channels for 16% (Hanek 1982; Bayley and Petrere Jr 1989). There is much local variability, such as near the mouth of the Rio Tapajós, where the area of the floodplain lake is as high as 25% of the total (Sippel et al. 1992).

The three principal habitats of the Amazonian floodplains are lakes, floating meadows, and seasonally inundated rainforest (figures 3.7 and 3.8). The exact

FIGURE 3.8
A floating meadow of the Amazon River floodplain.

ratios of these three features have not been calculated for most rivers in the Amazon. Estimates of the amount of floodplain in the Amazon range from about 150,000 to 200,000 km^2 (Junk 1985a; Sippel et al. 1992). Each of the three main habitats along the Amazon River is estimated to embrace 40,000–80,000 km^2 (Junk 1985b). Large-scale deforestation has occurred along most of the middle and lower Amazon River in Brazil, and in this region floating meadows, at least during the annual floods, have greatly expanded their natural area vis-à-vis the original floodplain forests (Goulding 1993).

Within the tambaqui's general area of distribution, floodplain lakes and seasonally flooded rainforest are usually present. Flooded forest is greatly reduced in the Orinoco system compared with the Amazon (Colonnello et al. 1986). The upper tributaries of the Orinoco, however, have some relatively large flooded-forest areas, as does the estuary. The tambaqui is also common in the savanna areas of eastern Bolivia. The headwaters of the Rio Madeira drain this region, but little is known about the tambaqui's seasonal movements in Bolivia or to what extent it depends on riparian vegetation for food and shelter.

Floating meadows are mostly associated with muddy-water rivers because of the higher nutrient levels present (Junk 1970; Junk and Piedade 1993). Some black-water and clear-water tributaries also have floating meadows, but these are much less developed than their white-water counterparts. The nursery habitats of young tambaqui are restricted to white-water floodplain lakes, and these almost always have floating meadows.

AIR AND WATER TEMPERATURES

In the Amazon Basin, air temperature largely determines average water temperature for the larger rivers and their floodplains. The waters from the thousands of relatively cool spring-fed streams have almost no effect on the average temperatures of the larger rivers into which they flow, though they can cool the lower layers of certain floodplain lakes. Average monthly air temperatures in the Amazon Basin below 200 m in elevation range from about 24 to 28°C. The lowest temperatures range from about 17 to 22°C, and highs occasionally reach 40°C (Salati and Marques 1984). Despite any variation in the high values, average monthly air temperatures change minimally from season to season.

In general, the average surface-water temperatures (first meter) in the Amazon are slightly higher than the average air temperatures (table 3.1), because water retains heat considerably longer than air. The greatest variation in water temperatures is found in floodplain water bodies because they have less mixing than river channels.

Higher water temperatures are from stagnant surface waters, but they are not characteristic of most of the floodplain. Temperature is more variable in lakes than in rivers and channels. High temperature peaks are normally associated with areas of floodplain lakes in which water circulation is minimal, such as along the shore zone and in floating meadows. Poor water circulation frequently leads to gradients, called thermoclines, with as much as a 13°C difference between temperatures at the surface and the bottom. River channels have only a weak thermocline, if any, because of the constant mixing caused by current and wind turbulence (Araujo-Lima 1984; Odinetz-Collart and Moreira 1989).

Surface-water temperatures in the central Amazon can drop to as low as 21°C when an Antarctic cold front, known locally as a *friagem,* invades the region (Brinkmann and Santos 1973; Odinetz-Collart and Moreira 1989). The rivers are in flood at this time, and cool surface waters in floodplain lakes and inundated forests can sink and cause a rapid turnover of bottom layers. This phenomenon is well known in the region, and the resulting hydrogen-sulfide poisoning leads to fish kills. As the cool water sinks, it disturbs bottom sediments where hydrogen-sulfide gas is trapped. The cooling effect, however, lasts only a few days, and temperatures return to normal soon after the cold front passes. In the southern part of the Amazon drainage where the tambaqui is found, water temperatures as low as 23°C have been reported for Bolivian floodplain lakes in the Rio Mamoré basin in May and June and in the pre-Andean area of the Peruvian Amazon (Loubens et al. 1992; Hanek 1982).

The tambaqui is being raised in regions where water temperatures are considerably lower than the averages for the central Amazon. For example, the tambaqui is now living, or has been found in, rivers and canals in Florida, Texas, and California (Fuller et al. 1995). Juveniles (>100 g) kept in ponds in southern Brazil also survived at temperatures below 20°C (Merola and Cantelmo 1987; Merola and Pagan Font 1988; Merola and Andreotti 1988); however, fish weighing less than

TABLE 3.1

Summary of Physical and Chemical Characteristics of the Main Habitats
Where the Tambaqui Is Found

River	River part	Habitat	Temp. (C)	Oxygen (mg/l)	Current (m/s)	pH	Trans. m	Cond. (uS/cm)
Amazonas (Br.)	river	mid-surf.	28.3-28.7	4.5-5.5	0.5-1.9	6.0-6.8	0.15-0.40	45-90
Amazonas (Br.)	river	mid-bot.	28.5-29.0	—	—	—	—	
Amazonas (Br.)	river	bank-surf.	25.0-31.0	2.2-12.0	0.1-0.4	6.0-6.9	0.30-0.50	—
Amazonas (Br.)	river	bank-bot.	28.5-29.0	1.8-6.2	—	6.0-6.9	—	35-70
Amazonas (Br.)	river	meadow-surf.	27.0-29.0	4.1-4.6	—	—	—	—
Madeira (Br.)	river	mid-surf.	28.9	—	—	6.9	0.32	50-60
Negro (Br.)	river	mid-surf.	28.0-31.0	>3	0.8	3.6-5.8	0.90-1.50	5-9
Mamoré (Bol.)	river	mid-surf.	26.0-29.0	—	0.7-1.4	6.8-7.1	0.03-0.40	87-260
Orinoco (Ven.)	river	mid-surf.	—	—	2	6.8	0.90-1.11	25
Marañon (Peru)	river	mid-surf.	22.5-28.9	2.6-6.9	—	5.4-7.5	0.05-0.3	102-169
Napo (Peru)	river	mid-surf.		7.5-8.4	—	7.4-7.7	—	—
Ucayali (Peru)	river	mid-surf.	24.0-32.0	2.4-7.5	—	6.0-9.1	.04-0.41	103-379
Amazonas (Br.)	chan.	mid-surf.	26.0-30.0	0.9-5.9	0-0.5	5.9-6.9	—	55-80
Amazonas (Br.)	chan.	mid-surf.	28.0-28.2	0.1-4.8	—	5.4-6.5	—	—
Amazonas (Br.)	chan.	mid-surf.	27.0-34.0	—	0-0.25	6.4-6.8	0.20-0.50	—
Amazonas (Peru)	chan.	mid-surf.	27.0-33.5	.70-12.4		6.4-8.3	.25-1.05	65-90
Amazonas (Br.)	lake	open-surf.	27.0-34.5	1.8-10.0	—	3.5-8.5	0.60-2.55	—
Amazonas (Br.)	lake	open-surf.	27.0-30.5	0.0-7.4	—	5.5-8.0	—	10-60
Orinoco (Ven.)	lake	open-surf.	27.2-31.5	5.5-9.0	—	6.6-7.1	—	—
Mamoré (Bol.)	lake	open-surf.	26.0-30.0	3.2-10.2	—	6.3-8.3	0.10-0.52	87-121
Mamoré (Bol.)	lake	open-bot.	23.9-28.6	1.7-6.2	—	—	—	65-218
Amazonas (Peru)	lake	open-bot.	25.8-37.0	1.2-13.5	—	5.4-8.4	.15-2.0	77-218
Orinoco (Ven.)	lake	bank-surf.	30.5-37.0	—	—	—	—	—
Orinoco (Ven.)	lake	bank-bot.	30.5-34.5	—	—	—	—	—
Amazonas (Br.)	lake	flooded forest-surf.	27.0-31.0	0.5-13.2	—	5.7-7.8	—	—
Amazonas (Br.)	lake	flooded forest-bot.	26.0-27.0	0.1-5.0	—	—	—	—
Amazonas (Br.)	lake	meadow-surf.	27.0-40.0	0-11.6	—	4.8-6.9	—	—
Amazonas (Br.)	lake	meadow-bot.	27.0-34.0	0-6.9	—	—	—	—

Sources: Fisher 1978; Richey et al. 1986; Forsberg et al. 1988; Oltman et al. 1964; Goulding et al. 1988; Schmidt 1973, 1976; Loubens et al. 1992; Lewis and Weibezahn 1981; Junk 1973; Araujo-Lima 1984; Odinetz-Collart and Moreira 1989; Alves 1993; Melack and Fisher 1983; Tundisi et al. 1984; Marlier 1967; Melack and Fisher 1990; Hamilton and Lewis 1987; Hanek 1982; Sanchez and Vasquez 1986, 1988; Guyot et al 1991. "surf."=surface; "bot."=bottom.

5 g died (Ferrari et al. 1991). Although the tambaqui can survive in considerably cooler waters than those found in the Amazon and Orinoco Basins, temperatures lower than 20°C affect reproductive success.

DISSOLVED OXYGEN

The large number of air-breathing fishes in the Amazon Basin suggests that low levels of dissolved oxygen have been characteristic since at least the time when Africa and South America were separated in the Cretaceous, some 65 million years ago. Neither high nor low oxygen levels directly correlate with the overall distribution of the tambaqui. Oxygen levels, however, are important to keep in mind when considering local patterns and the habitat where the species is found (e.g., Junk et al. 1983).

The greatest variation in dissolved-oxygen levels is found in floodplain lakes. At various times of the year anoxic waters (those lacking oxygen) are found in floodplain lakes, floating meadows, and flooded forests. Overall oxygen conditions appear to improve from the central Amazon to the peripheral areas of the tambaqui's distribution. For example, oxygen levels in the Rio Mamoré and Orinoco systems are generally better than those that have been recorded near Manaus (Loubens et al. 1992; Hamilton and Lewis Jr 1987).

In almost all floodplain habitats during the year little oxygen occurs below depths of 3 m. Subsequent to the peak of the annual inundation, floodplain waters can become stagnant because of the lack of circulation. Also, the decay of organic matter from floating meadows and forest materials leads to deoxygenation. At this time of year many fish species, including the tambaqui, can be seen taking in surface water to get enough oxygen. The fish often move out of flooded forests and floating meadows and into open waters where the wind's mixing of the water and the lesser amount of decay provide better breathing conditions.

Dissolved-oxygen levels in Amazonian lakes vary much more on a daily than seasonal basis. Due to algae production and wind-mixing, the first few meters of the water column are relatively oxygen rich during the daytime. The bottom is invariably anoxic. As surface water cools at night and sinks to the bottom, and warmer water rises, the entire water column can become devoid of oxygen. During the low-water period, wind-mixing "turns over" floodplain lakes (Melack and Fisher 1983). The trade winds that blow up the lower and middle Amazon seem to be especially important along the main river for injecting atmospheric oxygen into the water.

River channels are relatively rich in dissolved oxygen. They show minimal differences between surface and bottom layers on a daily or seasonal basis. Fluctuating river levels cause a seasonal interchange of water between the floodplains and river channels. During the rising-water period, when the floodplains are being heavily inundated, dissolved oxygen flows into the floodplains from the river channels. When the inflow stops, stagnation begins (Junk et al. 1983).

CURRENT SPEED

Current speed is an important factor influencing the distribution of many fresh-water fish species. The Amazon River falls only 300 m from the eastern edge of the pre-Andean area in Peru to the Atlantic Ocean, a distance of approximately 4,000 km. The midstream velocity of the Amazon River during the flood stage reaches a maximum of about 2 m/s; the average velocity is 1.4 m/s, or 5 km/hr. River water moving at 120 km/day takes about thirty-three days to travel from the eastern foothills of the Andes to the Atlantic. As discussed earlier, the main river dams the lower reaches of the tributaries of the central Amazon for several months each year, reducing the current speed. In the case of the Rio Negro, the current speed averages about 0.8–1.4 m/s, or 2.9–5.0 km/hr.

Only in the upper Rio Madeira, at the Cachoeira do Teotônio just above Porto Velho, has the tambaqui been found passing torrential waters. These migrations, however, are too modest to support commercial fisheries of any size. There are no known tambaqui populations in the torrential rivers of the Andes or Brazilian and Guiana Shields. In contrast, the tambaqui's relative, the pirapitinga (*Piaractus brachypomus*), commonly passes rapids and migrates as far as headwater areas (e.g., Rio Machado of Rio Madeira; Rio Itacaiunas of Rio Tocantins; and Rio Branco of Rio Negro).

CHAPTER FOUR

MIGRATION AND REPRODUCTION

The first studies of tambaqui migrations were made in the Rio Madeira, the Amazon River's largest muddy tributary (Goulding 1979, 1980, 1981; Goulding and Carvalho 1982). In this tributary adult tambaqui migrate to black-water and clear-water tributaries to feed on fruits and seeds found in flooded forests. After the floods they migrate down the tributaries and enter the Rio Madeira channel, where they spend the low-water season. When the river level begins to rise rapidly in November, tambaqui schools move upstream until spawning at the beginning of the floods. The cycle is completed when the fish return once again to the flooded forests.

Unlike the Rio Madeira, the Amazon River does not serve as a single axis for migratory fishes living in all of its tributaries. This is because schools living in the muddy tributary systems, such as the Rio Madeira, Rio Purus, and Rio Juruá, do not need to migrate as far downstream as the Amazon River to find turbid water in which to spawn. The muddy tributaries themselves provide satisfactory spawning habitats.

Fisheries data from the Rio Madeira clearly show that most of the adult tambaqui biomass enters the main river channel by the beginning of the low-water period. Experimental fishing in the western Amazon also confirms the movement of adults from the floodplains to river channels at the end of the seasonal floods (figure 4.1). Catches of adult tambaqui from floodplain lakes are minimal during the low-water period. Even before overexploitation became a problem, no large populations of adults inhabited the floodplain lakes during the low-water period, as is apparent from Petrere Jr's (1978a, 1983) excellent data sets on the tambaqui landed in the Manaus market in the mid-1970s. During the mid-1970s the tambaqui accounted for approximately 44% of the fish landed in Manaus. At that time only adult or nearly adult tambaqui were exploited on a large scale. Petrere Jr's (1978a) analysis of the fisheries of the two most important floodplain lakes—Lago

Janauacá and Lago do Rei—exploited for the Manaus market showed that the tambaqui accounted for only about 5% of the catch during the low-water period. At Lago do Rei on the island of Careiro adjacent to the mouth of the Rio Negro, the tambaqui was the most important species captured during the high-water period, and catches were nearly four times greater than those reported for the low-water period. If adult tambaqui remained in large numbers in floodplain lakes during the low-water period, the Manaus fisheries data would almost certainly reflect this presence.

The annual floods are constantly undercutting the soft alluvial banks of muddy rivers. When the water level falls, these banks often cave in, and the forest on them drops into the water. Most of the levee areas along the middle Amazon River, however, have been deforested, and woody shore areas are now rare. Woody shore areas are important low-water refuges for the tambaqui. The loss of this habitat along the Amazon River might be causing tambaqui populations in search of appropriate low-water habitat to enter muddy tributaries of the main stem to a greater extent than when the levee forests still remained.

Petrere Jr's (1983) length-frequency distribution data for the tambaqui sold in the Manaus market during the low-water season of 1978, when mostly large fish were exploited, show that 55 cm was the size at which they began to be captured on a significant scale. This might be only a reflection of the gill net's mesh size, but we would propose another reason. By four years of age, or about 55 cm, tambaqui begin to migrate from their nursery habitats in the muddy-river floodplains and to the river channels during the low-water period. In the Rio Machado, a clearwater tributary of the upper Rio Madeira, individuals as small as 44 cm were found; thus it is possible that some fish start migrating at about three years of age. No field measurements of discrete schools have determined the length-frequency distributions of size classes for different river regions. Petrere Jr's (1983) published data for the Manaus market represent an average over a broad area of the central Amazon Basin. The length-frequency distributions of fishes from discrete schools in river channels and from different areas is needed to determine how tambaqui are recruited into the main migratory reproductive populations. Cursory examination of catches suggests that mixed adult-size classes migrate together.

RECRUITMENT FROM THE RIO AMAZONAS (BRAZIL)

In Brazil the Amazon River is called the Rio Amazonas below its confluence with the Rio Negro. The Rio Amazonas floodplain is large and studded with numerous lakes. Young tambaqui are one of the most common fish stocks in this region and probably the most heavily exploited. Adult tambaqui are relatively rare in the markets of Santarém, Monte Alegre, Alenquer, and Óbidos (Isaac and Ruffino 1996; personal observation). When relatively large numbers arrive, they are invariably from the Rio Trombetas or farther up the Rio Amazonas. Fishermen in

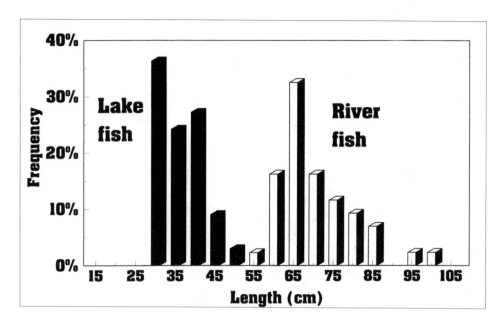

FIGURE 4.1

The size distribution of tambaqui captured at two sites of the middle Rio Solimões (Amazon River) during experimental fishing in November 1995.

the Santarém area report that adult tambaqui were abundant two or three decades ago. Veríssimo (1895) stated that tambaqui 50–60 cm in length were the most commonly exploited size classes at the end of the last century. It is possible that when the tambaqui was less exploited a century ago, most of the fisheries based on it were for first-year migratory stocks, that is, three- to four-year-old fish. The Rio Amazonas floodplain has been heavily deforested. It is, therefore, also possible that pre-adult and adult tambaqui do not stay in this region because they can find sufficient food in too few flooded forests. More will be said about this later.

The abundance of young tambaqui in the Rio Amazonas floodplain leaves little doubt that this area is a major nursery habitat for the species. Given the abundance of young fish and the poor showing of adults, we can assume that a large upstream migration of subadults occurs. A downstream migration does not occur, as tambaqui are rare in the far eastern region. No known fisheries based on tambaqui migrations exist in the Amazon River channels in the Santarém area. The river channels in this region are large, and the trade winds result in much rougher conditions than farther upstream. It is possible, however, that migrations—which for adults appear to be only in an upstream direction—go largely unnoticed.

Floodplain conditions along the Amazon River from near the mouth of the Rio Xingu to above Iquitos provide major nursery habitat for young tambaqui. The muddy tributaries greatly add to the total nursery habitat available for the species. Due to strong trade winds, the large size of water bodies, and constant water mixing, the floodplain lakes of the lower Amazon River region are better oxygenated

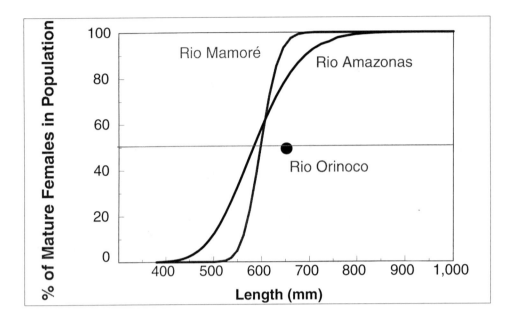

FIGURE 4.2

Percentage of mature female tambaqui in populations that have been studied from the Rio Amazonas, Rio Mamoré, and Rio Orinoco.

than those farther upstream, where climatic conditions are more stagnant. The relatively well oxygenated and extensive floodplain lakes of the middle Rio Amazonas region could be one of the principal reasons for the abundance of young tambaqui in this region.

SIZE AT FIRST SPAWNING AND SEX RATIO

Female tambaqui in the wild are known to mature as small as 45 cm, or about 3.5 kg (Pinheiro 1985). The size at which approximately 50% of the female population is mature is 58 cm, or about 6.3 kg. All females larger than 75 cm are mature (figure 4.2). Small differences in average maturity sizes have been reported from different river basins, but the great variability of habitat conditions within given regions makes it difficult to determine if the size differences are due to biological or sampling phenomena. Data for males are less detailed. In the Rio Mamoré Basin in Bolivia and the central Amazon in Brazil, half of the male population reaches maturity at about 63 cm (SUDEPE 1981; Loubens and Aquim 1986).

The numbers of males and females are roughly equivalent in the natural populations that have been studied in the central Amazon and Rio Madeira headwaters (Pinheiro 1985; Loubens and Aquim 1986). In the Rio Mamoré basin, however, female tambaqui outnumber males in those populations larger than 70 cm. Loubens and Aquim (1986) suggested that sexual differences in growth rate might be the cause.

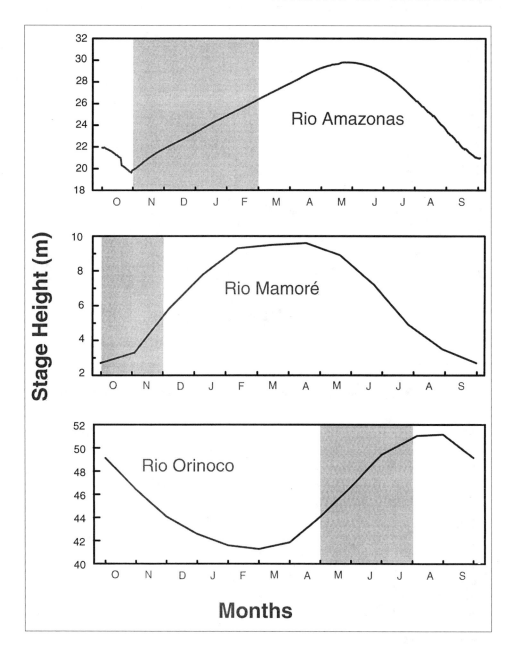

FIGURE 4.3

Shaded area indicates spawning season of tambaqui in Amazon and Orinoco Basins.

SPAWNING SEASON AND SITES

Tambaqui spawn during a two- to five-month period from the beginning to the middle of the annual floods (SUDEPE 1981; Pinheiro 1985). In the central Amazon these floods occur between November and April (figure 4.3). In the Rio Mamoré basin to the south of the central Amazon, the spawning season begins in October

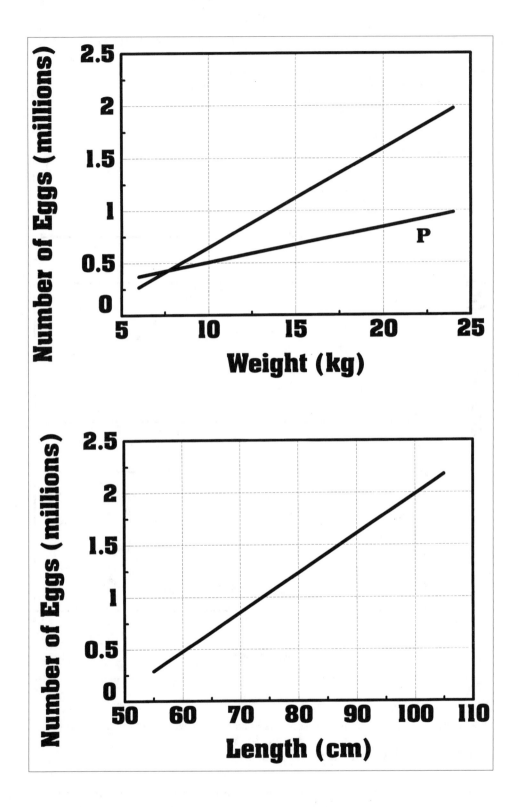

FIGURE 4.4

Tambaqui fecundity in relation to body weight and length (r = 0.7 for length and r = 0.65 for weight). Regression lines are based on ten females for weight and ten females for length. The line marked "P" shows the fecundity reported for Peruvian captive brood stock. (*Source:* Alcántara 1989.)

and ends in December (Loubens and Aquim 1986). To the north in the Orinoco region, it is from May to August (Novoa 1982).

Other than fishermen's reports, strong indirect evidence indicates that the tambaqui spawns in the river channels and not in the floodplain water bodies. Only fish older than seven days have been captured in floodplain water bodies, whereas four- to fifteen-day-old larvae have been captured in the Amazon River channel near Manaus and Tefé. Fishermen report that tambaqui spawn in woody shore areas or along levees with floating grasses. Experimental fishing in the open waters of the Amazon River channel failed to produce any yolk-sac larvae of tambaqui. The species apparently does not spawn in midchannel but somewhere along the levees. Possibly, the tambaqui chooses specific microhabitats along shore areas. These habitats would probably be where the fish could avoid turbulence and abrasive surfaces. This would allow fertilized eggs a better chance of survival.

FECUNDITY AND EGG SIZE

The tambaqui is a fecund fish (figure 4.4). The number of mature eggs per female increases linearly with fish size. In the central Amazon, a ripe 60-cm tambaqui has an average of 480,000 eggs; an 80-cm female will produce about 1.2 million eggs. The average number of eggs per gram of body weight, excluding the ovaries, is 78 (standard deviation = 37). The exact number of eggs produced is probably related to the amount of energy the fish was able to obtain during the high-water period when feeding in flooded forests. Well-fed brood stocks kept for fish culture can be even more fecund than wild populations (Woynarovich 1988). However, reduced fecundity in captivity has been reported as well (Alcántara 1989).

Fecundity is the first factor that determines the potential number of larvae. Egg size may also be important for the survival of individual larvae. The size of the yolk of an unfertilized egg determines the amount of fat and protein available to the larva. It also determines the size of the larva at first feeding (Araujo-Lima 1994). The olive-green, unfertilized egg of wild tambaqui averages about 1.31 mm in diameter and weighs 0.68 mg (table 4.1). The egg is rich in lipids, and more than half of its mass consists of water. Protein is the main determinant of larval growth. The high proportion of fat suggests that the egg favors metabolism instead of growth. This adaptation is necessary because larvae must resist starvation during the period they are drifting downstream (Araujo-Lima 1994).

TABLE 4.1
Summary of Size and Chemical Composition of Tambaqui Eggs

Measurements	# Females	Samples per female	Mean	Standard deviation
Diameter of unfertilized egg (mm)	4	18	1.31	0.09
Volume of unfertilized egg (cubic mm)	4	18	1.2	0.24
Wet weight of unfertilized egg (mg)	3	10	0.68	0.01
Dry weight of unfertilized egg (mg)	3	10	0.28	0.01
Water content of unfertilized egg (%)	3	10	41.37	
Ash content of unfertilized egg (%)	1	10	5.05	
Energy content of unfertilized egg (J/mg)	2	4	31.63	1.56
Protein content of unfertilized egg (%)	2	4	32.16	9.1
Lipid content of unfertilized egg (%)	2	4	59.84	9.1
Egg diameter fertilized egg (mm)	1	18	1.8	0.15
Volume of fertilized egg (cubic mm)	1	18	24.42	2.5
Volume of perivitelinic space (%)	1	18	94.63	

Calculations of chemical composition assumed 3% carbohydrate, 23.4 J/mg for protein, 40.4 J/mg for lipids, and 17.0 J/mg for carbohydrates. Protein, ash, and lipid contents are in percentage of dry weight.
Source: Heming and Buddington 1988.

REPRODUCTIVE INVESTMENTS

Although female tambaqui produce a massive number of eggs, the reproductive investment of the individual is relatively low compared with that of other species that spawn in river channels (Araujo-Lima 1990). No data for male gamete production exist, but with fish in general, gametes tend to be smaller than eggs. Although 1 g of testis represents the same energy investment as 1 g of ovary, the total weight of male gametes is much less.

The mass of eggs per female represents only 2–8% of body weight (figure 4.5). The eggs, however, are denser and richer in nutrients than body flesh, but not so dense or rich as those of other characin fishes. Egg mass represents about 5–12% of total body energy. Adult tambaqui feed very little during the low-water season; thus, gonad development relies on abdominal fat reserves. Abdominal fat can reach 10% of body weight (Castelo et al. 1980). This energy supply is more than enough to satisfy the fat requirement of the eggs. Larger fish spend slightly more energy and body mass per spawning than smaller individuals.

DOWNSTREAM DISPLACEMENT OF NEWBORN

Because adults are known to migrate only upstream in muddy rivers, young fish must move downstream (figure 4.6). Otherwise, the upstream migration would

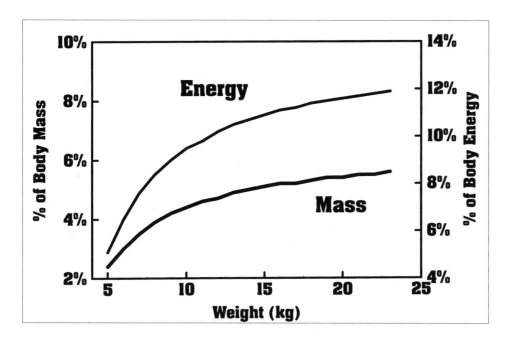

FIGURE 4.5

Relative mass (grams of egg/grams of fish x 100) and energy (expressed in joules in eggs/joules in fish x 100) expended for spawning in relation to fish size.

soon depopulate the downstream areas (figure 4.7). Using experimental fishing methods, Araujo-Lima captured tambaqui larvae in the Rio Amazonas channel at the beginning of the annual floods. Young larvae were found drifting in the river between the end of October and the beginning of March (samples taken in 1981–82 and 1984–85). Because newborn larvae are unable to swim during the first two days of life, they are passively carried downstream or remain resting on the levee bottom. Larvae four to fifteen days old are probably also passively carried downstream. Given an average current speed of 3.6 km/hr, tambaqui newborn (four to fifteen days old) could be carried about 400–1,300 km downstream from their spawning sites before entering a floodplain area. The possibility also exists that some eggs and nonswimming larvae are passively carried into floodplain waters relatively near to where spawning takes place, but their chances of survival would seem minimal because of adverse physical and chemical conditions (for embryos) and because of the large number of floodplain predators present, from which the young larvae could not actively escape.

Viewed geographically, the downstream displacement of eggs and fry outlined above indicates that adult populations spawning as far upstream as near the borders of Brazil, Peru, and Colombia, and perhaps from the middle Rio Madeira, could colonize the middle Amazon River floodplain. To what extent the Rio Purus might "export" tambaqui larvae to the Amazon River would be more problematic because of the extreme meandering nature of this muddy tributary. The numerous

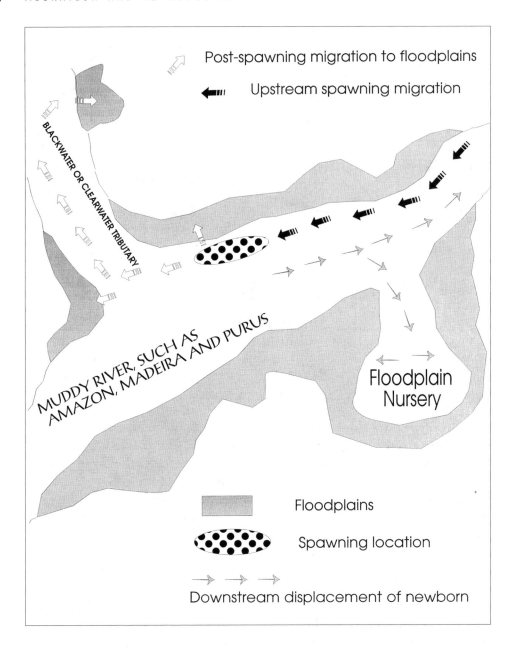

FIGURE 4.6

Generalized model of the reproductive migrations of tambaqui in the central Amazon.

loops and oxbows, and the slower speed, of the Rio Purus would appear to decrease the average downstream-displacement distance. The same would be true of the Rio Juruá farther to the west. Experimental sampling for larval tambaqui in river channels, however, is needed to test these hypotheses.

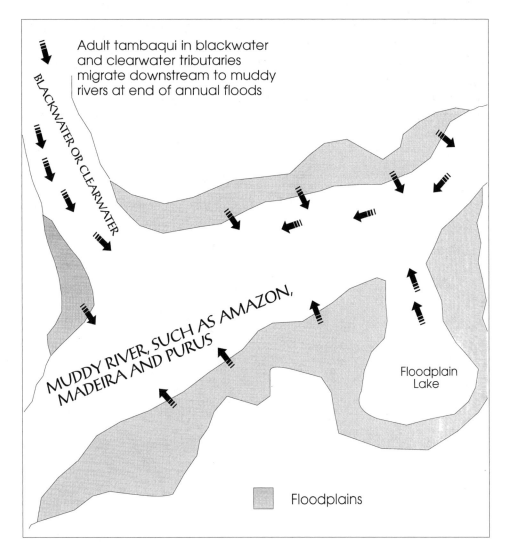

Adult tambaqui in blackwater
and clearwater tributaries
migrate downstream to muddy
rivers at end of annual floods

BLACKWATER OR CLEARWATER

MUDDY RIVER, SUCH AS AMAZON,
MADEIRA AND PURUS

Floodplain
Lake

Floodplains

FIGURE 4.7

Generalized model of the manner in which tambaqui in the central Amazon migrate to the channels of muddy rivers at the end of the annual floods.

OBSERVATIONS IN THE ORINOCO SYSTEM

The ecology of the tambaqui (cachama) has not been studied as intensively in the Orinoco as in the Amazon Basin. Comparisons between the two systems would be useful to analyze the ecological flexibility of the tambaqui. Machado-Allison (1982, 1987) reported that cachama migrate upstream in the Orinoco system in mixed schools and that spawning takes place in tributaries of the main river and the Rio Apure. Mixed schooling for the tambaqui has not been observed in the Amazon, but it perhaps takes place because natural hybrids with the pirapitinga (*Piaractus brachypomus*) are known to occur in the wild. Machado-Allison captured juveniles in the Rio Apure, Rio Meta, and Rio Portugueza. The Rio Meta and Rio Apure have higher sediment loads than the Orinoco (Meade et al. 1983)—a condition suggesting that Orinoco populations migrate from rivers with relatively low sediment and nutrient loads to those with higher levels, just as happens in the Amazon Basin.

CHAPTER FIVE

NURSERY HABITATS

Juvenile tambaqui populations in the Amazon Basin are restricted to the flood-plains of muddy rivers, such as the Amazon River, Rio Madeira, and Rio Purus. The waters of these floodplain areas are not always turbid and they often receive clear-water or black-water streams. In some cases the floodplain areas also contain black-water lakes. Nevertheless, nutrients injected into floodplain water bodies from the main river channels during the annual floods lead to relatively high pri-mary production in the form of algae and floating plant communities.

Tambaqui juveniles have adaptations to survive in floodplains with pro-nounced annual variability in water quality and habitat. During the flood season when all habitats are available, juveniles are concentrated in flooded forests and floating meadows (figure 5.1). In two well-surveyed floodplain lakes of the middle Amazon River region, Lago do Rei and Lago Grande de Manacapuru, 90–93% of the juveniles were found either in flooded forest or under floating plants. During the low-water period (October to December), almost no forest is flooded, and float-ing meadows are greatly reduced in size. Lago do Rei on the island of Careiro near the mouth of the Rio Negro, for example, shrinks nine to ten times its high-water size (Merona 1988). At this time of the year fish become concentrated in the open waters, reaching densities 5–17.5 times those recorded during the high-water period. Although space may be limited during the low-water period, juveniles nevertheless remain in floodplain waters rather than migrating to river channels.

FOOD FOR LARVAE

Tambaqui larvae change foods as they grow. The first food is the egg yolk, a swollen storehouse of fats, proteins, and nutrients. A young fish absorbs its yolk sac to grow rapidly during the first few days of life. By the time tambaqui larvae

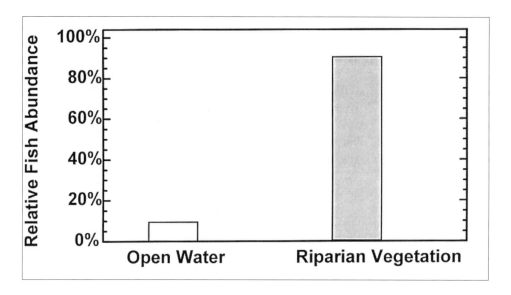

FIGURE 5.1

Abundance of juvenile tambaqui (200–1,000 g) in floodplain lakes is higher in riparian
vegetation than in open water during the flood season.

(Data based on the distribution analysis of 767 fish captured in 26 samples during 1986, 1987, 1990, and 1991
[ANOVA, p = 0.0014]. ORSTOM and Max Planck projects at INPA kindly provided raw data.)

reach 6.0 mm in length, only 10% of the yolk supply is left. Experiments have
shown that this is about 130 hours after fertilization when fish are kept at water
temperatures (28.7°C) similar to those of the Amazon River (Araujo-Lima 1990).
The yolk mass sustains the larval body until the second developmental phase,
when external food can be ingested.

Tambaqui larvae start to feed at 5.5–6 mm in length. This is 4.5–5.5 days after fertilization and 3.8–4.8 days after hatching in water temperatures of 27–29°C. A
slight overlap phase occurs when larvae are still absorbing the yolk and feeding
externally. The first external food eaten in the wild is still unknown. Tambaqui larvae in ponds initially eat micro-invertebrates, showing a preference for small
cladocerans and secondarily for rotifers and copepods (Zaniboni Filho 1992).

Because tambaqui larvae are relatively large by the time they first feed externally, and the mouth gape is 0.4 mm, they can choose from a wide spectrum of
potential foods. The larvae can swallow almost any food item up to 0.5 mm. Many
rotifer species in the Amazon River system are about this size (Koste and
Robertson 1983; Robertson and Hardy 1984). Also abundant are small cladocerans
(e.g., *Bosminopsis deitersi*, *Bosmina* spp., *Ceriodaphnia cornuta*, and *Moina minuta*) and
copepods (*Thermociclops minutus*). The above zooplankton species are plentiful in
the floodplain lakes at the same time tambaqui larvae are colonizing these nursery
habitats (Carvalho 1981; Hardy 1992; Robertson and Hardy 1984).

We also suspect that benthic cladocerans, such as various species of the families
Macrothricidae and Chydoridae, may also be important foods for tambaqui larvae.

These cladocerans are especially abundant in the floating vegetation (Junk 1973). Unfortunately, too few larval tambaqui under 6.0 mm have been captured in flood-plain water bodies for a quantitative analysis of their foods.

At seven days of age tambaqui larvae (7–8 mm) start to feed on cladocerans, small copepods, and chironomid fly larvae, the last measuring 0.4–1.0 mm in length. Young tambaqui also eat larger chironomid larvae of 2–5 mm in length and 0.2–0.5 mm in diameter. These larger chironomid larvae are probably manipulated in their mouths before being swallowed. The specific site where the fish larvae are swimming seems to influence the exact composition of the diet. Larvae in floating meadows prey heavily on copepods and chironomids; fish at the edge of meadows consume more cladocerans. Larval tambaqui diets remain relatively unchanged until the fish reach about 15 mm in length, at which time they are no longer considered to be larvae.

FOOD FOR JUVENILES

Juveniles 2–10 cm in length continue to prey on micro-invertebrates, but other food items, such as filamentous algae and wild rice, become increasingly important in the fishes' diet as they grow. Selecting larger items maximizes the energy gain per unit of foraging time.

The seasonal diets of juvenile tambaqui (13–50 cm) have been studied in detail in a large floodplain lake (Lago Manaquiri) of the middle Amazon River and a much smaller floodplain lake of the upper Rio Madeira (Calama floodplain opposite the Rio Machado in Rondonia) (table 5.1). To date no studies from any of the large lakes of the lower Amazon River have occurred. Comparisons are important because muddy-river floodplains have thousands of small lakes, often less than 1 km^2 in area, in addition to the immense open-water areas of the Amazon River. Juvenile tambaqui are known to be common both in small and large floodplain lakes during the low-water period (Carvalho 1981; Goulding and Carvalho 1982).

We will describe the Manaquiri floodplain area here because it represents the type of tambaqui habitat common along much of the Amazon River. During the floods Manaquiri becomes connected with adjacent floodplain areas of the right bank of the Rio Solimões (Amazon River above the confluence with the Rio Negro). This floodplain region is nevertheless geographically definable because of the presence of two large lakes that communicate with the Amazon River through a 35-km channel that cuts through the levees. At the peak of the floods, Amazon River channel water spills over the levees and inundates the entire floodplain. Except for their connections with the single channel that communicates with the river, the Manaquiri lakes and lagoons become isolated during the low-water period.

As Amazon River water travels up the Manaquiri channel, its sediments largely settle to the bottom. Lake transparencies reach 1.7 m, in contrast with the nearly opaque and highly turbid channel of the main river. Manaquiri lake waters are

TABLE 5.1
Principal Foods Eaten by Tambaqui in the Wild

Length	(1–2 cm)	(2.1–4 cm)	(7–10 cm)	(16–20 cm)	
Weight	(0.1–0.3 g)	(0.4–3.0 g)	(14–40 g)	(150–300 g)	
Season	Low water	Low water	High water	Low water	High water
Floodplain	Amazon	Amazon	Amazon	Amazon	Amazon
Zooplankton	73%	45%	20%	60%	50%
Insects	23%	20%	4%	—	—
Wild rice	0%	13%	22%	30%	31%
Fruits/seeds	0%	0%	0%	4%	15%
Algae	1%	0%	54%	—	—
Others	10%	20%	0%	5%	2%
Mean Fullness	60%	65%	68%		

dark (but not black) in color, and their pH is usually around 6.7. The Manaquiri floodplain is in constant ecological flux because of water-level fluctuation. Especially notable are the great biomass changes in floating plant communities. During the low-water period, wild rice (*Oryza* spp.) grows rapidly on the emerged lake and lagoon shores, forming verdant fields reminiscent of those of domestic, cultivated species. When the river level rises with the floods, the rice communities are inundated, and the rising water and the winds eventually extirpate the rice. Other aquatic plants, especially several grass species, the water hyacinth, and herbaceous groups from several other families, largely replace the rice communities and form dense floating meadows (Junk 1970).

The second study site, Calama of the upper Rio Madeira, was in a natural state with no deforestation. This area is studded with numerous small lakes and lagoons, many of which are quasi-oxbows or linear in shape. When the main river invades the Calama floodplain at the height of the floods, the lakes become highly turbid. As the water level falls, sediments drop to the bottom, and transparencies reach about 2.0 m. During the low-water period, the larger water bodies become turbid because wind mixes the bottom sediments. The high surrounding forest protects the smaller water bodies from the wind, so they remain relatively clear until the new floods. The Calama water bodies are slightly acidic to neutral in pH. For eight to eleven months each year they are landlocked. Many become choked with floating plants. Floodplain rainforest surrounds the numerous lakes.

Of the 150 central Amazon tambaqui juveniles (2–51 cm standard length) examined during the high-water period (March through August), only two had empty stomachs, and mean fullness was 62%. Zooplankton was always an important food item. Altogether, three food items accounted for 96% of the total bulk of food eaten. Of the 125 specimens examined during the low-water period (September through February), 14% had completely empty stomachs, and mean fullness

TABLE 5.1 (CONTINUED)

Sources: Goulding 1980; Goulding and Carvalho 1982; samples by first author near Manaus

(20-36 cm)			(>40 cm)			
(300-1,600 g)			(>2.1 kg)			
Low water	High water	High water	High water	Low water	Low water	High water
Amazon	Amazon	Madeira	Amazon	Amazon	Madeira	Madeira
58%	32%	42%	18%	55%	25%	<1%
—	—	—	—	—	12%	<1%
8%	32%	—	7%	6%	<1%	—
<1%	34%	42%	71%	71%	10%	94%
—	—	—	—	—	—	
34%	2%	18%	4%	38%	52%	5%
	60%	28%	60%	60%	<1%	72%

dropped to 34%. Zooplankton accounted for 70% of the total bulk consumed, while not one of the other nine items eaten represented more than 10%.

Young tambaqui have a preference for seeds but also eat considerable quantities of fleshy fruits. The smallest individual that was found to have eaten fruits or seeds from trees or shrubs at Manaquiri was 19 cm in length. However, specimens of less than 10 cm that had eaten seeds were captured in the floodplain forest of Janauacá, a site about 30 km downstream of Manaquiri. Because of deforestation, wild rice is undoubtedly now more abundant in the Manaquiri floodplain than formerly, when high forest was present around the margins. When the water level rises rapidly, the rice communities growing on the low, open shores of the lakes are flooded. Young tambaqui move into these areas to strip the seeds from the submerged stalks. Rice seeds were found in individuals ranging between 2.0 and 45 cm in length, though this food was dominant only in specimens smaller than 30 cm. Tree fruits and rice seeds are available in large quantities only during the floods, whereas zooplankton is an important food item during both the high- and low-water periods.

Of the nineteen tambaqui specimens (20–36 cm) examined during the high-water period (March through mid-May) at Calama of the Rio Madeira, none had empty stomachs, and mean fullness was 41%. Zooplankton and fruits accounted equally for 84% of the total bulk consumed by all specimens. Four items represented the remaining 16%. Of the fifty-nine specimens examined during the extended low-water period (mid-May through February), none had empty stomachs, and mean fullness was 31%. Tree fruits and seeds accounted for 49% of the total bulk consumed by all of the low-water specimens, followed by zooplankton with 24% and floating-meadow remains with 17%. The remaining 10% consisted of eight items.

Although the Calama floodplain forest is inundated for a shorter period (three to four months) each year, many fruits and seeds still fall into the water because of

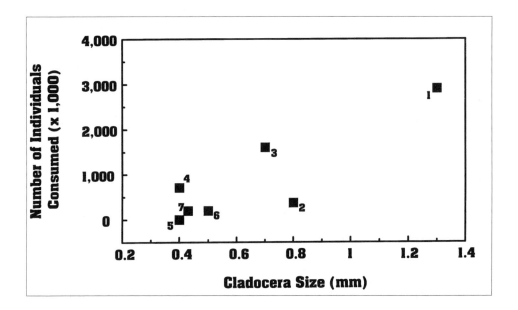

FIGURE 5.2

Size of Cladocera zooplankton and the number of individuals found in juvenile tambaqui stomach contents. 1. *Daphnia gessneri*; 2. *Diaphanosoma spp.*; 3. *Moina reticulata*; 4. *Ceriodaphnia cornuta*; 5. *Moina minuta*; 6. *Ceriodaphnia reticulata*; 7. *Bosmina* spp.

the large overhanging trees that completely surround the lake and lagoon margins. In deforested floodplain areas that are in secondary succession, such as most of the middle Amazon River, the large shore trees are often missing, and thus little over-hanging vegetation exists to supply fruits and seeds to the water bodies even before the onset of the main floods. Most of the fruit material eaten by the Calama specimens was seeds, and these were almost all masticated.

TAMBAQUI AND ZOOPLANKTON

About 92% of the bulk of zooplankton eaten consisted of cladoceran crustaceans, with *Daphnia gessneri, Ceriodaphnia cornuta, Moina reticulata,* and *Ceriodaphnia reticulata* being the most important species (figures 5.2 and 5.3). The other 8% consisted of copepods and ostracods. During the low-water period, *Moina reticulata* was the most important species eaten, followed by the copepod *Notodiaptomus amazonicus;* the latter were barely consumed during the floods (Goulding and Carvalho 1982).

As at Manaquiri, *Daphnia gessneri* (Cladocera) was the most important zoo-plankton eaten by young tambaqui at Calama during the floods. *Daphnia gessneri* was eaten throughout the year, but during the low-water period was less impor-tant than *Notodiaptomus* spp. (Copepoda).

The standing stock of zooplankton can be relatively high in the floodplain water bodies of Amazonian muddy rivers (table 5.2). Measurements of standing crops

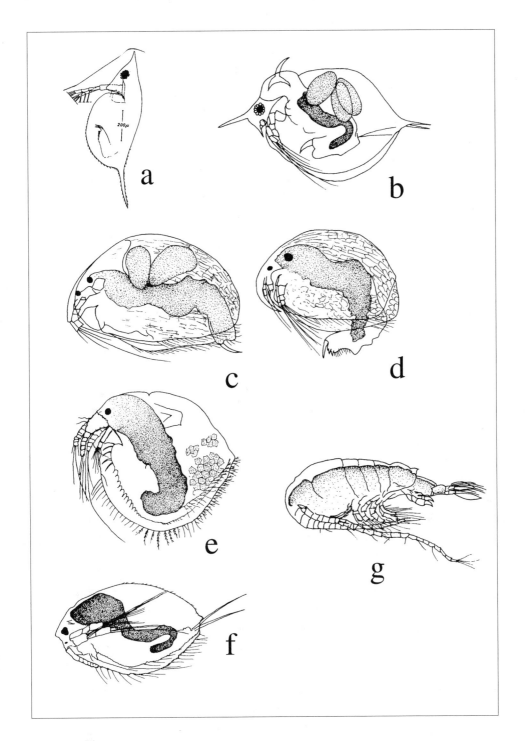

FIGURE 5.3

Zooplankton eaten by tambaqui. A. *Daphnia gessneri*; B. *Ceriodaphnia*; C & D. Chydoridae; E & F. Macrothricidae; G. Calanoida.

TABLE 5.2

Characteristics of Micro-crustaceans Eaten by Tambaqui

Species	Size (mm)	Dry weight (µg)	Lake	Max. Den. ind./ll	Avg. Dens. ind./ll	Season	Reference
Daphnia gessneri	1.3	—	Manaquiri	12	—	flood	Carvalho 1981
Daphnia gessneri	—	—	Calado	553	171	flood	Fisher et al. 1983
Daphnia gessneri	—	—	Jacaretinga	19.7	3.7	flood	Hardy 1992
Moina reticulata	0.7	—	Manaquiri	9.5	—	low water	Carvalho 1981
Moina reticulata	—	—	Jacaretinga	79	26.6	flood	Hardy 1992
Ceriodaphnia reticulata	0.4	—	Manaquiri	42	—	low water	Carvalho 1981
Ceriodaphnia cornuta	—	—	La Orsinera	—	7.2	flood	Twombly and Lewis 1987
Ceriodaphnia cornuta	—	—	Jacaretinga	78.9	9.8	flood	Hardy 1992
Ceriodaphnia reticulata	0.5	1.6	Manaquiri	4	—	flood	Carvalho 1981
Bosmina spp.	0.4	—	Manaquiri	80	—	low water	Carvalho 1981
Bosmina sp.	—	—	La Orsinera	—	5.1	flood	Twombly and Lewis 1987
Diaphanosoma sp.	0.8	—	Manaquiri	6.6	—	flood	Carvalho 1981
Notodiaptomus amazonicus	1.7	—	Calado	15.9	—	low water	Santos Silva 1991
Oithona amazonica	—	—	La Orsinera	—	313	flood	Twombly and Lewis 1987
				Max. Den. ind/m²	Avg. Dens. ind/m²		
Benthic Cladocera	—	3.5	Calado	50 000	—	low water	Junk 1973
Benthic Cladocera	—	3.5	Manacapuru	220 000	—	low water	Junk 1973
Benthic Cladocera	—	3.5	Xiborena	136 000	—	low water	Junk 1973
Benthic Cladocera		3.5	6 lakes	150000	49000	flood	Junk 1973
Conchostraca	—	38	Calado	10 000	—	flood	Junk 1973
Conchostraca	—	38	Manacapuru	10 000	—	flood	Junk 1973
Conchostraca	—	38	Xiborena	2700	—	flood	Junk 1973
Chironomids	—	—	Redondo	657	260		Marlier 1967

can underestimate zooplankton production, since planktivorous fishes such as the tambaqui consume a considerable part of it. Bayley's (1983) fish-production data from the middle-Amazon floodplain area suggest that young tambaqui are among the most important zooplanktivorous species in muddy river-floodplain water bodies. The zooplankton species eaten by juvenile tambaqui can reach standing densities of 500 ind./l of water during the flood season. The densities of zoo-plankton that have been measured in Amazon River–floodplain water bodies are similar to those reported for aquaculture ponds (Zaniboni Filho 1992).

Tambaqui eat zooplankton 0.4–1.7 mm in length, with a preference for larger species. The most common zooplankton eaten are the cladocerans *Daphnia gessneri, Diaphanosoma* sp., and *Moina reticulata* and the copepod *Notodiaptomus amazonicus* (figure 5.2). All of these species are larger than 0.7 mm. The main small zooplankton species (0.4 mm) consumed in relatively large quantities is the cladoceran *Ceriodaphnia cornuta*. This species is common in floodplain lakes, but its seasonal abundance varies greatly. In a detailed study, Carvalho (1981) showed that clado-cerans are eaten during most of the year, while copepods show the greatest occur-rence in tambaqui diets during the low-water period. The spatial distribution of zooplankton is probably not uniform. Adult *Daphnia gessneri,* for example, are con-centrated in patches at depths of 3–4 m, and they can reach densities as high as 500 ind./l (Fisher et al. 1983).

Fish capture zooplankton either by particulate- or filter-feeding. The first mode is visual and selective. The fish sees the particulate matter before ingesting it. Filter-feeding consists of passing large quantities of water across the gill rak-ers to remove zooplankton (Hyatt 1979; Lazzaro 1987; Gibson and Ezzi 1985, 1992). The exact foraging strategy of the tambaqui is not yet known. Small juve-niles (<16 cm in length) can probably select individual prey, but this does not seem possible for larger fish. The highest biting rate reported for any young juve-nile fish species is only about two bites per second (Gibson and Ezzi 1992). If indi-vidual zooplankton were selected at this rate, then only two could be eaten per second. The average number of zooplankton found in juvenile tambaqui from the middle Amazon River floodplain was about 87,000 individuals (Carvalho 1981). Experimental evidence has shown that small organisms do not remain in fish stomachs for more than five hours at water temperatures of 25–30°C (Fange and Grove 1979). A fish catching two zooplankton per second would consume 7,200 ind./hr, or 36,000 in five hours. At least 50% of stomach contents contain-ing zooplankton is digested in two hours. At these rates, then, a planktivore par-ticulate-feeding could never accumulate an average of 87,000 zooplankton in its stomach.

A selective-feeding strategy between particulate acquisition and filtering is gulping. Selective-feeding juvenile tambaqui would visually select and then gulp patches of preferred zooplankton species, thus taking in a much larger quantity of prey than random filtering or selecting individual prey.

WILD RICE

Wild rice (*Oryza grandiglumes* and *Oryza glumaepatula*) is common in floodplain water bodies of the muddy rivers of the Amazon Basin. *Oryza glumaepatula* is also found in some areas of black-water and clear-water tributaries. Both species fruit during the floods. *Oryza glumaepatula* fruits between February and May in the central Amazon, and *Oryza grandiglumes* from April to June (Rubim 1993). The seed crops do not have sharp peaks, but fruiting takes place over a relatively long period. Seed production can reach 1.2 tons/ha (Rubim 1993).

CHAPTER SIX

FRUITS AND SEEDS

Only in South America have fish communities evolved fruit- and seed-eating as a major part of the food chain. The availability of fruits and seeds as a major fish food in the Amazon Basin is due to the presence of large floodplain forests subject to long periods of seasonal inundation (figure 6.1). The flooded forests of the diverse river types vary considerably in plant species composition and physiognomic structure. We would, therefore, expect variety in the preferred fruits and seeds selected by fishes in specific floodplain regions. Our lists of the fruits and seeds eaten by fishes are still incomplete as only a few areas have been studied (Canestri 1970; Goulding 1980; Gottsberger 1978; Goulding et al. 1988; Ziburski 1991; Kubitzki and Ziburski 1993).

An excellent study of an island (Ilha da Machantaria) of the middle Amazon River showed that, at least to some extent, fish eat almost all fruit and seed species that fall into the water (Kubitzki and Ziburski 1993; Ziburski 1991).

Fruit- and seed-eating fishes of the Amazon belong almost exclusively to the characin and catfish families. Fruit-eating among other families, such as some cichlids, appears to be minimal. Most fruit-eating fishes that have been discovered are medium to large as adults, or larger than 20 cm. Some of the smaller (<15 cm) deep-bodied tetras (e.g., *Moenkhausia*) also feed heavily on seeds, but few data are yet available (Goulding et al. 1988). Of the characins, the main deep-bodied fruit- and seed-eaters are the pacus (including the tambaqui) and various piranha species. Several important genera (*Triportheus, Brycon,* and *Chalceus*) of elongate characins are also highly frugivorous. Headstanders (Anostomidae) are the second most important family of fruit- and seed-eating characins. Fruit-eating catfishes belong to the three species-rich families Pimelodidae, Doradidae, and Auchenipteridae. Fruit-eating fishes in these families range from large species reaching more than 1.3 m and 50 kg to some catfishes of the families Pimelodidae and Auchenipteridae reaching less than 20 cm in length.

FIGURE 6.1

Flooded forest of the Amazon River. Tambaqui and other fish migrate to this type of habitat during the floods to feed on fruits and seeds that fall into the water.

FRUIT- AND SEED-EATING BY TAMBAQUI

As seen in the previous chapter, the dietary preference of the tambaqui shifts from zooplankton to seeds and fruits as the fish grows. Adults are known to feed to some extent on zooplankton, but this food becomes of minor importance compared with that of fruits and seeds (table 6.1). Theoretically, considerable competition exists among the vegetarian fish species for the fruits and seeds they eat, though showing this statistically is difficult. Where floodplains have been deforested, fruit and seed production has undoubtedly decreased. Fish populations have also decreased because of fishing and floodplain deforestation; thus, competition for food would be reduced as well. To date no study has been made of the entire community of fruit- and seed-eating fishes in a muddy floodplain area. Several studies of individual fish species from the middle Amazon region suggest that young tambaqui, pacus (*Mylossoma* and *Myleus*), brycons (*Brycon*), and sardinhas (*Triportheus*) all eat many of the same fruit and seed species (Honda 1974; Almeida 1980; Paixão 1980; Borges 1986; Ziburski 1991; Kubitzki and Ziburski 1993).

The river level is the principal factor influencing the availability of fruits and seeds for fish. Most flooded-forest tree species fruit during the high-water period so that water or fish can disperse their seeds (Gottsberger 1978; Goulding 1980; Ayres 1993; Kubitzki and Ziburski 1993). Only a few species fruit during the low-water period, and seeds of these species, such as the enormous kapok tree (*Ceiba*

TABLE 6.1

Average Tree Densities and Fruit/Seed Characteristics of Species Eaten by Tambaqui in Flooded Forests

Species	Part Eaten	Width Diam. (cm)	Fruiting Season	# Months Fruiting	Floats?	Trees/ha. (Várzea)	Trees/ha. (Igapó)	Fish Size (cm)
Embaúba (Cecropia sp.) Moraceae	flesh	0.2 W	all year	2–3 mo	yes	31.5	—	20–36
Munguba (Pseudobombax munguba) Bombacaceae	flesh/seed	0.5 D	peak	2 mo	yes	—	—	20–30
Capitarí (Tabebuia barbata) Bignoniaceae	seed	1.0 W	peak	4–5 mo	yes	3.6	—	20–40
Taquarí (Mabea sp.) Euphorbiaceae	seed	0.6 D	begin.	3–4 mo	yes	0.3	30	>40
Tarumã (Vitex cimosa) Verbenaceae	flesh/seed	1.0 D	begin.	2 mo	yes	20	—	>25
Seringa barriguda (Hevea spruceana) Euphorbiaceae	seed	2.5 W	begin.	3–4 mo	yes	12.4	10	44–75
Seringa (Hevea brasiliensis) Euphorbiaceae	seed	1.5 D	peak	2–3 mo	yes	5	—	44–75
Jauarí (Astrocaryum jauary) Palmae	flesh/seed	3.0 D	peak	2–3 mo	no	5–7	8	44–75
Abio (Neolabatia sp.) Sapotaceae	flesh	3.0 W			yes	2.8	—	44–75
Supiarana (Alchornea schomburgkiana) Euphorbiaceae	seed	0.6 D	peak		yes	14.1	—	44–75
Piranheira (Piranhea trifoliata) Euphorbiaceae	seed	0.6 D	peak		yes	6.4	2	44–75
Castanharana (Eschweilera sp.) Lecythidaceae	seed	2.0D	end			6.9	—	44–75
Arapari (Macrolobium acaciaefolium) Leguminosae	seed	—	—	—	yes	—	50	44–75
Jenipapo (Genipa americana) Rubiaceae	seed	5.0D	—	—	yes	—	—	44–75
Cachinguba (Ficus sp.) Moraceae	seed	—	—	—	—	0.5	—	44–75
Goiaba araçá (Eugenia inundata) Myrtaceae	seed	2.0D	begin.	—	yes	—	—	>25
Araçá (Myrcia fallax) Myrtaceae	seed	—	—	—	—	—	—	—
Camuri (Gymnoluma glabrescens) Sapotaceae	—	—	—	—	—	—	—	—

Sources: Smith 1979a; Goulding 1980; Carvalho 1981; Piedade 1985; Rankin-De-Merona 1988; D'Oliveira 1989; Campbell et al. 1992.
Várzea = flooded forest of muddy-water rivers; Igapó = flooded forest of black-water and clear-water rivers; begin = beginning of flood.

FIGURE 6.2
The munguba tree
(*Pseudobombax munguba*)
during the high-water
season on the Amazon
floodplain.

pentandra)—which has now largely been destroyed along the Amazon River—are mostly wind-dispersed. Few floodplain tree species produce fruit throughout the high-water period. Most species have an intense fruiting period of two to three months, and floodplain animals are adapted to this short harvest (Ziburski 1991; Kubitzki and Ziburski 1993; Ayres 1993; Goulding 1980, 1989).

Floodplain tree species vary greatly in their distribution and abundance. Although pure stands of individual or few species are rare, communities with dominant species often have densities of a dozen or more individuals per hectare (figure 6.2). These dominants are often the favorite of fruit- and seed-eating fish. At the local level, resistance to average seasonal flooding appears to be one of the factors that influence the distribution and densities of individual plant species. Those species able to tolerate submerged roots for long periods will often be the most abundant species (Ferreira 1991).

The tree species producing fruits and seeds used by the tambaqui are relatively abundant in flooded forests compared with the pervasiveness of other species in the community. One hectare of black-water-flooded forest, for example, would

FIGURE 6.3

Munguba seeds are embedded in a cottonlike material that disperses the seeds with the help of the wind.

contain two to fifty medium to large fruit trees (table 6.1). The abundance is even higher in muddy-river-flooded forests, where 45–83 fruit trees/ha have been reported (Rankin-De-Merona 1988; Campbell et al. 1992). Few data are available on fruit and seed production per tree, which would be a better measure of food availability. One species that has been measured is the munguba (*Pseudobombax munguba*), a relative of the kapok tree (figure 6.3). On the Amazon River floodplain, the munguba was reported to have densities of 5 trees/ha (Rankin-De-Merona 1988; Campbell et al. 1992). An average tree produces about 1.2 kg of seeds (dry weight) (Rogério Gribel, INPA personal communication). If the above quantities are representative of the Amazon River, then its flooded forests produce at least 105,000 tons of munguba seeds annually.

Although exact data are not yet available, other species are more common and have much larger fruit or seed crops than the munguba. The total fruit and seed production of the Amazon River's flooded forests probably exceeds 1 million tons. If flooded tributary forests are added, then the total must be in the tens of millions of tons.

In the 1970s at least 2 million adult tambaqui were sold annually in the Manaus market (extrapolated from Petrere Jr 1978). Adult tambaqui feed almost exclusively on fruits and seeds. These fish add at least 1 kg of flesh for every 10 kg of fruits and seeds eaten. An average adult (6 kg) might grow 1.3 kg/yr; thus it would

TABLE 6.2

Estimates of Seed Production of Three Species Commonly Eaten by Tambaqui
on Amazon River Floodplains

Species	kg/tree	trees/ha	kg/ha	Total Fruit Production (t)	Potential Fish Production (t)
Munguba (*Pseudobombax*)	1.4	6.0	8.4	105,905	10,591
Seringa/rubber (*Hevea*)	2.8	12.4	34.9	441,162	44,116
Jauari (*Astrocaryum*)	6.6	5.7	37.6	475,885	47,589
Total				1,022,953	102,295

Potential fish production from the total biomass of the three fruit species is based on a conservative conversion ratio of 1 kg of fish per 10 kg of fruit eaten.
Calculations are based on data from Piedade 1985; Sippel et al. 1992; Gribel personal communication; Campbell et al. 1992; Ayres 1993; Rankin-De-Merona 1988.

consume 13 kg of fruit and seeds annually. Two million adult tambaqui would eat at least 26 million kg of fruits and seeds in a year (table 6.2).

Heavy molarlike dentition and strong jaws allow the tambaqui to crush hard nuts. Fish are unable to digest hard nut walls and would not be able to use a large percentage of the fruit crop that falls into the water if they did not have the ability to crush nut walls. No known nut in the flooded forest is too hard for the tambaqui to crack (Kubitzki and Ziburski 1993). Only a few common species are too large for ingestion, such as the common macucu (*Aldina latifolia* [Leguminosae]). Nuts of the jauari palm (*Astrocaryum jauari*) require a crushing force of 200 kg/cm^2; a rubber tree seed requires a crushing force of 24 kg/cm^2. Neither species is a problem for the tambaqui.

The tambaqui, like other fruit-eating fishes, does not feed heavily on all seeds that are abundant and of appropriate size to be crushed. Several species of legumes produce huge seed crops each year, but the tambaqui only occasionally attacks them. We suspect that some of these might be toxic, but experimental evidence is needed to test this hypothesis. Turtles are known to feed heavily on legumes, and possibly a major ecological separation evolved between fish and these reptiles. Before they were overexploited, side-necked turtles (*Podocnemis* spp. [Pelomedusidae]) were abundant in the Amazon. Like fish, these turtles migrate to the flooded forests to feed on fruits and seeds.

Although tambaqui seem to prefer seeds, they also eat large quantities of fleshy fruits. Some of these fleshy fruits have large seeds, such as those of the family Sapotaceae. Only occasionally does the tambaqui crush the seeds of these fruits (Goulding 1979; Kubitzki and Ziburski 1993). Instead, the fleshy fruit is swallowed whole, and the viable seeds are defecated. Most fleshy fruits are berries or fig syconia (a special type of fruit), and the seeds are minute and escape mastication. It is probable that the fish select a variety of species that include a mixture of seeds and fleshy-fruit material to get the best balance of protein, carbohydrates, fats, and vitamins.

Most of the fruits and seeds on which the tambaqui feeds float (Kubitzki and Ziburski 1993), so the fish must rise to the surface to grab them. Observations in the wild and in large tanks reveal that the tambaqui rises in a diagonal position, and the mouth reaches to within a few centimeters of the surface. The floating fruit or seed is then sucked downward and into the mouth. When a hard nut is ingested, the tambaqui descends several meters below the surface, assumes a horizontal position, and then crushes the nut wall. The cracked nut of rubber tree seeds is often expelled, grabbed in another position, and then bitten anew. This process can be repeated several times until the shell is discarded. Fishermen paddling in the flooded forest often hear the sound produced by this feeding activity. In the water the sound travels much farther than through the air, and it alerts other tambaqui of the presence of food. In large tanks tambaqui attempt to define feeding areas, and the fish spend much time and energy chasing one another about, even when large quantities of food are available. This behavior can sometimes be observed in the wild, though it is much more difficult to see there because of the poor transparency of most flooded-forest waters.

SENSORY LOCATION OF FRUITS AND SEEDS

Flooded forests are vast habitats where the availability of the preferred fruits and seeds can be highly patchy. The shade of the forest and the low transparency of most Amazonian rivers means that there is little light penetration into the water. Tambaqui have various sensory capacities for locating food and use a combination of them to find fruits and seeds.

As discussed earlier in reference to migration, subsequent to spawning in muddy-river channels, tambaqui migrate to flooded forests of either clear-water or black-water tributaries, or to the adjacent floodplain areas of the muddy rivers. Various factors could affect the choice of a specific area for high-water feeding. Obviously, there must be extensive flooded forest, at least in the central Amazon where the species is most abundant. The presence of large areas of flooded forest is not always correlated with river size, however, and the tambaqui must instinctively know this. Some of the smaller tributaries of the middle Amazon River, for example, have extremely large floodplains, such as the Rio Manacapuru system west of Manaus. Tambaqui are known from fisheries data to be abundant in these areas.

Some fish species are already well known to have an extremely keen olfactory sense that is used for navigation. The most famous example is adult migratory salmon, which are able to recognize home streams by olfaction (Hasler and Scholz 1983). Tambaqui have large nares with external flaps, and their presence suggests that the fish has a highly developed olfactory sense (figure 6.4). It is possible that they use olfaction to detect floodplains rich in fruits and seeds. Amazonian rivers are highly charged with organic compounds originating from trees. Most of these compounds, however, are derived from nonflooded vegetation, though it is rea-

FIGURE 6.4

Tambaqui eating rubber tree seed. Note large nares.

sonable to believe that each river has its own unique "bouquet" as a result of the diversity of plant communities and the varying geology of the drainage systems. With the coming of the floods, inundated forests might release enough plant chemicals to be detectable in river channels by the tambaqui and other fish. These chemicals might not necessarily be from the same species on which the fish feed, but they would hypothetically be associated with them in the flooded forest.

Even if the tambaqui is unable to detect flooded-forest chemicals in the river channels, the olfactory sense could still be important for locating trees once the fish is in floodplain waters. Each tree species has a distinct smell because of its unique chemical composition of resins, alkaloids, phenols, and other organic compounds. It is quite possible that the tambaqui and other fruit- and seed-eating fishes are able to locate the desired tree species by following olfactory trails composed of molecules released into the water by flooded-forest trees. Fallen fruit would also release chemical signals into the water, to attract fish to them to have their seeds dispersed. Fish disperse the seeds of many floodplain trees and shrubs, and in some cases a mutualistic relationship has evolved (Gottsberger 1978; Goulding 1980; Ziburski 1991; Kubitzki and Ziburski 1993).

Tambaqui undoubtedly use vision and sound to locate fruits and seeds. In deep flooded-forest waters not much can likely be seen on the bottom. Since some fruit sinks, we would suspect that smell is used to locate it. We might also hypothesize that the fish "feel around" on the bottom with their snouts, but this type of activity could be dangerous, especially in jauari palm (*Astrocaryum jauary*) patches, where pungent spines from fallen fronds are common. No spine wounds have been observed on the snouts of tambaqui feeding on jauari palm fruits; thus they likely do not locate this food by tactile means.

Tambaqui have large stomachs and relatively long intestines. Individuals of more than 10 kg can have more than 1 kg of fruit and/or seeds in their stomachs and intestines. The freshness of the stomach contents of fish captured in flooded forests leaves little doubt that tambaqui can obtain a kilogram or more of fruit or seeds in a day. The full stomachs that most tambaqui have in areas where flooded forests have not been destroyed suggests that the fruit and seed supply does not limit the production of adult fish. The main exception would be in the rare years when the floods arrive late or are of less than normal duration.

FRUIT AND SEED DIVERSITY IN TAMBAQUI DIETS

The plant diversity of distinct floodplain areas has been studied at several sites in the Amazon Basin. The greatest diversity yet reported is for the muddy Rio Manu area of southeastern Peru, where approximately 1,372 plant species have been registered from the low-lying floodplain (Foster 1990). The Manu floodplain is considerably higher in elevation than most of the Amazon River floodplain. The Manu study showed that about half of the total plants is trees and shrubs, or nearly 70% of the entire flora when lianas are added. The Mamirauá floodplain at the confluence of the Amazon River and Rio Japurá is probably just as diverse. Ayres (1993) recorded nearly three hundred tree species greater than 10 cm in diameter in white-water and black-water areas of the Mamirauá floodplain region.

From a botanical perspective, it is important to compare the floristic composition and distribution frequency of the plant species in various river types whose fruits and seeds are eaten by the tambaqui. Given that adult tambaqui migrate to black-water and clear-water tributaries, the possibility exists that more food can be found in the flooded forests of these types of rivers than in muddy-river areas. Differences in species composition or abundance could be the reason. Tree biomass is reported to be considerably lower in black-water than muddy-river forests (Prance 1978). To what extent fruit and seed biomass might also be less has not been demonstrated. Whatever the case, tambaqui are, or were, so abundant in the clear-water and black-water flooded forests of the central Amazon that fruit and seed biomass can be dismissed as a limiting factor to their distribution in these areas.

Most of the tree and shrub genera on which tambaqui are known to feed are found in all the major river types. The most drastic differences in species composition are between muddy-water and black-water flooded forests, even in areas of close proximity (Ayres 1993). The fruits and seeds of species in the same tree or shrub genus are usually similar morphologically. To a tambaqui or other fish, then, species are probably less important in nutritional differences than genera. In this context we can hypothesize that the seasonally flooded forests of the central Amazon are ecologically similar in regards to the tambaqui's diet.

FIGURE 6.5
Most of the fruits and
seeds on which the tam-
baqui feeds float, such as
illustrated by these uxi
(*Licania* sp., Chryso-
balanaceae) drupes.

VISUAL ESSAY ON FRUITS AND SEEDS EATEN BY TAMBAQUI

The following visual essay is designed to give the reader a feeling for the great
diversity of fruits and seeds that are present in flooded forests and on which the
tambaqui feeds. One or two examples have been chosen from each of the main
plant families. Some if not many of these plant species might one day be cultivated
on Amazonian floodplains for fish food (see chapter 14). (figures 6.5, 6.6, 6.7, 6.8,
6.9, 6.10, 6.11, 6.12, 6.13, 6.14, 6.15, and 6.16).

FIGURE 6.6

A Spruce's rubber tree (*Hevea spruceana* [Euphorbiaceae]) capsule beginning to dry out so that the three seeds inside can be ejected and dispersed by water.

FIGURE 6.7

An exploded rubber tree capsule that has ejected its seeds.

FIGURE 6.8
A rubber tree seed floating in the waters of a flooded forest.

FIGURE 6.9

The family Euphorbiaceae has many flooded-forest tree and shrub species on which the tambaqui feeds. The piranha-tree *(Piranhea trifoliata)* produces huge seed crops and might be a potential candidate for "fish orchards" for aquaculture.

FIGURE 6.10

Shrublike trees often get inundated before their fruits have had a chance to mature. Tambaqui and other fish can literally "pluck" these flooded fruits. Shown here is *Alchornea* sp. (Euphorbiaceae) that grows along riverbanks and floodplain lakes.

FIGURE 6.11

The famous Brazil-nut tree is not found on Amazonian floodplains, but there are many other species of its family (Lecythidaceae) on which the tambaqui feeds. The large seeds of *Lecythis* species fall into the water after the fruit's capsule opens its hatch.

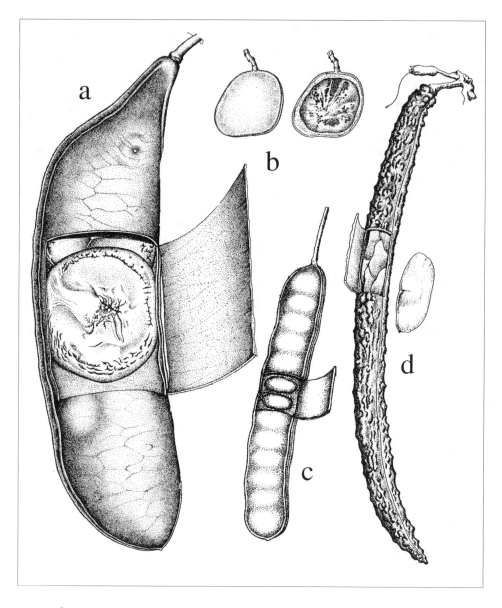

FIGURE 6.12

The families Leguminosae and Bignoniaceae produce a wide variety of flooded-forest capsular fruits whose seeds float and are thus easily accessible to the tambaqui.
A. *Campsiandra comosa* (Leguminosae); B. *Macrolobium acaciifolium* (Leguminosae);
C. *Inga* sp. (Leguminosae); and D. *Tabebuia barbata* (Bignoniaceae).

FIGURE 6.13

Examples of the types of berries or berrylike fruits eaten by the tambaqui. A. Passion fruit (*Passiflora* sp. [Passifloraceae]; B. Wild soursop (*Annona* sp. [Annonaceae]); C. *Cecropia* sp. (Moraceae); D. Wild guava (Myrtaceae); E. Melon family (Cucurbitaceae); and F. Fig (*Ficus* sp. [Moraceae]).

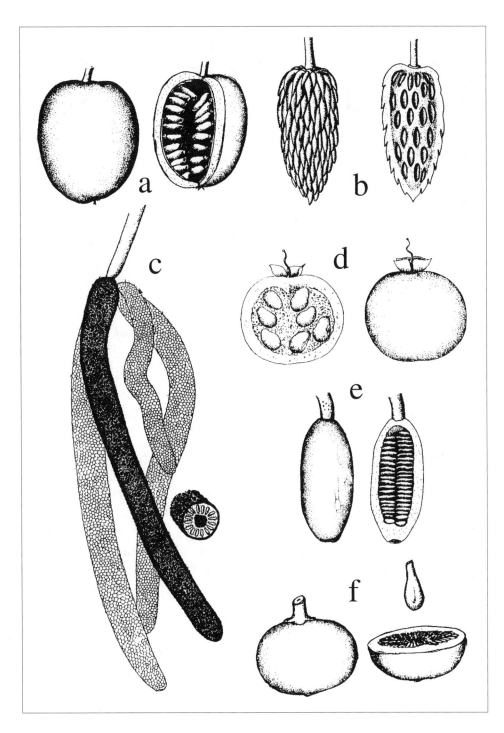

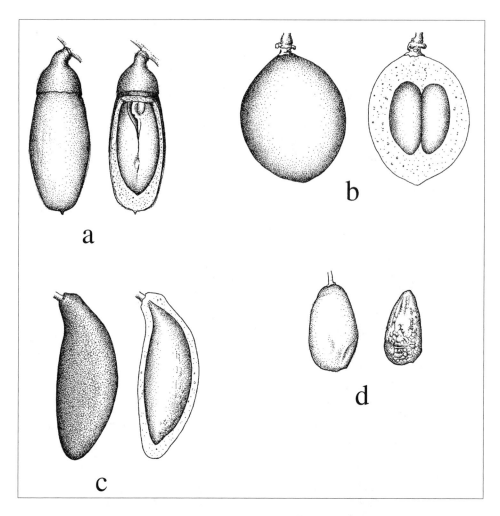

FIGURE 6.14

Examples of the types of drupes eaten by tambaqui. A. Louro (Lauraceceae). B. Sapotaceae; C. Uxi (*Licania* sp. [Chrysobalanaceae]); and D. Cajurana *(Simaba* sp. [Simubaraceae]).

FIGURE 6.15

The jauari (*Astrocaryum jauari*) is one of the most common palms on Amazonian flood-plains. Its fruits sink to the bottom, often in thick growth where there are many spines. The tambaqui has unknown adaptations for finding these fruits without getting wounded by jauari spines.

FIGURE 6.16

Catoré (*Crataeva benthami* [Capparidaceae]), a small tree, is one of the largest fruits on which the tambaqui feeds. The small seeds are rarely crushed and are thus dispersed by tambaqui. Catoré fruits are also widely used in the Amazon for bait to catch tambaqui in flooded forests. This species might be promising for "fish orchards."

CHAPTER SEVEN

The first step taken to determine what a fish eats is to analyze its stomach contents. Field data reveal what a fish eats but not necessarily the relative nutritional contribution of each type of food ingested. Interpreting the nutritional value of diets from stomach-content analyses alone must be done with care. The digestion rates of various food items can differ significantly. For example, small items might pass rapidly through the stomach and thus would not be noted in sufficient quantity to indicate their importance in the diet. The following discussion is based on both stomach-content analyses and laboratory investigations such as stable-isotope analysis.

The foods eaten by the tambaqui are chemically quite diverse. Compared with fruits and seeds, zooplankton, insects, and algae have a high water content (figure 7.1 and table 7.1). Nuts, such as those from rubber trees (*Hevea*), mungubas (*Pseudobombax*), piranha-trees (*Piranhea*), and tarumã (*Vitex*) are rich in proteins and lipids. Other fruits and seeds are high in carbohydrates. The relative proportion of nutrients and water in foods ingested by tambaqui changes as the fish grow, mostly because juveniles and adults consume more seeds. Seeds have a considerably lower water content than zooplankton and other foods eaten by larval tambaqui.

The relative protein intake decreases with fish size. The average protein content of preferred foods drops from 42% for larvae to only about 20% for juveniles and adults. On the other hand, the amounts of carbohydrates and lipids consumed by juveniles and adults are inversely related. Young juveniles of the central Amazon floodplain eat large quantities of rice seeds. These seeds are lean compared with the fatty rubber-tree seeds eaten by adults. The result is a marked change in the amount of energy in the diet. Adults maintain a diet that supplies 23 kJ/g of food consumed, whereas the juveniles' diet provides only 18–20 kJ/g (a kilojoule—kJ—

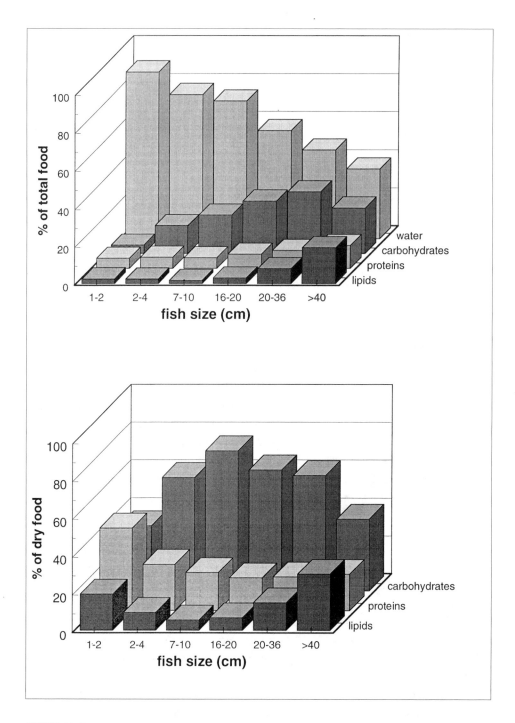

FIGURE 7.1

Average nutritional value of the diet of wild tambaqui. Data are expressed as percentages of food total weight (above) and of food dry weight (below).

TABLE 7.1

Nutritional Characteristics of Common Foods Eaten by Wild Tambaqui

	Water %	Protein %	Carbo-hydrates %	Lipids %	Ash %	Fiber %	Energy J/g
ANIMALS							
Aquatic insects (larvae of chironomids)	84	58.3	—	10	10	—	24,243
Cladocera	94	52.6	15.2	10.7	18.2	—	21,800
Rotifera	90	40	40	15	5	—	—
Zooplankton	88	61.5	64.8	1		—	—
PLANTS							
Algae (*Chlorella* + *Scenedesmus*)	—	42.8	27.4	7.2	1	—	15,000
Algae (Pond populations of Phytoplagellates)	88	33.3	16.7	10.8	6	3.5	—
Embaúba (*Cecropia*) (whole)	51.7	4	68.1	0.9	4.9	22	13,125
Genipapo (*Genipa*) (flesh)	80.2	2.6	77.8	2.7	—	—	—
Jauarí (*Astrocaryum*) (flesh)	60	8	78.5	8	5.5	—	6,988
Jauarí (*Astrocaryum*) (seed)	42.4	5.6	71.4	25.5	1.4	—	16,296
Munguba (*Pseudobombax*) (seed)	14.3	21.3	25.7	31.9	5.2	15.9	22,024
Piranheira (*Piranhea*) (seed)	49.8	15.9	—	—	—	—	—
Rice (*Oryza*) (seed)	15.7	8.1	88.2	2	2	0	17,974
Seringa (*Hevea*) (seed)	4.1	19.2	24.4	44.2	2.9	9.3	26,125
Seringa barriguda (*Hevea*) (seed)	39	15.9	—	—	—	—	—
Tarumã (*Vitex*) (seed)	71	17	43	7.5	4.5	3	—

All nutrients are related to food dry weight. Energy = J/g of dry weight.
Sources: Aguiar personal communication; Dias et al. 1988; Esteves 1988; LaNoue and Choubert 1983; Peters 1987, Piedade 1985; Prus 1970; Roubach 1992; Waedoff 1991; Zarnecki 1968.

is a standard unit used to measure energy). Adults need higher-energy foods to meet their heavier metabolic demands.

Because the tambaqui is omnivorous, it has adaptations for digesting both plant and animal food. There are obvious advantages to eating fruits and seeds. Low water content and larger particle size suggest that fruits, but especially seeds, offer a much higher gain of energy per volume of ingested food than other items. This advantage may explain why early in life tambaqui have a high percentage of seeds in their diets.

A cladoceran crustacean measuring 0.6 mm represents approximately 3.0% of the body mass of a 6.0-mm tambaqui larva. This would be the equivalent of a 1.5-kg meal for a person weighing 70 kg. Because volume increases to the cube of linear dimensions, a 12-mm tambaqui larva would receive ten times less food biomass from a single cladoceran than would a 6.0-mm fish; for a 20-mm larva, one hundred times less relative biomass. The point is that if the tambaqui were to depend solely on zooplankton, it would have to eat greater relative and absolute quantities of this food to satisfy its nutritional demands as it got larger. The large size of the tambaqui means that it cannot rely solely on zooplankton in Amazonian waters to sustain itself. Other foods are more rewarding. For example, a single rice seed contains the energy equivalent of approximately 4,000 cladoceran zooplankton.

Even when juvenile tambaqui are feeding heavily, the average number of zooplankton in their stomachs would still provide less energy than a rubber-tree nut (zooplankton estimates based on Carvalho 1981). Thus, if the swimming costs of foraging for seeds and gulping zooplankton are considered nearly equal, then the net gain from seeds would be much higher. This estimate is conservative because finding patches of zooplankton, and then ingesting them, requires more energy than handling a seed.

The quantity of food consumed is not the only important aspect of feeding. Animal flesh provides a complete range of amino acids, some of which may be important in fish nutrition. Plant items are usually less digestible than animal. The structural and chemical composition of plant cell walls inhibit the hydrolytic rate of enzymes (Tacon and Cowey 1985). The feeding metabolism consequently increases, and the energy gain decreases. Fruits, however, are also rich in vitamins, especially vitamins A and C, in addition to being good sources of energy and protein. The fruits of the family Myrtaceae, for example, have one of the highest vitamin C contents of any plants recorded.

By selecting fruits and seeds, tambaqui feed on the most nutritious parts of flooded-forest plants. The digestion and assimilation of different fruit and seed species may in part depend on the size of the tambaqui. For example, young juvenile tambaqui (<20 cm) grow well when fed munguba (*Pseudobombax*) and wild rice (*Oryza*) seeds. On the other hand, they do poorly when fed triturated rubber-tree seeds (*Hevea*) (Roubach 1992). The opposite must be the case with adult tambaqui because they feed so heavily on rubber-tree seeds and select them when given a choice of several species on which they feed (Goulding personal observation in filming tanks, Santarém). Young juveniles may not be able to digest rubber-tree seeds fully, or perhaps some essential nutrients are missing.

FOOD ASSIMILATION AND BODY COMPOSITION

The analysis of stomach contents and their chemical composition reveals only part of a nutritional evaluation. The ingested food is transformed into usable energy and building blocks. The various food items usually have a different residence time in the stomach, and these times can be measured only through experiments. Once food reaches the stomach, it is inundated with gastric fluids, especially hydrochloric acid and pepsin. The gastric fluids cover the surface of the food and, along with the peristaltic movements of stomach muscles, break the ingested material into smaller particles to start the digestive process (Jobling 1986). Mechanical friction during feeding stimulates the production of gastric fluids. Pepsin activity in the tambaqui remains independent of protein quantity and quality but increases with stomach fullness (Kohla et al. 1992). Food particles pass to the gut when they are of sufficiently small size and when the pyloric valve aperture is opened. Large items, such as unbroken palm nuts (*Astrocaryum jauari*), are the last to be expelled in the digestive process.

In the intestine (duodenum) pancreatic juice produced in the hepato-pancreas attacks the food. This juice is rich in enzymes and will further advance the digestion of proteins. Trypsin, chymotrypsin, amylase, and lipases, among other enzymes, will break down proteins, carbohydrates, and fats (Halver 1989). Intestine-produced enzymes will further break food into smaller components, which will then be assimilated. In tambaqui digestion, trypsin activity increases with the protein content of the food. When tambaqui eat large quantities of fruits and seeds, however, trypsin activity decreases (Kohla et al. 1992). According to the above argument, a reduction of the enzyme substrate due to the incomplete digestion of plant material, or to enzyme inhibitors normally found in seeds, would cause the decreased rate of trypsin activity.

Once the food energy is assimilated, it is used for metabolism to sustain body functions. Fish are able to burn protein, carbohydrates, and lipids to produce energy. Lipids are the highest in energy, followed by protein and carbohydrates (Jobling 1994). Stored fat is important for metabolism during periods of low food availability, as well as for the production of eggs that are rich in lipids. Only about 1.5% of an adult tambaqui's fat is stored in muscles. Juveniles (about 35 cm) are even leaner, with only about 0.2% fat in their muscles (Castelo et al. 1980; Saint-Paul 1984c; Junk 1985a). Another 10% is stored in the peritoneal cavity. Other characin species from the central Amazon have 5–15% of their total fat stored in their muscles (Junk 1985a).

CARBON ISOTOPIC COMPOSITION OF TAMBAQUI

As emphasized above, field studies of the foods eaten by tambaqui do not provide a quantitative evaluation of how the various components are assimilated. Fish-feeding experiments can yield the necessary data but are time consuming and expensive. An alternative method is carbon-isotope analysis. Every chemical element on earth has two or more forms caused by different numbers of neutrons in the nucleus—that is, different atomic weights. Carbon-isotope analysis has been

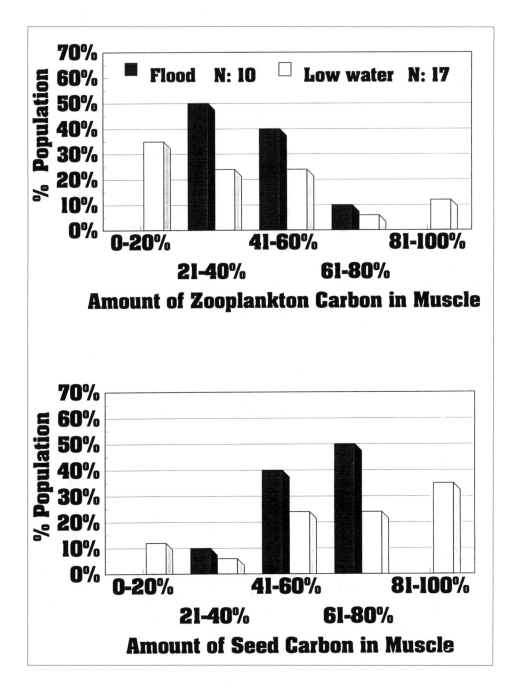

FIGURE 7.2

Amount of fruit /seed and zooplankton carbon in the flesh of central Amazon tambaqui populations during the low- (October–January) and high- (February–September) water periods.

used in the last decade to determine the importance of different types of foods that are assimilated into animal flesh. The method consists of identifying the plant carbon sources from which the flesh was built. After carbon is fixed during photosynthesis by a plant, the ratio of carbon-13 (C-13) to C-12 isotopes remains relatively stable as they move through the food chain from plant to animal. When relatively few isotopically distinct plant groups are involved, it is often possible to identify the plant carbon sources directly from the carbon-isotope ratios (Araujo-Lima et al. 1986; Forsberg et al. 1993). Carbon-isotope ratios are measured in the laboratory by using a machine called a mass spectrophotometer.

Most of the plants of the Amazonian floodplains can be divided into either C-3 or C-4 photosynthetic pathways. C-3 plants are considerably depleted of C-13. These plants include phytoplankton, trees, and some floating plants. Phytoplankton can further be distinguished from the above by their isotope ratios (Araujo-Lima et al. 1986). Floodplain C-4 plants are mostly herbaceous species, or the floating meadows, which are often highly productive communities (Junk 1985b). The contribution of C-4 plants to tambaqui flesh, however, is negligible.

Seeds and zooplankton have distinct isotope ratios because zooplankton receive carbon from phytoplankton (Forsberg et al. 1993). Therefore, the relative contributions to fish flesh can be estimated (figure 7.2). Carbon-isotope measurements show that about 65% of a tambaqui's flesh is derived from fruits and seeds (Araujo-Lima et al. forthcoming). The seventeen samples tested showed minimal variation (<5%) in relation to either fish size or river-level period. The average contribution of zooplankton carbon was 35%. Carbon from seeds is even more important for juvenile sizes. The conclusion is that fruits and seeds are the main foods assimilated by both juvenile and adult tambaqui.

CHAPTER EIGHT

AGE, GROWTH, METABOLISM, AND BIOMASS

Growth is usually measured in a defined period. Time implies that something is known about age. Measuring the age of tambaqui in the Amazon has been accomplished mostly by indirect means. Bayley (1983, 1988) and Isaac and Ruffino (1996) showed that young tambaqui reach 290–313 g in the wild in the first year of life (figure 8.1). The tambaqui's growth rate during this period is similar to that reported for other large river fishes of Africa and South America (Welcomme 1985; Bayley and Petrere Jr 1989; Bayley 1988; Worthmann 1983). Wild jatuarana (*Brycon cephalus*), a common characin food fish that is omnivorous but relies heavily on fruits and seeds, has been shown to reach 550–750 g in one year (Villacorta-Correa 1987). More studies of wild populations of various species are needed to determine the range of growth rates, especially their differences between natural and disturbed areas. Both Bayley and Villacorta Correa carried out their studies in highly disturbed floodplains.

The tambaqui reaches at least 30 kg and 1 m in length after thirteen years (Goulding and Carvalho 1982; Petrere Jr 1983b; Isaac and Ruffino 1996). There are fishermen's reports of tambaqui weighing 40 kg, and Goulding has seen a photograph of an individual captured in the Rio Mamoré that might have been this large. There are no estimates of how old a fish this size might be. The average age at which tambaqui become sexually mature in the middle Amazon is 3.5–4.0 years, or approximately 6.3 kg (see chapter 4). The absolute growth rate is highest at four to five years of age; at this time fish weight increases 3.3 kg/yr. Growth is then progressively reduced, but a nine-year-old fish still grows 2 kg/yr.

Growth rates can be expressed in absolute or relative terms. Both rates depend on fish size. As the fish increase in size, absolute growth rate increases, but relative growth rate decreases. The absolute growth rate is strongly dependent on fish size, and sometimes it is not the best parameter to use for comparisons (figure 8.2). A large slow-growing fish, for example, may have the same absolute growth rate as a small

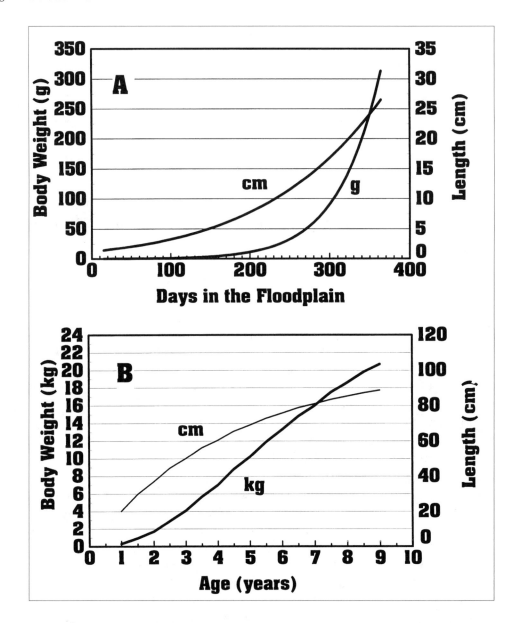

FIGURE 8.1

Predicted average weight and length of the tambaqui during its first year in floodplains (A) and until ten years of age (B).

(Data for the first year were calculated from Bayley 1988, and for ten years from Isaac and Ruffino 1996.)

fish growing fast. Relative growth rate is thus more meaningful. Bayley's (1983, 1988) data from the middle Amazon River can be used for estimates of absolute growth rate. From these data relative growth weights can also be determined (table 8.1). As with most fishes, the relative growth rate of the tambaqui is high for young stages and then decreases exponentially with size. Larvae with yolk sacs grow

37%/day (Araujo-Lima 1990). Juveniles grow 3.3%/day in the first year (Bayley 1988). Adults grow less than 0.16%/day (Petrere Jr 1983b; Isaac and Ruffino 1996). As fish increase in size, the amount of new tissue formed in relation to body size decreases exponentially. One explanation is that the increase in the maximum rate of food consumption with growth is less than the increase in the metabolic demands of the fish (Brett 1979). Genetic constraints can also be important (Jobling 1986).

ENVIRONMENTAL INFLUENCE ON GROWTH RATES

Temperature affects the rates of food consumption, metabolism, and, therefore, fish growth (Wootton 1990; Ricker 1979). These effects have not been studied in wild tambaqui populations but are apparent in experimental situations. Growth seems to stop at temperatures below about 22–24°C (Merola and Souza 1988; Merola and Pagan-Font 1988; Lovshin forthcoming). Water temperatures in the Amazon and Orinoco floodplains ranges over 26–34°C (see chapter 3). Relatively low temperatures may occur occasionally at the water surface, such as in a rainstorm, or during the passage of cold fronts (Odinetz-Collart and Moreira 1989).

TABLE 8.1
Growth Rates for Wild Tambaqui

Period	Final weight	Relative growth rate (%/day)	Sources
0-2 days	0.00026	37.00	Araujo-Lima 1990
2-4 days	0.00055	14.10	Araujo-Lima 1991
0-2 months	1.2	2.60	Araujo-Lima
0-6 months	62.5	2.30	Isaac and Ruffino 1996
0-1 year	300	2.70	Bayley 1983
1-2 years	1716	0.47	Isaac and Ruffino 1996
2-3 years	4100	0.24	Isaac and Ruffino 1996
2-3 years ?	4790	0.11	Petrere Jr 1983
3-4 years	6974	0.15	Isaac and Ruffino 1996
3-4 years ?	7220	0.11	Petrere Jr 1983
4-5 years	10,190	0.10	Isaac and Ruffino 1996
4-5 years ?	10,332	0.10	Petrere Jr 1983
5-6 years	13,287	0.07	Isaac and Ruffino 1996
5-6 years ?	13,112	0.07	Petrere Jr 1983
6-7 years	16,055	0.05	Isaac and Ruffino 1996
7-8 years	18,569	0.04	Isaac and Ruffino 1996
8-9 years	20,737	0.03	Isaac and Ruffino 1996

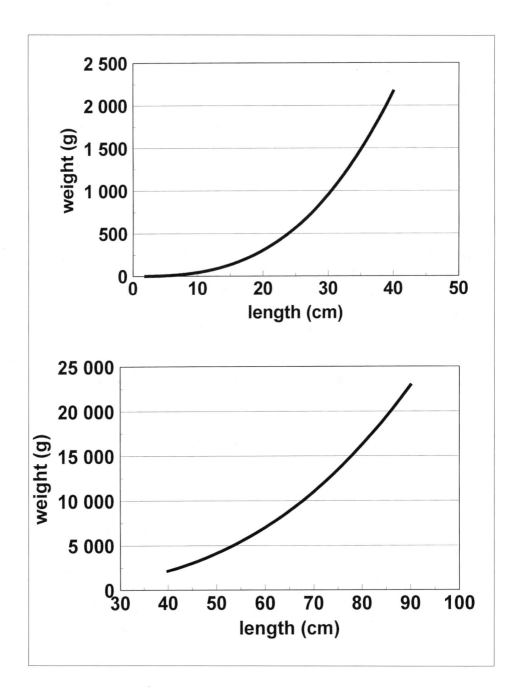

FIGURE 8.2

The length-weight relationship for juvenile and adult tambaqui.

(Based on data from Carvalho 1981 and Isaac and Ruffino 1996.)

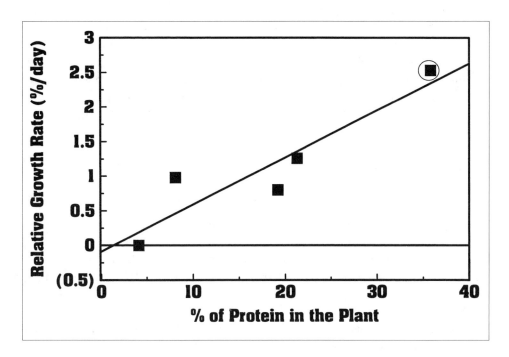

FIGURE 8.3

Dependence of the relative growth rate on the relative amount of protein in the diet
($r = 0.9$; $p < 0.05$). Data points indicated by squares consisted of pure plant material (*Hevea brasiliensis, Pseudobombax munguba, Oryza* spp., and *Cecropia* spp.). The square-in-circle data point was a balanced diet of 25% fish meal and various flour mixtures.
(Source: Rouback and Saint-Paul 1994)

These ephemeral temperature drops, however, are local and do not significantly affect the growth rates of central Amazon tambaqui populations. On the other hand, relative growth rate increases steadily with temperature. At 25°C the average growth rate of juvenile tambaqui reared in tanks is 0.8–1.4%/day, and at 29°C it reaches 4.2%/day.

Growth rate depends to a certain extent on the protein quantity and quality of the diet (Tacon and Cowey 1985) (figure 8.3). Tambaqui juveniles in a controlled study, for example, did not grow on a diet of 4% plant protein, based on *Cecropia* seeds at quantities of 4% of body weight/day. With foods richer in protein, they grew at 0.8–1.6% of body weight/day (Roubach 1992). The above experiments suggest that growth in the wild would also depend heavily on both the quality and quantity of food available.

Bayley (1988) checked for the effects of food availability on the growth rates of juvenile fish in Amazon River floodplain water bodies. The rate of rise of the annual floods seemed to be the principal factor that led to increased growth rates. Isaac and Ruffino (1996), however, found that growth is higher at the beginning of the flood and during the high-water months; during the low-water period, growth rate is slower. The cause is probably the reduced availability of food, especially seeds, as revealed by mean stomach fullness (see table 5.1). Saint-Paul (1984b) reported that during the low-water season, mean fullness of gut drops to half of its maximum value during the floods. Further evidence of the effect of food scarcity during the low-water period is reduced fish weight. Fish of the same length are 5–30% heavier during the flood season compared with their weights during the low-water period (Saint-Paul 1984b; Isaac and Ruffino 1996; also this study).

RESPIRATION

Like most fishes, the tambaqui uses oxygen removed from the water. The first ten to fourteen days of life are spent in oxygen-rich river channels. During its early larval development the tambaqui absorbs oxygen through its epidermis. At this time blood circulation in the yolk and body trunk is moderate, a condition suggesting that oxygen deprivation is not a problem in river channels. Gills become functional only when the fish reach their first feeding size, at which time they have entered the floodplain lakes.

Concentrations of dissolved oxygen are highly variable in floodplain water bodies during the course of the year. Levels often fall to below 1 mg/l for weeks and even months in some areas. In these waters juvenile and adult tambaqui show morphological, physiological, and behavioral adaptations in response to long-term low-oxygen levels.

Low availability of oxygen is known to limit food consumption and growth performance, even when food is abundant (Hayashi and Zuim 1981; Jobling 1994). In temperate-latitude ecosystems, fish growth is compromised when oxygen concentration in the water reaches the critical level of about 5 mg/l (Brett 1979). Below this level, growth rates and the efficiency of food conversion decrease. Many tropical species can use oxygen concentrated at the surface (Junk et al. 1983). The tambaqui is known to do so.

The gill area of the tambaqui is moderately sized when compared with that of other fish species (Gray 1954; Saint-Paul 1984a). The total gill area increases thirty-three times from 300-g to 20-kg fish. Given that oxygen consumption for growth and metabolism increases only four to ten times in the same size range, the respiration area does not appear to limit growth rate. Saint-Paul (1984a) found that tambaqui start to show the effects of hypoxia at oxygen concentrations of 2 mg/l. During short-term hypoxia, and at oxygen concentrations above 0.5 mg/l, the tambaqui increases the ventilation rate to increase gas exchange. At concentrations below 0.5 mg/l, the tambaqui enters what might be called "aquatic surface respiration" mode. The lower lip, which is naturally large and fleshy, becomes even more swollen, and this condition is thought to be an adaptation for channeling more oxygen-rich surface water into the mouth (Braun 1983). The deformed lip is an edema of the hypodermis and has a mechanical respiratory function. Although the surface film is rich in oxygen, it is also thin, and the fish must be precise in col-

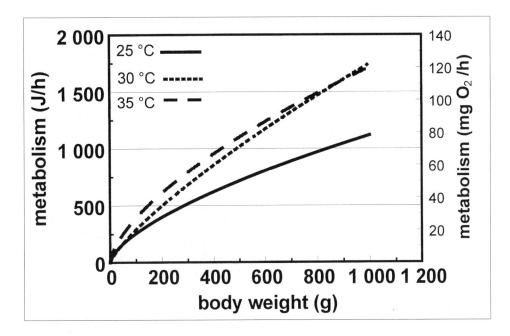

FIGURE 8.4
Routine metabolism of tambaqui.
(Data from Saint-Paul 1983.)

lecting the water that it pumps into its gills. The lower lip can change shape in a
few hours. When better oxygen conditions return, the lip assumes its normal shape
(Braun 1983). During long seasonal periods of low oxygen availability, tambaqui
can also improve their respiratory efficiency by increasing the hemoglobin concentration and number of erythrocytes in the blood (Saint-Paul 1984c).

METABOLISM

Metabolism measurements provide data for studying the energy budget of an animal. Estimates of the routine metabolism of the tambaqui have been made in tanks
with various water temperatures (Saint-Paul 1983). Routine metabolism, mostly a
function of size, is measured when activity is low to moderate and the animal is
not expending energy for food processing. At equivalent temperatures, routine
metabolism in tanks and in the wild are approximately the same (Saint-Paul 1983).

The routine metabolism of the tambaqui increases until the water temperature
reaches 30°C (figure 8.4). Even at 35°C, the metabolic rate is very close to this maximum for fish 2.5–40 cm in length (Saint-Paul 1983). Smaller fish have higher relative metabolic costs than larger individuals. For example, a tambaqui weighing 1
kg is thirty-three times heavier than a 30-g fish but needs only ten times the energy
the juvenile uses to satisfy routine metabolic costs.

Saint-Paul (1988) has shown that tambaqui metabolism is lower at night than during the daytime. In tanks, tambaqui appear to be most active in the morning. Routine metabolism also drops at low oxygen concentrations. At dissolved oxygen levels below 2 mg/l at 30°C water temperature, tambaqui begin to reduce their metabolic rate. The fish thus reduce their oxygen consumption exponentially. At oxygen levels of 0.5 mg/l tambaqui begin to show behavioral responses to hypoxia, and routine metabolism is reduced to 40% of its normal level.

The active and feeding metabolisms of tambaqui are unknown, but we can glean approximations from the literature (Gray 1954; Holeton and Stevens 1978; Brett and Groves 1979; Caulton 1982; Saldaña and Venables 1983; Wootton 1985; Priede 1985; Jobling 1994; Val and Almeida Val 1995). The feeding metabolism depends largely on food quality and ration and usually averages 1.7 times the routine metabolism. The active metabolism varies with fish activity and swimming performance. Depending on the fish's activity, it can reach 1.3–8 times the routine metabolism. The active metabolism of *Triportheus angulatus,* another characin, is two times higher than its routine metabolism when it is swimming at four body lengths per second (Holeton and Stevens 1978). The tambaqui has a relatively modest gill area for oxygen absorption; thus, it is probably not a particularly active species. Therefore, we may conservatively assume that its active metabolism is three times greater than its routine metabolism.

DAILY RATION AND AN APPROXIMATE ENERGY BUDGET

We do not have data on energy loss through feces, but such loss is usually 20–50% for other fish species (Brett and Groves 1979; Jobling 1994). Considering the general metabolic demands mentioned above and the assimilation efficiency of food, we estimate that a one-year-old tambaqui (300 g) requires daily rations of 3.7–5.0% of its body weight. Young adults (6.3 kg) and nine-year-old adults (20 kg) require average daily rations of 0.4–0.5% and 0.3–0.4%, respectively, of their body weights.

Based on the data available, a rough first approximation of the energy budget of the tambaqui can be made. During the first year of life 62% of the energy assimilated is used for growth; metabolism uses 38% (figure 8.5). Four- to nine-year-old fish use less than 22% of their energy for growth and less than 6% for reproduction. Investments in growth and reproduction would reach a maximum of 37% and 11%, respectively, if only the measured metabolism (routine) were considered. The actual value is probably intermediate. Metabolism uses a relatively large percentage of the energy intake of an adult tambaqui, probably because of high water temperatures in the Amazon and the large size of the fish. Annual investments for reproduction are lower for the tambaqui than for many fish species that have been studied (Brett and Groves 1979; Wootton 1985; Dabrowski 1985). When considered on a seasonal basis, however, the reproductive energy costs are relatively high.

The tambaqui appears to modulate the use of its body-energy reserves and

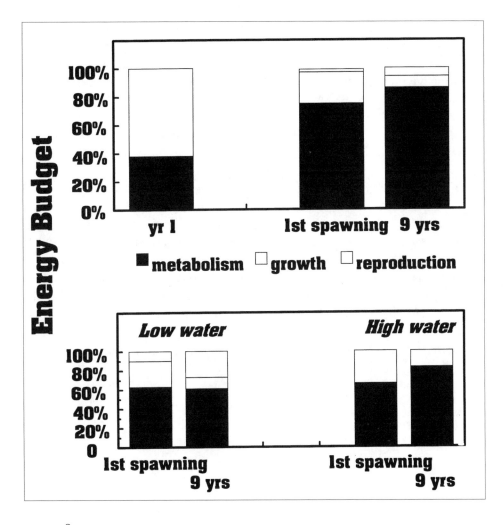

FIGURE 8.5

A first approximation of the annual energy budget of tambaqui. Growth is fastest during the high-water period, and reproductive costs are highest during the low-water period.

nutrients between the high- and low-water periods. Energy is accumulated during the high-water season and then drawn on for body maintenance and gonadal development during the low-water period. Gonadal development uses up to 10% of the energy assimilated by a four-year-old adult during the low-water season; for nine-year-old adults it can be as high as 27%. During the low-water period the tambaqui must rely on body reserves since less food is available. For example, the 20,000 kJ of energy accumulated as fat in a 6.3-kg fish at its first year of maturity is enough to supply the lipids needed for the development of the gonads. Eggs are approximately 40% protein. Egg protein is probably derived from muscles and seasonal foods ingested by the adults. Small adults use up fat reserves more quickly than older fish. After spawning, only 0.2% of the body weight of a 6-kg adult is fat.

In comparison, more than 2.0% of the body weight of a 20-kg fish can be fat. These data suggest that young adults are subject to greater food stress than older individuals. Finally, the amount of energy that can be stored in the body limits the reproductive investment for young adults. Because older fish store more energy, they are able to invest more in egg production.

BIOMASS

Bayley (1983, 1988) carried out biomass experiments for Amazonian fish in the wild in the floodplain areas of the Amazon River near Manaus. Bayley used a small net to sample fish communities. His samples consisted mostly of juveniles and species of relatively small size. Juvenile tambaqui represented nearly 1% (0.9%) of the total biomass captured. This estimate must be considered the minimum tambaqui biomass present. The tambaqui is one of the largest fish species found in Amazon River floodplain waters, and size classes larger than 2.0 kg could not be captured with the small net Bayley used. The total tambaqui biomass in muddy-river floodplains along much of the Amazon River is probably 2–3% of the total fish present, or at least it was before overfishing became a problem.

CHAPTER NINE

TAMBAQUI FISHERIES

The tambaqui has probably been a popular food fish for as long as people have been in the Amazon. Although Indians did not have metal hooks, metal-tipped harpoons, or gill nets, they were undoubtedly capable of killing large tambaqui. Archaeologist Ana Roosevelt has found tambaqui remains in ancient Indian sites along the Amazon River (personal communication). Wooden spears and bow and arrow were probably the two main methods Indians used to take large tambaqui, as this fishing gear was widely used at the time of the arrival of Europeans.

As stated in chapter 2, the first mention of the tambaqui appears in the 1699 chronicles of the German Jesuit João Filippe Betendorf. The priest arrived in the Amazon in 1661 and was soon dispatched to establish a mission in the Rio Tapajós region (Betendorf 1901; Hemming 1978). Betendorf also had contact with Jesuits who were sent to explore and proselytize in the Rio Madeira region. Commenting on the exploration of the Rio Madeira, and specifically on the Iruriz tribe, Betendorf wrote that "there are various kinds of fish available to them, such as manatee [sic] and piraíba catfish, but that the Indians do not eat them. Instead they sustain themselves on a kind of fish they call tambaquiz [sic], which are very delicious."

A century later the Portuguese explorer Alexandre Rodrigues Ferreira indicated that the tambaqui was a food fish, though he commented in his notes that it was very spiny (Ferreira 1972). The Bavarian naturalists Johann Baptist von Spix and Carl Friedrich Philipp von Martius traveled widely in the Amazon in the late 1810s and recorded various observations of indigenous fishing. For reasons that are not clear the tambaqui was not listed as a food fish exploited by Indians at this time (Spix and Martius 1823). Agassiz (1829) later described the fishes collected by Spix, but the tambaqui was not among them. Agassiz, however, was undoubtedly aware of Cuvier's (1818) description of the fishes, including the tambaqui, collected by Alexandre Rodrigues Ferreira. By the 1850s the tambaqui was being exploited regularly, as Alfred Russel Wallace (1853) mentioned eating it with the local peoples

FIGURE 9.1
José Veríssimo, the first
person to write something
substantial about the tambaqui.

in a floodplain area near Manaus. By the turn of the century, with the Amazon rubber boom in full swing and Manaus and other towns growing, the tambaqui
became one of the most important food fishes.

In 1895 José Veríssimo, who was a native of Óbidos on the middle Rio
Amazonas, and who was to become one of Brazil's outstanding scholars of the
period, published a book called *A Pesca na Amazônia* (*Fishing in the Amazon*) (figure
9.1). Veríssimo (1895, 1970) was the first to synthesize in writing the economic and
historical importance of fish in the Amazon region, and the need to manage fisheries. That a literary scholar should write a book on Amazonian fisheries is in itself
an admirable feat, especially at the turn of the last century. One of his chapters is
titled "Small Fisheries," and it is highly revealing of the tambaqui. After discussing
the importance of flooded forests as a seasonal refuge for fish, Veríssimo stated the
following:

> Of the small fisheries, that of the tambaqui comes in first place. The tambaqui is large,
> fleshy and delicious. It reaches 50–60 centimeters, with a maximum height of 22–30 cen-
> timeters. During the months of the main floods, which are July and August in the upper

Amazon and August to September in the Lower Amazon, tambaqui are very fat and greatly desired. Tambaqui fat is also used to make lighting and cooking oil. It is fished in considerable quantities in lakes and channels during those months, and is prepared not only fresh but also dried or smoked. Conserved in this way, we found it for sale in village shops. According to local opinion it also makes the best piracuí [fish flour]. Its abundance during this period is so great that it is almost without value, as fishermen arrive in Manaus with canoes full of the fish; after selling it at a minimum price, the rest is given to prisoners in the local jail.

Veríssimo then goes on to describe how the tambaqui is fished:

There are various skilled ways that it is fished. Other than commonly used gear such as nets, line, cast net, weirs and traps, there are also some peculiar methods for tambaqui fisheries. . . . It [the tambaqui] feeds on diverse tree and shrub fruits—catauarí, jauarí, tarebá, taquari, taquarirana—that grow in the shore areas and fruit during the floods. These are generally called tambaqui fruits. When mature the fruits detach themselves from the branches and fall, and they produce the characteristic sound of a small spherical object penetrating the water from high above. This sound alerts the fish that is waiting nearby and, with a speed peculiar to fishes, the tambaqui shoots at the fruit and swallows it. The locals take advantage of this habit to catch tambaqui. We might give some credence to stories in which exaggeration and marvel frequently stand as equals with the truth. In this case it is believed that the jaguar is the master of this type of fishery. The jaguar is said to take a position on a log at the river's margin or in a shaded recess inside the flooded forest. With the end of its tail it beats the water in order to imitate falling tambaqui fruits. When the fish rushes to this sound, the predator, with its great agility, shoots at it and will even follow it to the bottom if necessary, because the jaguar swims as if it were a fish.

Not being able to imitate the cat in every way, the native invented a type of fishing pole, to the end of which is attached a small rock or other round object made from manatee bones, instead of a hook. The water is beaten with this ball in order to imitate falling fruit. . . . A second pole is also prepared, but this one has a fish hook which is baited with the same fruit that is falling nearby. The bait is placed in the water. . . . Along with the hook is a small float to keep heavy fruits from sinking. This pole is placed on the bottom of the canoe with the hook in the water. With the gaponga—the name given to the pole with a ball—the fisherman produces the characteristic sound of falling fruit near the baited hook. The delicious but hungry tambaqui appears with its dark back at the water's surface. As the fish rapidly shoots at the fruit that does not betray the hook, it swallows it. The fisherman quickly grabs the pole and suspends the beautiful catch.

Veríssimo observed tambaqui in the late 1890s when the rubber boom was in full swing, the floodplains were once again becoming colonized subsequent to the decimation of the Indians several centuries before, and the city of Manaus was growing. The large quantities of tambaqui that Veríssimo reported in Manaus at the turn of the century were in part a reflection of the rubber boom and the growing population. By 1900 Manaus claimed approximately 50,000 inhabitants, and there was an active money economy (Burns 1965). That tambaqui fat was being used for cooking and lighting oil may have been a result of the overexploitation of turtle eggs and manatee, the two main animal sources of oil in nineteenth-century Amazonas (Smith 1979b; Best 1984).

Veríssimo implied that the size classes of tambaqui exploited at the end of the nineteenth century were 50–60 cm. He evidently thought that this was the average adult size. We now know that the average adult size, at least before heavy exploitation took place, was larger than this (Petrere Jr 1983). If these sizes were in fact the average for tambaqui exploited commercially, then young adults or subadults made up most of the catch at the time. It is possible that large tambaqui of more than 60 cm were difficult to catch with the nets, lines, weirs, and traps used in the late nineteenth century.

With the decline of the rubber economy after about 1915, Manaus entered a period of stagnation and decline until the creation of the Free Trade Zone in 1967 (Mahar 1976). The only important innovation in fisheries technology was ice, which became regularly available in the 1950s. No accurate fisheries data were collected prior to the 1970s, but local fishermen have told us that the tambaqui was an important food fish in the 1950s and 1960s. After 1967 Manaus grew rapidly, and its population exceeded 600,000 inhabitants by 1980 (IBGE 1992). Accompanying this growth was an explosive expansion of the until then relatively underexploited fisheries. Manaus's population exceeded 1 million in the late 1980s. In 1996 the estimated population was about 1.5 million.

In response to large-scale development projects and scientific interest in the 1970s, the military government of Brazil began to increase funding for the National Institute of Amazonian Research (INPA) in Manaus. One of the principal aims of INPA was to study the aquatic resources so that they could be managed and developed. During the latter half of the 1970s, the Manaus, Itacoatiara, and Porto Velho fish markets were investigated as part of INPA's effort.

Petrere Jr's (1978a) studies of the Manaus market showed that the tambaqui was by far the most important species being exploited in the central Amazon in the mid-1970s. In 1976 it accounted for 44% of all fish landings recorded in Manaus. Nutritional studies of various neighborhoods in Manaus showed that the average per capita consumption of fish was in excess of 150 g/day (Giugliano et al. 1978). This statistic was startling because it demonstrated quantitatively that the average citizen in Manaus was more than sufficiently supplied with animal protein. One species—the tambaqui—accounted for an extraordinary amount of this animal protein. Petrere Jr's (1978a) data revealed that most of the tambaqui catch was taken with gill nets. Other than gill-net technology, a reliable supply of ice was the main technological factor that allowed Manaus fishermen to focus their efforts on the tambaqui.

By the mid-1970s there were approximately five hundred fishing boats in the Manaus fleet with iceboxes, though most of these were of less than 2 tons. In the central Amazon, the ice-to-fish ratio is approximately 2:1. With ice and larger boats, Manaus fishermen could travel as far as 1,500 km in search of new stocks of tambaqui. By the end of the 1970s the Manaus fishing fleet was exploiting tambaqui in the lower and middle Rio Madeira, nearly all of the middle and upper Amazon River in Brazil, the lower and middle Rio Purus, and the Rio Juruá. The Manaus

TABLE 9.1

Per Kilogram Prices ($US) of Tambaqui for Various Markets

Market	Type	JUVENILES			ADULTS		
		Average	Minimum	Maximum	Average	Minimum	Maximum
Manaus	fresh	2.00	0.50	4.32	2.57	1.05	6.80
Adolpho Lisboa	fresh	2.20	1.21	4.32	2.60	1.44	4.26
Panair	fresh	2.40	1.00	3.00	3.40	1.75	6.80
Feira livre	fresh	1.82	1.40	2.90	2.34	1.05	4.07
São Jorge	fresh	1.43	0.50	1.90			
Alvorada II	fresh	2.14	1.00	3.90			
Walter Rayol	fresh	2.01	1.34	3.24	2.32	1.39	3.64
Senador Cunha Melo	fresh				2.16	1.09	3.14
Japiimlandia	fresh	2.07	1.23	3.01			
Cajual	fresh	1.41	0.67	2.13			
Coroado II	fresh	2.86	1.44	3.60	3.04	1.09	5.73
São José II	fresh	1.63	1.08	2.12	2.14	1.29	2.88
Rio de Janeiro	fresh	2.01					
Casas Sendas	fresh	2.41					
Casas Sendas	live	4.22					
Carrefour	fresh	1.60					
Northeast Brazil	fresh	1.43					
Colombia							
Street markets	fresh	1.60					
Panama							
No name	fresh	2.16	1.97	2.34			
No name	live	4.69					
Peru							
Iquitos	fresh	3.09					

fleet began to compete with fishermen based in smaller towns. This might explain why the tambaqui was relatively unimportant in smaller towns, such as Itacoatiara on the middle Rio Amazonas (Smith 1979a, 1981).

The upper Rio Madeira basin is the farthest region from Manaus where there is an active tambaqui fishery. In the 1970s the tambaqui was one of the ten most important species captured for the Porto Velho market (Goulding 1979, 1981). Fishermen had also begun to exploit populations of tambaqui in the Rio Mamoré, Rio Guaporé, and Rio Beni (Bolivia), all of which are headwaters of the Rio Madeira. In the 1980s the tambaqui was reported to be either one of or the most important species captured for the Porto Velho market based on the middle and upper Rio Madeira (Santos 1986; Boischio 1992). The tambaqui, or gamitana as it is called locally, is of less importance in Peru (Eckmann 1985; Guerra Flores et al. 1990).

TECHNOLOGY OF TAMBAQUI FISHING

The gear used in tambaqui fishing is a combination of modern and traditional. Because the tambaqui is migratory and lives in floodplain and river-channel waters, no single gear is satisfactory for all habitats. Within the last two decades traditional gear has greatly declined in importance because of the widespread introduction of various kinds of nets made from synthetic materials. The knowledge used to find the tambaqui at different times of the year, however, is largely based on traditional oral-natural-history folklore.

Gill nets have been used in the Amazon since the nineteenth century, but their importance until the 1960s was minimal because of the expense of purchasing or making them. In Amazonian waters piranhas also cause much damage to gill nets, thus increasing the expense of using this method. Portuguese fishermen evidently began to use gill nets commercially in the Manaus area in the 1930s, mostly for large tambaqui caught in flooded forests. At that time gill nets were made mostly from cotton line. By the mid-1970s gill nets, or various types of synthetic line to make them, became readily available in Manaus (figure 9.2). Gill-net technology spread rapidly, and by 1980 fishermen and riparian peasants throughout the central Amazon were using this gear. Gill nets are now one of the most commonly seen food-procurement technologies in floodplain settlements.

Gill nets are used mostly in quiet waters. Drifting deep-water gill nets are used in the river channels, but they are employed mostly for catfishes and are not effective for capturing tambaqui. Some fishermen use seinelike nets with large mesh that can function like gill nets, circling the fish when they are migrating in the river channels and trapping them when they try to escape.

Most gill-net fishing for large tambaqui takes place in flooded forests. The gill net was the first gear, other than explosives—which have also been widely used—that enabled fishermen to catch large numbers of fish in flooded forests. In general fish become widely dispersed in floodplain forests during the four- to six-month

FIGURE 9.2
Construction of a tambaqui gill net.

high-water period each year. Because of its fruit- and seed-eating behavior, the tambaqui becomes more concentrated than most fish species in the flooded forests. Fishermen know what fruits and seeds the fish are feeding on in a particular area. Gill nets are placed near the tree sources of these foods. For example, when rubber-tree capsules are exploding and hurling their seeds into the water, fishermen can be fairly sure that tambaqui will be feeding in this area.

Gill nets used in flooded forests for large tambaqui range in length from 25 to 50 m (figure 9.3). An individual commercial fisherman might use up to thirty nets spread over several kilometers of flooded forest. The nets are usually stretched between tree saplings or vines. The flexibility of these plants gives the gill net "play" when a large fish is enmeshed and trying to escape. This prevents the fish from breaking the line, as might happen when fishing with a pole and reel.

Manaus fish market data for the mid-1970s clearly reveal the effectiveness of gill nets in capturing tambaqui in flooded forests (Petrere Jr 1978a). Tambaqui alone accounted for 95% of the total gill-net catches recorded for Manaus. The monthly distribution of these catches suggests that at least 70% of the tambaqui had to have been taken in flooded forests, as this is the only habitat where these fish are found in large quantities during the floods.

In the 1980s fishermen began to decrease the mesh size to catch smaller tambaqui. Lake populations, which consist mostly of fish under 30 cm, were heavily attacked during the low-water period with gill nets ranging in mesh size from

FIGURE 9.3

Capturing tambaqui with gill net in flooded forest.

about 10 to 15 cm. The large quantities of juvenile tambaqui now seen in Amazonian markets are captured mostly with gill nets. The average yield of the Manaus fleet dropped from more than 80 kg/fisherman/day in the early 1980s to 40 kg/fisherman/day in the mid-1980s (Merona and Bittencourt 1988). In the Santarém region gill nets account for 70% of the tambaqui catch. The average yield in the middle Rio Amazonas region in 1995 was 15–48 kg/fisherman/day (Isaac and Ruffino 1996).

Lampara and beach seines are common gear in Amazonian fisheries. A lampara seine is a type of pull-net used to encircle a school of fish. Once the fish are encircled, the net is pulled together by lines on either end. A large bag is formed, and the fish are unable to escape. A beach seine is similar in construction but much longer. Manaus fishermen sometimes use beach seines as long as 300 m. Seines can be used during either the high- or the low-water period. The tambaqui, however, does not migrate during the high-water period, and seines are of no use in flooded forests.

During the low-water period and at the beginning of rising water, tambaqui schools are encountered in muddy-river channels. Smaller groups can also be found in wooded shore areas. Lampara seines are used for these small groups. Fishermen will often use motorized canoes to scare fish from woody areas to open waters where they can be seined. When large schools are migrating upstream, especially at the beginning of rising waters in preparation for spawning, fishermen can attempt to encircle a school when it moves along a beach area. The unobstructed nature of beaches allows the long seines to be pulled ashore, and fish are much easier to capture than in midstream.

In the 1970s fishermen reported catching up to 10 tons of tambaqui, or perhaps 700–800 individuals, in one beach haul with a seine. This is the only indication we have of the minimum known size of tambaqui schools migrating in river channels. Schools are probably much larger than this, as only a portion of them can be captured.

A trotline is a line ten to several hundred meters in length to which are attached a series of shorter lines. Only the shorter lines have hooks. In Amazonian fisheries trotlines are used mostly in river channels and flooded forests. Trotlines used in river-channel fisheries have a weight on the end to carry the hooks to the bottom. Large tambaqui are found mostly in river channels during the low-water period, and they are difficult to catch at this time of year with trotlines, probably because of reduced feeding. Adult tambaqui, unlike the predaceous catfishes captured in river-channel fisheries, do not actively seek food during the low-water period.

Trotlines are effective for catching large tambaqui in flooded forests. The flooded-forest trotline is usually 10–30 m long and has five to ten hooks. These devices are stretched between saplings or vines, and the hooks are baited with the same fruit or seed species that are falling into the water where the lines are stretched. The favorite species are rubber-tree seeds and jauari palm fruits, though many more are also used (Smith 1979a, 1981). After the flooded forest's main fruiting season, crabs and mollusks are also used as bait. In the mid-1970s tambaqui accounted for 96% of the fish captured with trotlines for the Manaus market (Petrere Jr 1978b).

The pole and line is seldom used to catch large tambaqui. Smaller size classes, or the so-called ruelos and bocós, are commonly captured in flooded forests with fruit- or seed-baited hooks. The gaponga device, described earlier in this chapter, is employed to imitate falling fruits and seeds to lure tambaqui to the baited hook of the fishing pole.

The harpoon in Amazonian fisheries is used mostly for killing the pirarucu (*Arapaima gigas*). Skilled harpoon fishermen can also spear tambaqui surfacing to take fruits and seeds in the flooded forests. Harpooning was widely practiced before gill nets became available and also when large tambaqui were still abundant (Magalhães 1931). In the mid-1970s the tambaqui was the second most important species taken with harpoons for the Manaus market, though it was far behind the pirarucu, each representing about 11% and 87%, respectively, of the total catch taken with this gear (Petrere Jr 1978b).

ESTIMATES OF ANNUAL TAMBAQUI CATCHES

Tambaqui catches have been recorded for three cities along the Amazon River and for Porto Velho on the upper Rio Madeira in the state of Rondonia (figure 9.4). The

FIGURE 9.4

Main urban markets in the Amazon Basin where the tambaqui is sold.

Manaus fishing fleet captures more tambaqui than all other Amazonian towns and cities combined because of its large fishing fleet, the historical popularity of the species in the city, and attractive market prices.

Manaus is the largest fish market in the Amazon Basin based on freshwater species (figures 9.5). Quantitative sampling of the Manaus market began in 1975 under the direction of Miguel Petrere Jr and the Fish Division of INPA (Petrere Jr 1978a, 1978b). At the time of the first studies in the mid-1970s, all large fish markets in Manaus were located on the Rio Negro riverfront. In 1975 Manaus had a population of approximately 450,000. In the period from July 1977 to June 1978, Petrere Jr was able to build a huge and pioneering database on Manaus landings, species, effort, size classes, and other data. These data represent the only quantitative view of central Amazon fisheries in what might be called the pre–heavy exploitation period. All studies now and in the future will undoubtedly use Petrere Jr's data as a baseline.

Manaus has nearly tripled in population since 1975, and the urban geography of the city has expanded greatly. Fish markets have become more spread out, and waterfront activity no longer dominates the retail end of the business. There are now at least forty street markets and several dozen supermarkets and freezer businesses selling fish in Manaus. Fishing boats, as well as the freight and passenger boats that are used to transport catches from cities along the middle and upper

FIGURE 9.5
Two- to three-year-old tambaqui being sold on the Manaus waterfront.

Amazon River in Brazil, the Rio Purus, and the Rio Madeira, supply the Manaus markets. Manaus buyers operating from freight and passenger boats pay higher prices than those offered in the smaller cities and towns, so local fishermen sell their catches to the Manaus buyers.

The most striking statistic revealed by Petrere Jr's (1978a) studies was the overwhelming importance of the tambaqui in Manaus's total catch. This species alone represented more than 40% of all fish sold in the Manaus market. The largest annual catch recorded was in 1976, in which 13,314 tons of tambaqui were sold in Manaus. Catches fell in 1977 to 9,030 tons and in 1978 to 8,217 tons (Petrere Jr 1983). The fishing effort was also measured for the tambaqui fisheries at this time. In retrospect, Petrere Jr's study appears to have been coincidental with an explosive growth in the fishing effort aimed at the tambaqui. Using the number of tambaqui fishing trips as a measure of effort, there was an overall decline in catch per unit of effort from 1976 to 1978.

As mentioned earlier, nearly all of the tambaqui catch in the 1970s consisted of adult fish. In the Manaus market these fish averaged about 9.0–15 kg (Petrere Jr 1978a). Because measurements were not made of the tambaqui in the Manaus market in the 1980s, it is not possible to pinpoint the year or years when the fishing effort switched from adults captured in flooded forests and river channels to immature fish taken in floodplain lakes. Our personal observations suggest that there was not a "crash" in adult tambaqui populations, but rather that adult catches declined steadily throughout the 1980s. Fishermen turned to immature

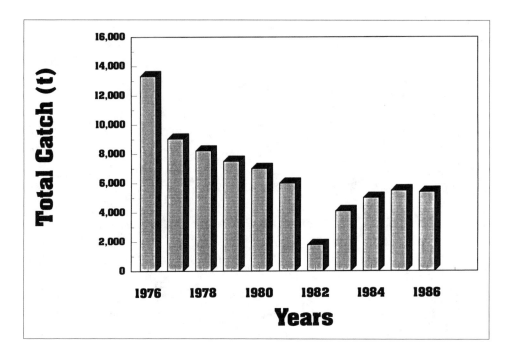

FIGURE 9.6

Annual catch of tambaqui in the Manaus market between 1976 and 1986.
(Data from Petrere Jr 1985 and Merona and Bittencourt 1988.)

tambaqui, but the total catches of these smaller-size classes have never reached the peaks recorded for adults in the 1970s (figure 9.6). Merona and Bittencourt (1988) reported that tambaqui catches in the Manaus market ranged from 4,000 to 6,000 tons between 1979 and 1986 and that the species dropped to second place behind jaraqui (*Semaprochilodus* spp.).

In 1995 Tefé, a city located on the middle Rio Solimões (upper Amazon River of Brazil), had a population of about 30,000. The Tefé region is now being intensively studied as part of a program to protect the largest floodplain reserve in the Amazon (J. Ayres 1993; D. Ayres 1994). The Mamirauá Ecological Reserve is an 11,000-km^2 area embracing the delta of the lower Rio Japurá and the contiguous Rio Solimões (Amazon River) floodplain, which is just upriver of Tefé. The state of Amazonas created the reserve in 1990. Ronaldo Barthem of the Goeldi Museum has collected fisheries data in the Tefé market to assess the resource base and economic pressures affecting the Mamirauá Ecological Reserve.

The average annual catch of the Tefé market is about 2,000 tons, of which young tambaqui represent about 20% (Barthem forthcoming). Most of the large tambaqui delivered to Tefé are sent to Manaus in passenger boats because of the higher prices paid in the capital. There are few historical data for the Tefé fisheries, though the second author lived in the area in 1973. At that time only large tambaqui (12–20 kg and >60 cm) were being captured for the Tefé market, and they were selling for less than the equivalent of $3.00 for the entire fish. Pinheiro (1985) reported that the average tambaqui sizes in the Tefé area in the 1980–1984 period ranged from 50 to 65 cm. Barthem's recent data show that only 11% of the tambaqui sold in Tefé are now larger than 55 cm. Young tambaqui sold in the Tefé market are captured in nearby floodplain lakes, including those of the Mamirauá Ecological Reserve, and the average size is 39 cm.

With 300,000 inhabitants, Santarém is the second largest city in the state of Pará. It is located at the confluence of the Rio Tapajós and the Amazon River. Most of the commercial fishing sustaining Santarém takes place in the floodplain lakes of the Amazon River. Annual catches are about 3,700 tons. The tambaqui is among the ten most important commercial species, though catches have declined in recent years. Ruffino and Isaac (1994) have shown that at least 90% of the tambaqui catch from the Rio Amazonas near Santarém consists of immature fish.

Porto Velho is the main market for the middle and upper Rio Madeira fisheries. This market was first studied in the 1977–1979 period. During that period the tambaqui was the sixth most important species, and adult fish accounted for more than 95% of the total catch of tambaqui (Goulding 1979, 1981). The Porto Velho fishing cooperative, known as the Colônia de Pescadores Z-1, has historically been one of the most effective groups in the Amazon in collecting fish data. The cooperative collects data mostly for taxation purposes, though catches by species are also recorded. Boischio (1992) reviewed the Porto Velho data for the 1984–1989 period and found that the tambaqui was the most important species recorded by the cooperative. Goulding's (1979, 1981) data included catfish catches sold to freezer plants in Porto Velho, and that data showed the dourada (*Brachyplatystoma filamentosum*) the most important species during the late 1970s. Gold-mining operations in the Rio Madeira during the 1980s appear to have reduced the importance of the dourada catfish, which many people thought had become contaminated with mercury. This may in part explain why the tambaqui was more heavily attacked in the Rio Madeira in the 1980s.

By 1984 the total Porto Velho catches of tambaqui more than doubled from the late 1970s average. During the entire period two seasonal peaks could be detected. The largest catches were taken at the beginning of the floods, that is, during the spawning period when adults are in the river channel. The second peak was during May, June, and July, when the river level was rapidly falling. We suspect that these catches were mostly immature fish captured in floodplain lakes. By the late 1980s tambaqui catches in the middle and upper Rio Madeira had begun to decline from the 1987 peak year (310 tons).

TAMBAQUI PRICES

Since July 1993 we and Efrem Ferreira of INPA have collected weekly data on tambaqui prices in various markets in Manaus (figure 9.7). Adult tambaqui are the

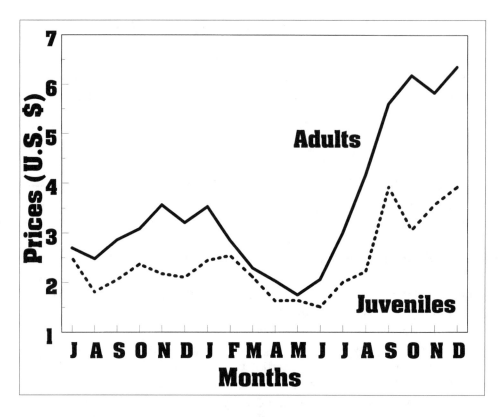

FIGURE 9.7

Average US$ prices of tambaqui in Manaus from July 1993 to December 1994.

most expensive fish sold in Manaus. Mid-1990 prices varied between about $5.00 and $8.75/kg for fish larger than 50 cm. In May 1995 large individuals (20–22 kg) were selling for at least $100, though these sizes are relatively rare. As mentioned earlier, most of the catch is now made up of juveniles less than 40 cm in length (figure 9.8). Between July 1993 and May 1994 the average price paid for juveniles was about $2.60/kg.

Fishermen receive about one third of the retail value of the fish they catch. In May 1994 the Brazilian government greatly strengthened its currency and renamed it the real. The stabilization of the real led to a sharp increase in fish as well as other food prices in Manaus. In October 1995 juvenile tambaqui of 20–40 cm were selling for $4.00–5.00/kg. Despite the high prices, demand remains high for tambaqui. Tambaqui raised in fish culture are now cheaper than those sold on the Manaus market.

FIGURE 9.8
Juvenile tambaqui are
now being heavily
exploited along the
Amazon River, and little
has been done to control
this exploitation.

CHAPTER TEN

INDUCED SPAWNING AND FRY CULTURE

Brazilian interest in fish culture since the 1930s has resulted in important technological innovations (Bardach et al. 1972; Silva and Gurgel 1989). Geographically,
these innovations have been inversely proportional to the aquatic resources and
fish diversity present. Poor areas with little water, especially in northeastern Brazil,
were the first to develop fish culture on a significant scale. The northeast, well
known for its periodic droughts and food-shortage problems, needed protein-pro-
duction systems since the local rivers, with the exception of the highly modified
Rio São Francisco, are too small to support commercial fisheries of any significant
scale. Most effort was focused on reservoirs fed by small streams. Several
Amazonian species, such as tucunarés (*Cichla spp.*), pirarucu (*Arapaima gigas*), and
oscar cichlids (*Astronotus ocellatus*), were imported to the northeast in the 1930s and
1940s. The tambaqui was not included among these early experimental species,
though in the 1930s it was recommended by the famous Brazilian zoologist
Rodolpho von Ihering (Silva and Gurgel 1989). Most attention focused on predators because they were thought to be better tasting and would command higher
market prices. Exotic species, such as *Tilapia* and common carp, also received much
attention.

In 1966, in the northeastern state of Ceará, the "Valdemar C. de França"
Aquaculture Station of the late National Department of Works Against Droughts
(DNOCS) obtained twenty-four tambaqui shipped from Manaus. The DNOCS's
researchers considered the possibility of introducing the species in northeastern
dam reservoirs and rivers. In 1974 the cultured stock was transferred to the Unit of
Intensive Aquaculture Station (UEPI) in Pentecoste, Ceará. The imported tam-
baqui reportedly grew fast, and by 1974 they were weighing more than 7 kg (Lopes
and Fontenele 1982). These fish, however, were never used for induced spawning.
In the same year an additional seventy-four juvenile tambaqui were obtained from
Iquitos, Peru. Almost certainly, brood stocks used in northeastern and southern

Brazil were derived from the Peruvian Amazon. Colombian and Venezuelan brood stocks were derived from fish captured in the Orinoco system (Hernández 1989).

Documented feeding experiments with the Peruvian tambaqui reared in Brazil began in 1974 (Silva et al. 1974; Lovshin et al. 1974). Beginning with about two thousand fry per hectare, with an average weight of 6.0 g, these early experiments produced 2.2 tons/ha/yr. The relatively fast growth rate was encouraging.

The UEPI research group's first attempts to induce reproduction were unsuccessful. In 1977 Silva and his collaborators succeeded in reproducing tambaqui for the first time in captivity (Silva et al. 1977). Using an extract of the pituitary glands from the mud-feeding characin *Prochilodus cearensis* induced spawning. The survival rate, however, was very low (Lopes and Fontenele 1982; Silva and Gurgel 1989). By the end of the 1970s, tambaqui had also been induced to spawn in captivity in Venezuela (Bermudez and Kossowski 1979). In the 1980s fish farms in several South and Central American countries, North America, and Asia were breeding tambaqui in captivity (Silva et al. 1984; Morais Filho et al. 1983; Mendonça 1984; Moncayo et al. 1988; Hernández 1989; Castillo 1986). Most of the brood stock used in Brazil was acquired from the DNOCS's aquaculture stations.

INDUCING SPAWNING IN CAPTIVITY

As discussed in earlier chapters, the tambaqui is a migratory species, and water levels and other factors induce it to spawn in the wild. There are few reliable reports of tambaqui spawning spontaneously in captivity. A brood stock kept by the Aquaculture Station of the Lisandro Alvarado Central-West University in Venezuela reportedly spawned in two consecutive years in small tanks of only 6.0 m^2 in surface area. Spawning reportedly took place during the same period as it did locally in the wild (Kossowski et al. 1986).

For the tambaqui to be farmed successfully, it must be induced to spawn in captivity. A brood stock must be maintained and individuals chosen for spawning. This step is perhaps the most important in the whole induced-spawning process. Females should be sufficiently mature, that is, capable of producing progesterone, to have a high probability of ovulating as a result of hormonal injections (Carosfeld 1989).

Hormonal injections are used to achieve the final maturation of the oocytes, since ovulation rarely occurs in ponds without this stimulus. The most commonly used hormone is an extract from the pituitary gland (hypophysis). This extract contains the gonadotropins that are needed to stimulate the gonads (Stacey 1984; Carosfeld 1989; Bernadino et al. 1988; Bernadino and Alcântara 1988). Glands from donor fish are removed from the brain and then dried, pulverized, and dissolved in a saline or glycerin solution for use. Fresh glands can also be preserved in pure ethanol. Most glands come from carp and South American curimatá (*Prochilodus* spp.), but a wide variety of other species can be used as well. Synthetic hormones alone or mixed with pituitary extracts have also successfully induced spawning in fish. LHRH (gonadorrelin), a commonly sold gonadotropin-releasing hormone, can stimulate ovulation (Castangnolli et al. 1988; Hernández 1989). Little is yet known about the chemical pathway of this drug, though it is reportedly as efficient as pituitary extracts (Stacey 1984). Human corionic gonadotropin (HCG) is another commercially available hormone employed in a few cases to induce tambaqui to ovulate (Valencia et al. 1986; Saldaña and Ascori 1986, 1988; Rojas and Ascon-Dionisio 1988).

The techniques using pituitary extracts to stimulate tambaqui ovulation are now well established, and success rates are greater than 80% (Hernández 1989). Procedures reported from different laboratories show only slight variations in the number, frequency, and intervals of extract doses injected into brood stock (Lopes and Fontenele 1982; Alcántara and Gerra 1986). Most stations today are using only two injections of pituitary extract to induce spawning (Hernández et al. 1992).

Fish farms use a total dose of 5.5 mg of dry pituitary gland per kilogram of female tambaqui (figure 10.1). The first dose (preparatory) is only 0.5 mg/kg. The second, and final, dose is injected twelve to twenty-two hours later and consists of 5 mg/kg. Pinheiro et al. (1988) recommended an increase in the final dose when the female is heavier than 7.0 kg. The dry glands are macerated and mixed in a saline solution (0.6% NaCl) at 1 mg of pituitary gland per 0.1 ml of solution. The solution is injected from below the ventral fin and into the peritoneal cavity. Females respond to the treatment 200–300 "degree hours" later. A "degree hour" is the sum of the hourly temperatures of the water in which the fish are kept and is a good measure because of the importance of temperature on reproduction. Venezuelans are reported to use slightly higher doses of up to 6.0 mg/kg. Colombians have also successfully experimented with five doses of 1.5 mg/kg during a 72-hr period (Hernández et al. 1992).

Males are injected with two pituitary doses of 0.5 and 2.5 mg/kg. The time interval is the same as for females (Pinheiro et al. 1988). Satisfactory results have also been obtained with two equal doses of 1.0–1.5 mg/kg (Woynarovich 1988).

Spawners are normally kept in small tanks to improve handling. Some laboratories keep fish in cloth bags until the gametes are released. Water temperature should be kept stable within the range of 26–30°C. An anesthesia is sometimes used to calm the spawners at the time of gamete release. Quinaldine at a concentration of 0.5 ml/100 l of tank water is effective (Ross and Ross 1984; Woynarovich 1988). A fish weighing 7.0 kg can be hard to handle and control. To avoid the premature liberation of ovules (unfertilized eggs), some laboratories sew the genital papilla until proper ovulation time.

Fertilization is normally done through a "dry" procedure. The fish and hands of the technicians are dried to avoid any potential dripping water. The ovules are then collected in a bowl. After the collection of the ovules, the sperm is added, and the combination is mixed for a few minutes. Water is then added slowly. The water, eggs, and sperm are then kept in constant movement for five minutes. After the eggs have "hardened" from water absorption, the water is carefully changed, and the fertilized eggs are transferred to incubators.

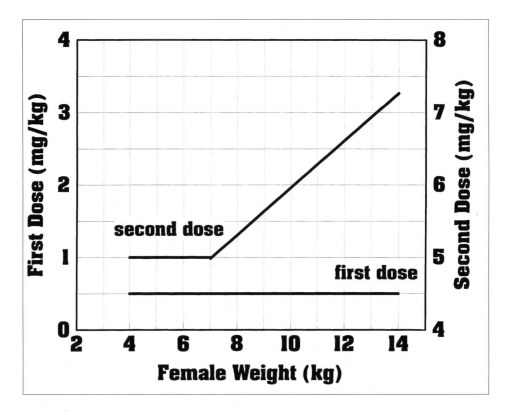

FIGURE 10.1

Pituitary dosages given to tambaqui to induce spawning in captivity (based on weights).

BROOD-STOCK MANAGEMENT

Proper brood-stock management is important to achieve successful spawning. Most laboratories keep fish in monospecific ponds at a stocking density of 50–300 g/m^2, but in some cases densities are allowed to reach 1 kg/m^2. Floating cages with 0.5–1.0 kg/m^2 have also been successfully used in Venezuela.

Tambaqui brood stock are fed daily rations averaging 2.3% of body weight; the minimum is 1.5%. The average protein content of pellets is about 28%; the minimum is 21% (figure 10.2). Unfortunately, no quantitative analysis is available on the effect of different feeding regimes on brood-stock growth and health.

Manure or chemical fertilizers added at 0.25–3.0 tons/ha/month can stimulate algae and zooplankton production in ponds. The use of snails as a protein supplement is also a common procedure. In some regions the ration is maintained at the same level throughout the year. In central and southern Brazil rations are reduced 100% during the winter (cool) months. At CODEVASF (Brazil), UCLA (Venezuela), and La Teraza (Colombia) rations are reduced 33–66% during the two to three months before spawning. This reduction simulates natural conditions.

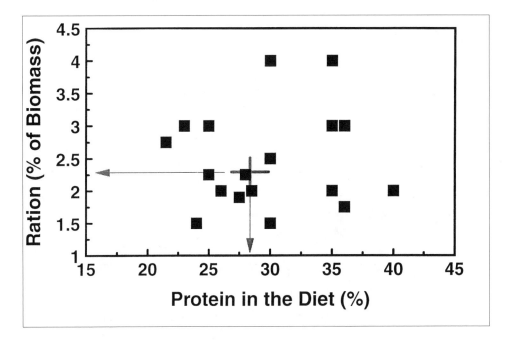

FIGURE 10.2

Size and protein content of the brood stock ration in eighteen Latin American aquacultural plants. The arrows indicate average values.

Management of feeding, stocking, and hormone treatment can result in multiple spawnings per year. Pinheiro and Silva (1988) stocked 4–7-kg brood stock at a relatively high density of 4–8 kg/m². These fish were fed pellets containing 35% protein at a daily rate of 3% of body weight. To enhance productivity in tanks, mollusks and manure from cattle, pigs, and ducks were also added on a regular basis. This feeding regime was rich in protein. By separating the mature from the immature fish and treating them separately, larvae were produced year round.

EGG INCUBATION

The fertilized eggs of tambaqui should be transferred to incubators ten minutes after fertilization. The incubators most commonly used are the Woynarovich type of 60- or 200-l capacity. Other types include square tanks with aeration and small conical vessels. The Woynarovich incubators achieve the highest stocking densities. Eggs are stocked at 0.5–3.5 g/l of water; this is equivalent to 800–6,000 eggs/l. Most laboratories use average egg densities of 2 g/l or 3,000 eggs/l (figure 10.3). At these densities the hatching success is expected to be 60–90% (Hernández et al. 1992). Egg-stocking densities above 1.5 g/l of water are difficult to manage in 60-l incubators (Zaniboni Filho 1992). At these high densities the top net of the incubator will tend to clog because of the increased flow of water needed to keep the eggs

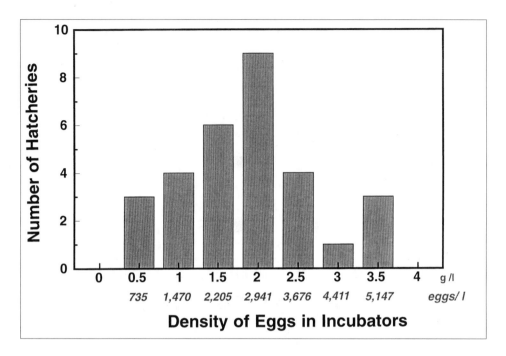

FIGURE 10.3

Stocking density of tambaqui eggs in thirty laboratories and aquaculture plants in Latin America.

afloat. Clogging can cause egg mortality rates as high as 80%. Zaniboni Filho (1992) recommends that stocking densities of 60-l incubators be less than 2,500 eggs/l.

A recent experiment found that egg incubation in concrete tanks leads to rates of hatching only marginally inferior to those reported for Woynarovich incubators (Zaniboni Filho 1992). In contrast, however, egg densities in concrete tanks must be kept at less than 160 eggs/l. Despite the necessity of stocking at lower rates, concrete tanks might be preferable because they can be put to other uses, such as serving as holding areas for fry and brood stock.

Tambaqui eggs should be incubated at 26–29°C. Temperatures above 30°C have been reported to cause heavy egg mortality (Valencia et al. 1986; Pinheiro et al. 1988). The hatching time measured since fertilization is known to decrease mostly as a function of temperature (Eliott et al. 1987; Pauly and Pullin 1988). From average temperatures of 26–29°C, incubation time decreases from eighteen to thirteen hours (figure 10.4).

CARE OF LARVAE

Newborn larvae live on yolk reserves for four to six days before they develop adaptations to feed on external items. The exact length of this period depends most

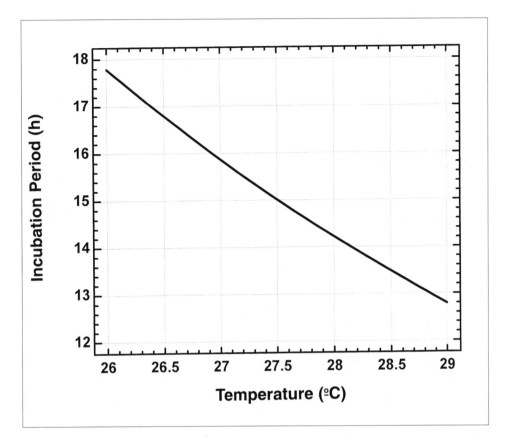

FIGURE 10.4

Duration of incubation period in relation to average water temperature.

(Sources: Silva et al. 1977; Lopes and Fontenele 1982; Woynarovich 1988; Alcántara and Gerra 1988; Valencia and Puentes 1989; Bello et al. 1989; Araujo-Lima 1994.)

often on water temperature. The initiation of external feeding is perhaps the most sensitive phase of the entire cultivation process. At this phase heavy larval mortality can occur due to predation or unsuitable food. Published survival rates for cultivated tambaqui larvae are 0–66%, though the exact causes of mortality are not always reported (Silva et al. 1977; Lopes and Fontenele 1982; Senhorini et al. 1988; Woynarovich 1988; Alcántara and Gerra 1986; Valencia and Puentes 1989; Bello et al. 1989; Zaniboni Filho 1992). For the majority of cases mortality seems to correlate most with stocking densities. High survival rates are expected with low stocking densities, which reduce competition for food and predator-prey encounter rates.

Two major procedures are used for rearing tambaqui larvae. First, post-yolk-sac larvae are kept in controlled conditions and fed intensively on nonliving food. After a few days the larvae are transferred to zooplankton-rich tanks or small ponds where the live diet is supplemented with fine-grained dry food. Second, ready-to-feed larvae are transferred directly to zooplankton-rich tanks or ponds supplemented with additional food. The first procedure seems to be the most effective (Woynarovich 1988; Pinheiro et al. 1988; Silva and Gurgel 1989; Malca 1989; Hernández et al. 1992).

Larvae kept in incubators or small concrete tanks receive some combination of micro-encapsulated egg and/or powdered-milk mixtures three to four times a day. In some cases zooplankton sieved from ponds or purchased brine shrimp (*Artemia nauplii*) are also supplied (Malca 1989; Hernández 1989). Reported stocking densities are highly variable, ranging from 100 to 2,000 ind./m^3 in tanks. After four to five days in incubators, tambaqui larvae are siphoned to buckets and transferred to recently fertilized ponds at densities of 10–700 ind./m^3. Zooplankton production must be high to supply an adequate food supply. Special care must be taken to avoid thermal shock. Early-morning hours are often the best as incubator and pond temperatures are similar.

POND TREATMENT, ZOOPLANKTON PRODUCTION, AND PREDATION

Fry ponds usually vary in size from 100 to 200 m^2. Before use, ponds should be dried out, exposed to the sun for five to seven days, treated with lime at 50–100 g/m^2, and fertilized with chicken (50–100 g/m^2) or cattle manure (100–300 g/m^2). Chemical nutrients can also be used. In the Amazon, where temperatures are high, ponds should be refilled two to four days before tambaqui larvae are placed in them; cooler areas require more time (Woynarovich 1988; Pinheiro and Silva 1988; Senhorini et al. 1988; Fim 1992). Pond fertilization with pig sewage has also been used with success (Pinheiro et al. 1988). Zaniboni Filho's (1992) data show that total larvae production in ponds improves slightly by increasing the quantity of chicken manure within the 50–228 g/m^2 range. On the other hand, the biological demand for dissolved oxygen also increases because of organic overload. Low oxygen levels can lead to high fry mortality. A balance must, therefore, be reached between the quantity of manure used and water quality.

Predators, such as dragonfly nymphs (Odonata) and small unwanted fishes, prey on tambaqui larvae. As mentioned above, ponds need to be dried out and treated with lime. If ponds are connected to surrounding waters, predators can easily recolonize. Ferraz de Lima (1989) claims that a single dragonfly nymph can destroy up to thirty-one tambaqui larvae per day. Treatment with insecticides has been tried, but the results are not encouraging (Ferraz de Lima 1989; Valencia and Puentes 1989). Zaniboni Filho (1992) also experimented with organo-phosphate insecticides (Neguvon), but these did not reduce mortality rates in ponds. We should also mention that the general tendency is to avoid insecticides in favor of mechanical means to prevent predators from colonizing ponds (Hernández et al. 1992).

LARVAL FEEDING IN CAPTIVITY

One-week-old tambaqui can reach impressive growth rates of 40%/day when feeding on zooplankton in waters at 27–28°C (Zaniboni Filho 1992). At this rate of growth, larvae double their weights every two to three days. Young captive larvae prefer to prey on small cladocerans but will also consume copepods and rotifers (Zaniboni Filho 1992). As the larvae grow, they add, if available, ostracods and chironomids to their diets. This feeding behavior is similar to that of wild larvae (see chapter 5).

Young larvae will also eat brine shrimp (*Artemia*), and satisfactory growth rates have been achieved with this food. On the other hand, diets based on rotifers produce lower growth rates (Fex de Santis 1991). Comparative studies of the efficiency of these mass-cultivated prey in relation to pond-reared Cladocera and copepods are still lacking. Twenty-day-old larvae grow equally well (10–15%/day) when fed on zooplankton diets rich in rotifers or cladocerans (Sipaúba-Tavares 1983, 1988; Zaniboni Filho 1992). At this age, however, tambaqui larvae accept dry artificial food, which can then account for an important part of the diet.

Despite optimal growth on live food, tambaqui larvae accept artificial diets early in life. Newborn larvae fed pure dry powder attain survival rates above 47% in controlled conditions (Fex de Santis 1991). Mixed diets, however, provide higher survival and growth rates.

Small particles with crude protein content as high as 40% usually characterize dry foods for larvae. Dry foods should be stable in water for at least thirty minutes (Cantelmo and Senhorini 1989). These qualities are often difficult to achieve in "homemade" larval feeds used with tambaqui. Egg microcapsules, fine-grained dry food, and egg-milk mixtures are the most successful feeds used (Pinheiro et al. 1988; Malca 1989).

CHAPTER ELEVEN

DISEASE AND PARASITES

Protection from disease is one of the principal goals of aquaculture. Thus far no epidemic diseases have been reported for either wild or cultivated tambaqui, so it has gained a reputation as a robust species (Hernández et al. 1992). It would not be surprising, however, considering the history of fish culture, if problems begin to appear with the intensification of large-scale farming of this species. Investing in disease control is extremely important and is best approached through preventative measures, such as maintaining uninfected stocks and proper diets, rather than relying unrealistically on medicines (Thatcher 1991).

One of the principal problems in the Amazon is that tambaqui breeding stock and fry are often kept in ponds or tanks that use the same water. Furthermore, the same gear is often used to handle adults and fry. Parasites are thus transferred through the circulating water or on the gear. Complete isolation of adults and fry is probably the most significant step that could be taken to reduce parasitism. Even experimental fish farmers in the Amazon have yet to learn this lesson (Thatcher personal communication).

In the Amazon Basin, fish parasitology is a young discipline, but thanks to Vernon Thatcher and his group at INPA, a critical mass of information has become available. Since 1979 Thatcher and his colleagues have described more than two hundred new species of fish parasites and organized the available information into comprehensive monographs and books (e.g., Thatcher 1991). Fortunately, one of the fish species on which the INPA parasitology laboratory has focused is the tambaqui.

Parasites do not attack fish indiscriminately. Most parasites are host specific, so preventing infection is possible if strict precautions are taken. The danger, however, is that exotic fish species, such as carp, will introduce cosmopolitan parasites into the Amazon Basin. The tambaqui has ten known macroparasites, of which six are known only from this fish. The number of macroparasites reported for the tambaqui is relatively small compared with the totals for temperate-latitude fish species (Wootton 1990). The number of macroparasites attacking herring, stickle-backs, lake sturgeon, and some species of croakers can be more than double the number of species thus far reported for the tambaqui (Wootton 1990; Choudhury and Dick 1993; Thoney 1993).

Under poor environmental conditions, age and stress largely determine disease intensity. In general, young fish are the most susceptible, as they have not had time to build up resistance. Stress, commonly caused by mishandling, excessive crowd-ing, or inadequate feeding, or some combination of these, also greatly increases the chances of heavy parasitism. An ill fish may develop many different types of infec-tions due to weakened resistance, so the common parasites tend to appear together. Incubator hygiene is also of major importance to keep eggs and newborn larvae healthy (Conroy 1989).

Treatments to reduce parasite infection, and hence disease, can be taken on either the group or the individual level. The exact methodology chosen depends on the type of parasite and to some extent on how the fish are kept. Many of the methods now used for the tambaqui are still experimental and, though reported to work, often yield variable results. Since no single panacea exists, continued experimentation is imperative. Support of the Fish Pathology Laboratory of INPA will be essential if local aquaculturalists are to keep abreast of new species and pathologies.

The most important diseases reported for the tambaqui are columnariosis (a bacterium), dermatosis (usually fungi), ichthyophthiriosis (a protozoan), and unnamed infections caused by the monogenetic trematode *Linguadactyloides brinkmanni* and the copepod *Perulernaea gamitanae* (Thatcher and Kritsky 1983; Thatcher and Paredes 1985; Conroy 1989; Hernández et al. 1992). Other parasites, such as nematodes and branchiuran crustaceans, can also be problems, but thus far to a lesser extent. Infection of tambaqui by microparasites, such as fungi, bacteria, and protozoans, has received less attention.

BACTERIA

Bacteria attack eggs and newborn larvae and can cause severe mortality (Bermudez 1980; Conroy and Mujica 1985). They adhere to the walls of the incu-bators and egg capsules and can rapidly reach dangerous densities.

Flexibacter columnaris is a long bacterium known for its peculiar habit of stack-ing to form distinctive columns (Ceccarelli and Oliveira 1986). It is a common inhabitant of soil, water, and fish skin. A low natural resistance of the fish caused by stress and injuries facilitates infection. Most commonly this bacterium causes external infections, but it can also occur internally without visible signs. Externally, the disease is first apparent as small gray lesions on the surface of the body and/or fins; as the infection increases, muscle tissue may also be affected. The margins and

FIGURE 11.1
Ichythyophthirius multifilis.

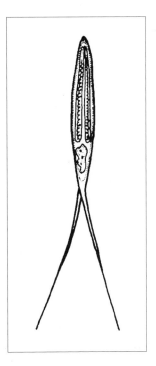

center of the lesion often have a yellowish color due to the accumulation of bacteria. The bacteria can be identified microscopically by the many long slender cells (0.5–10 microns) that move by flexing or creeping movements and form stacks.

Flexibacter columnaris attacks most freshwater fish, including tambaqui of all ages (Bermudez 1980; Conroy 1989). This bacterium can be especially common in mishandled young fish when water temperatures are above 20°C and/or when the fish are kept at high densities (Ceccarelli et al. 1990). In tropical areas *Flexibacter columnaris* has been reported in the cages and ponds of many institutions (Conroy 1989).

FUNGI

Species of *Saplogenia* are the most important fungi that have been reported to attack tambaqui. They can cause secondary infections when established in wounds. Eggs are also attacked. Infection spreads over the entire body and eventually gives the impression of cotton wool. The end result is necrosis. Stress due to poor environmental conditions or mishandling can cause fungal dermatosis.

PROTOZOANS

Ichthyophthirius multifilis causes ichthyophthiriosis. This protozoan is a large ciliated parasite (figure 11.1). It penetrates beneath the skin's surface and branchial filaments. When fully grown to 1 mm, the parasite can be seen without the aid of a microscope. It is reminiscent of a gray-white grain. Positive identification of this parasite in fish tissue is based on the large size of the protozoan, its ciliated form, and its horseshoe-shaped macronucleus. Although the protozoan is known to attack all age groups of fish, in tambaqui it is much more common in individuals less than four months old (Bermudez 1980; Mujica 1982). Ceccarelli et al. (1990) report that ichthyophthiriosis is one of the main causes of tambaqui mortality in southern Brazil.

Walliker (1969) and Paredes (1984) have reported finding protozoans of the genus *Myxobolus* in fish from the Amazon River, in both Brazil and Peru. *Myxobolus colossomatis* was recently described scientifically as a new species from infected tambaqui populations in the northeastern Brazilian state of Ceará (Molnár and

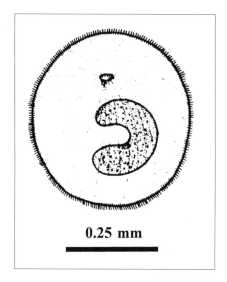

0.25 mm

FIGURE 11.2
Henneguya sp.

Békési 1993). *Henneguya* sp., another proto-zoan, is often found in gill filaments (Thatcher personal communication) (figure 11.2). All of these protozoans could turn out to cause serious problems in the future when large-scale fish farming occurs.

TREMATODES (FLATWORMS)

The monogenetic trematode *Linguadactyl-oides brinkmanni* has been reported in many aquaculture stations, and in some instances it is the most frequent parasite (Mujica 1982). It is a small wormlike creature that can reach 6 mm in length (figure 11.3). The parasite attaches itself to gill filaments, sometimes anchoring in the cartilaginous rod tissue. The infected tissue may overgrow the parasite, thus permanently fixing it to the site. Once fixed, the parasite eats gill tissue and blood cells, causing inflammation and finally the destruction of the gill filament. Branchial infes-tation also triggers the production of mucus, which can hinder gas exchange and ultimately lead to asphyxiation. Parasitologist Vernon Thatcher has counted up to seventeen *Linguadactyloides brink-manni* parasites on a single gill filament (personal communication).

Another monogenetic trematode that is fre-quently found on the gills is *Anacanthorus spatulatus* (Kritsky et al. 1980) (figure 11.4). Mujica and Armas de Conroy (1985) have reported as many as five trematodes per branchial filament, of which four were *Anacanthorus spatulatus*. This parasite has been widely spread to other areas with the export of tam-baqui juveniles to aquaculture stations (Pietro et al. 1986).

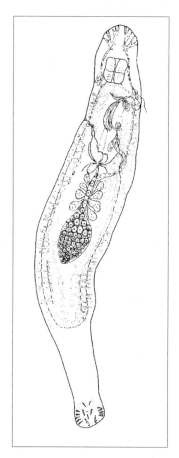

FIGURE 11.3
Linguadactyloides brinkmanni.

FIGURE 11.4
Anacanthorus spatulatus.

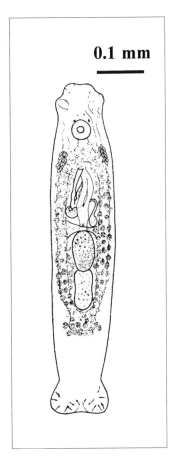

0.1 mm

ACANTHOCEPHALAN WORMS

Neoechinoryhnchus buttnerae, a parasite 15–32 mm in length, lives in the intestinal lumen (Golvan 1956). It does not have a digestive system per se, but rather through its skin it directly assimilates digested food from the fish's intestines. This parasite's life cycle includes one or two intermediate hosts. The first host is an ostracod, which is a tiny animal with a shrimplike interior but enclosed in a shell. Ostracods get infected when ingesting fish feces contaminated with the parasite's eggs. Tambaqui become infected when ingesting ostracods. Ostracods are most commonly found in or near floating plants. The parasitic worm's constant consumption of gut fluids affects the infected fish's growth, metabolism, and resistance to other pathogens.

NEMATODES

Chaubadinema americana is a common nematode species in wild stocks (figure 11.5); it has also been reported in captive fish in both cages and ponds (Conroy 1989). The pathology of this parasite and its effect on pond populations are still unknown. *Cucullanus colossomi* is an intestinal nematode that sucks blood. Thus far it has been reported only in tambaqui populations in Venezuela (Diaz-Ungria 1968; Thatcher 1991).

COPEPOD AND BRANCHIURAN CRUSTACEANS

Four crustaceans, all of which are ectoparasites (living on the exterior of the host), parasitize tambaqui. At least one more species has been discovered but awaits description (Thatcher personal communication). *Argulus multicolor,* a branchiuran, is an ellipsoid-shaped parasite; males reach about 4 mm and females 10 mm in width (figure 11.6). In the wild, *Argulus multicolor* seem to be more common during the high-water season, especially during June and July in the Amazon (Malta 1983, 1984). The parasite's eggs are fixed to various substrates. Newborn and

FIGURE 11.5
Chaubadinema americana.

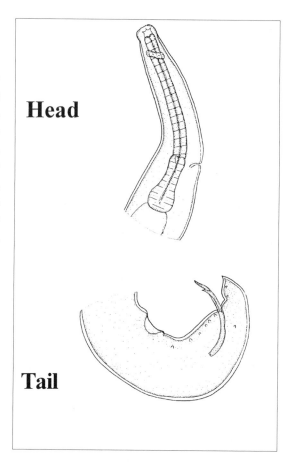

adults of both sexes attack tambaqui. They perforate the fish's skin with their mouth parts and inject anticoagulant and digestive secretions. Both blood and skin tissue are ingested. Heavy infestation can lead to death, especially in young tambaqui, as a result of anemia or secondary infections at the perforation sites in the mouth.

The males of *Dolops carvalhoi,* another branchiuran, are 5–6 mm in width; females are 6.9–7.3 mm (figure 11.7). The life history of this species is similar to that of *Argulus multicolor,* with the important exception that *Dolops carvalhoi* usually attaches itself only to the outer body of the fish. Once on the host, it moves about until finding a site, usually a sparsely scaled area, where it can perforate the skin to suck blood. This parasite mimics tambaqui scales, perhaps as an adaptation against predation from invertebrate-feeding fish. Finally, *Dolops carvalhoi* is able to leave its host and move to another fish (Malta and Varella 1983).

Perulernaea gamitanae, a copepod, is an extremely important parasite affecting captive stocks (figure 11.8). In the Amazon there are reports of juveniles with up to eighty parasitic copepods in the mouth. This parasite

FIGURE 11.6
Argulus multicolor

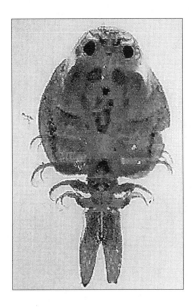

FIGURE 11.7
Dolops carvalhoi.

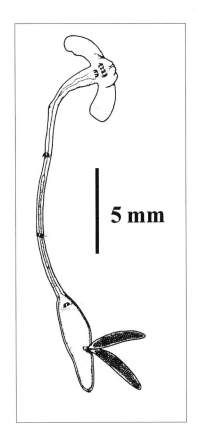

FIGURE 11.8
Perulernaea gamitanae.

fixes the end of its head in the fish's nostrils, under its tongue, in the esophagus wall, or in the inner wall of the operculum. At these various points the parasites suck blood. Other copepods, such as *Learnaea* sp., may turn out to be problems as well (Ceccarelli 1988; Varella personal communication). *Gamidactylus jaraquensis*, for example, has been found in the nares of tambaqui. An isopod (*Braga* sp.) in which both males and females inhabit the branchial chamber and browse on gill filaments also exists.

CHAPTER TWELVE

INTENSIVE FISH FARMING

Tambaqui have been reared successfully in tanks, ponds, and cages. Farming operations use cages and ponds, whereas experimental aquaculture favors tanks. When used in rivers and reservoirs with good circulation, open systems, such as cages and rafts, require less attention for the maintenance of water quality. On the other hand, they are more exposed to predation and poachers. Ponds offer better protection against predators but suffer the consequences of crowding, such as diseases and water-quality degradation. All of the systems mentioned above require that fish be fed intensively, as population densities are much higher than the natural production of food can support. At present a cheaper food supply is the main limiting factor to the expansion of tambaqui fish farming in the Amazon. Now that induced spawning and fry culture have been accomplished, more experimentation in the development of alternative food supplies is needed. The following discussion gives an overview of what is known about farming systems and the foods that can be used to raise tambaqui.

TRADITIONAL FOOD SOURCES

Farmed tambaqui are usually fed with pellets and zooplankton. Pellets can be either purchased commercially or home made. Zooplankton produced naturally in ponds is an important nutritional source for the tambaqui. In intensive and semi-intensive fish-culture operations, zooplankton is of more importance qualitatively than quantitatively. Zooplankton can provide fish with amino acids that are lacking in pellets and plant materials. The presence of zooplankton may in part be responsible for the better growth rate of tambaqui raised in ponds compared with that of tambaqui in cages. In cages, zooplankton is quickly depleted due to high fish densities. In ponds, the addition of nutrients, such as from animal manure, can increase zooplankton production.

Pellets are expensive and usually account for more than 50% of the ongoing costs in tambaqui farming (Herculano 1987; Merola and Pagan-Font 1988; Chabalin et al. 1989). Pellets are attractive to many fish farmers because they have an established quantity of nutrients, thus making possible the prediction of costs and yields. Furthermore, as the most common type of artificial food used in aquaculture, pellets are widely and regularly available, in numerous commercial brands and types with varying proportions of protein (table 12.1). Tambaqui have been fed commercial chicken pellets (19% protein) as well as frog pellets (40% protein); the energy content of these pellets ranges from 2,500 to 3,500 kcal/kg, or 11–14 kcal/kg of protein (Carneiro Sobrinho et al. 1989; Andrade et al. 1993). Protein content and the price of pellets are directly related. Considerable research effort has been aimed at finding the best compromise between protein content and cost.

The most common ingredients of pellets used to feed tambaqui are soybean meal, fish meal, meat meal, blood meal, yellow maize, wheat, and rice bran. Commercial pellets made from these ingredients are 18–40% protein, 3–10% fat, 20–50% carbohydrates, 7–20% fiber, and 7–13% ash. Water content normally varies from 7 to 15%. During the first year, pellets are fed at a rate of 3% of the fish's weight per day. After tambaqui reach one year of age, feeding is reduced to 1–2% of the fish's weight.

Many scientific experiments have studied the effect of protein content on

TABLE 12.1

Price ($US/kg) and Protein Content of Various Fish Pellets Sold
in Manaus and São Paulo in 1993

Product	Manufacturer	City	Type	Price US$	% Protein
Avimazon 3	Moageira	Manaus	poultry	0.2	17
Avimazon 2	Moageira	Manaus	poultry	0.5	19
Extraovo	Guabi	Manaus	poultry	0.29	16
Galetão	Guabi	Manaus	poultry	0.33	19
Crescimento	Agroceres	Manaus	poultry	0.36	16
Postura	Purina	Manaus	poultry	0.36	14
Corte final	Agroceres	Manaus	poultry	0.37	17
Postura	Agroceres	Manaus	poultry	0.38	17
Corte Inicial	Agroceres	Manaus	poultry	0.43	22
Piratropical	Guabi	Manaus	fish	0.58	28
Piratropical	Guabi	São Paulo	fish	0.31	28
Nutravit - e	Vitanutri	São Paulo	fish	0.66	35
Nutravit - m	Vitanutri	São Paulo	fish	0.46	30
Peixe	SIBRA	São Paulo	fish	0.5	27

growth. Fish protein usage depends on age, temperature, ration size, and protein quality (Wilson 1989). Comparisons are somewhat difficult to make because experimental conditions have been highly variable. In general, young juveniles (5–15 g) show a faster growth rate when protein content is increased (Macedo 1979; Eckmann 1987; Luna 1987; Hernao and Grajares 1989). Experiments with larger juvenile tambaqui, however, suggest that pellet protein content higher than 18% does not greatly improve growth rate, though there are some reports that it does (Macedo 1979; Merola and Cantelmo 1987; Kohla et al. 1992; Valencia 1985, 1988a, 1988b; Valencia and Puentes 1989; Campos Baca 1994). Differences in protein quality may in part explain the contradictory results.

Kohla et al. (1992) found that tambaqui fed pellets with 50% protein of animal and plant origin grew better than those fed pellets containing only animal protein. The same effect, however, was not found at lower protein concentrations. Several studies have shown that growth is improved when feed is rich in plant protein (Werder and Saint-Paul 1979; Hernao and Grajares 1989; Valencia and Puentes 1989). Pellets whose protein content consisted of 75–85% plant material yielded the highest growth rates. The lowest performance occurred when fish were fed exclusively either plant or animal protein.

At present the recommended protein concentration of tambaqui pellets is 18–25% (Carneiro 1981; Hernández et al. 1992; Vidal Jr et al. 1994). The energy content of pellets ranges from 12 to 17 kJ/g (2,500–3,500 kcal/kg), or 53 to 67 J/g of protein (Carneiro Sobrinho et al. 1989; Andrade et al. 1993). The diets of wild tambaqui are about 20–30% protein, 75% of which is of plant origin; energy levels, however, are lower in the wild.

The optimum growth per unit of feed can be calculated by what experimental aquaculturalists call apparent feed conversion efficiency (AFC). AFC is the ratio of the weight of pellets fed to the weight of fish produced and relates directly to production costs. Aquaculturalists want to achieve the lowest AFC possible. The average AFC is less than 2 for tambaqui smaller than 500–600 g (figure 12.1). It increases progressively to 4 in 2-kg fish. Carneiro Sobrinho et al. (1989) and Ferrari et al. (1991) found similar variation in AFC with body size at water temperatures of 25 and 27°C.

After the first six months of feeding, supplemental foods such as nuts, vegetables, and surplus human food may have a dramatic effect on the final costs of farming tambaqui. Alternatively, one can improve the AFC ratio by rearing another species with tambaqui. The conversion efficiency in relation to fish size is half in polyculture compared with monoculture. The result is an improvement in total investments in feed and total pond production.

ALTERNATIVE FOOD SOURCES

Farmers sometimes use foods other than pellets as either a supplementary or the main energy source. Domestic and wild fruits and vegetables, such as guavas,

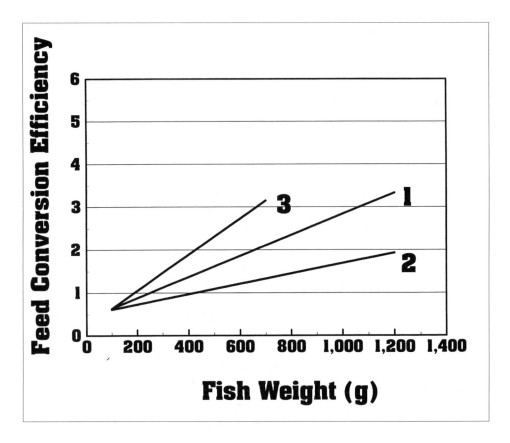

FIGURE 12.1

Conversion efficiency (weight of pellets/weight of fish) for tambaqui: 1. monoculture ponds (Carneiro Sobrinho et al. 1989; Ferrari et al. 1991); 2. polyculture ponds (Silva et al. 1984); and 3. fed only corn (Silva et al. 1993).

mangoes, potatoes, cabbages, pumpkins, bananas, rubber-tree seeds, munguba seeds, rice, corn, and manioc, have been used to feed tambaqui. Restaurant leftovers and organic residuals from food factories, such as popcorn, pasta, biscuits, and bread, have also been used as feed. In some cases this material is ground and made into pellets, though usually it is fed to the animals in the form in which it is collected (Ferraz de Lima et al. 1992). The substitution of local or readily available cheaper foods has been tried a few times. For example, fruits from the pupunha palm (*Bactris gasipaes*), a species now widely planted in South America, have been substituted for corn in pellets; fish silage has also been used as a substitute for fish meal (Carneiro 1991; Mori 1993; Pereira Filho 1995). Planorbid snails have been used to supplement pellets, especially for brood stock in the CODEVASF stations in northeastern Brazil.

Animal protein can be derived from a variety of sources as well. For example, farms in central Brazil raising fish and poultry have used chicken feces, surplus pellets, and meat from slaughterhouses to produce a pastry. This feed is placed in wooden boxes that are allowed to sink to the bottom of ponds. Adequate fish growth was obtained with an extreme reduction in the feeding costs.

A few experiments have been reported using foods other than pellets for tambaqui feed. Thus far most of these experiments have reported lower growth rates than those achieved with pellets containing a balanced mixture of the necessary dietary elements. Fish fed pellets made with pupunha fruit, corn, babaçu palm cake, and wild fruits from Amazonian floodplains resulted in lower growth rates compared with those from conventional pellets (Mori 1993; Silva et al. 1983; Silva et al. 1987; Roubach 1992; Valencia and Puentes 1989).

Less-than-optimum growth rates should not discourage the use of fruit material and other alternatives to pellets. Farmers should consider both growth rates and cost reduction when using alternative foods. Few studies have addressed the long-term cost effectiveness of using alternative food sources. One study that did dealt with the pacu (*Piaractus mesopotamicus*), a species with nutritional requirements similar to those of the tambaqui. Although pacu grew slower when fed agricultural litter, the experiment nevertheless reduced the total rearing cost by 55% compared with that for pellet-fed fish (Chabalin et al. 1992).

FISH ORCHARDS

To date, aquaculturalists have been quite conservative in their approach to food supply. Most pellets are imported from outside the region. These feeds are expensive and will greatly reduce profits if they are depended on in the long run. The rich and unique flavor of wild tambaqui is due mostly to a fruit and seed diet. The ecology of the tambaqui suggests that fruits and seeds could, and should, be one of the principal sources of food for intensive and extensive aquacultural operations in the Amazon. Similar to aquaculture, fish orchards could be used in intensive operations.

Within the last decade, entrepreneurs have increasingly invested in fruit farming in the Amazon as one viable or complementary alternative to cattle ranching (Smith et al. 1995). Virtually all orchard farms are located on terra firma, such as in eastern Pará near Belém, where oil palms, oranges, passion fruits, papayas, and black peppers have been planted in large tracts. Orchard fruits or seeds are not used on any significant scale as animal food anywhere in the world. Grains, such as wheat, maize, and oats, are cheaper to produce and preferred by livestock. Pigs feed heavily on acorns in Mediterranean oak woodlands, and they are the only animals with feeding habits in any way similar to those of the fruit- and seed-eating fishes of South America. South America, however, offers much greater opportunities for raising orchard-fed animals because of the presence of the tambaqui and its relatives.

Tree farming on the Amazon River floodplain is confined mostly to home gardens of the peasants (Goulding et al. 1996). Interestingly, many of the fruit and seed species planted or left near houses are fish baits, especially along the middle Amazon River where floodplain deforestation is so advanced that fruit and seed bait is often difficult to find. These "bait" trees, as with other floodplain species, are adapted to the annual floods. They fruit during the high-water season. In form they range from shrubs to trees. Many produce huge fruit or seed crops. Experiments would be needed to determine which home garden species might be most appropriate, in the sense of providing large yields and high nutritional value, for fish raised in captivity. An even greater variety of fruit and seed species in the flooded forests could be selected for potential cultivation. Some of these, such as sapucaia nuts of the Brazil-nut tree family, are also valuable as human food. Others, such as palm fruits, can also be used to feed pigs. Rubber trees produce one of the favorite foods of the tambaqui, and they can be tapped for latex as well. Many of the fruit and seed species that would be appropriate for fish could also be used to feed turtles, another Amazonian resource that should soon be produced in captivity.

The number of fruit and seed species that the tambaqui is known to eat suggests that mixed orchards would be the best bet. Having mixed orchards would offer greater protection against years when any particular species might produce poor crops and also a buffer against disease problems. Not all species fruit at the same time, and depending on their exact fruiting period, enough species could be planted to ensure that a food supply was available for the longest period possible. Some species whose fruit or seeds store well could also be selected; thus they could be used several months after harvest when the food supply might be short.

The rich soils of the muddy-river floodplains would provide the fastest growth rates for fruit trees. Since large parts of the Amazon River floodplain have already been deforested, there would be no need to clear natural habitats for fish orchards. The fruits of some upland trees would undoubtedly also serve as fish food. For example, the babaçu palm, a species that rapidly dominates cleared upland areas, commonly produces more than 1,000 kg/ha of fruit in disturbed areas. The 250-g nuts are too large for fish to crush, but the technology already exists for producing livestock press-cake and meal from the energy-rich kernels (Anderson et al. 1991). Many other palm species are also potentially usable in this way, and ecological information is available on them (Kahn 1988, 1991). Only experimentation is lacking.

MONOCULTURE IN PONDS

At present, earthen ponds are the most common system used to rear tambaqui. The natural production of zooplankton contributes to the food supply for tambaqui in ponds. Small fish are kept at 2–5 ind./m³. When juveniles reach approximately 100 g, the stocking density is reduced to 0.2–1.0 ind./m³. Fish kept at higher densities require increased water circulation and forced aeration.

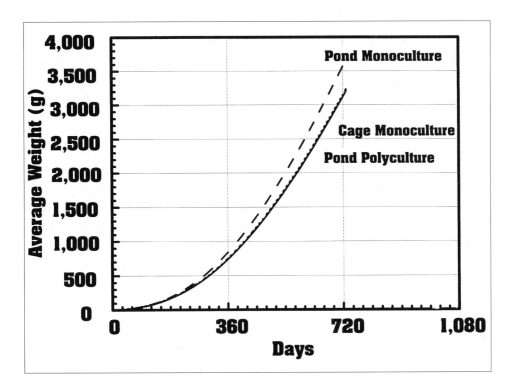

FIGURE 12.2

Average weight gains of tambaqui in ponds, cages, and polyculture.

The average weight gain of pellet-fed tambaqui reported for ponds in the first year ranges from 500 to 1,400 g (Silva et al. 1984; Forte 1982; Carneiro Sobrinho et al. 1989; Valencia and Puentes 1989; Bello et al. 1989; Ferrari et al. 1991) (figure 12.2). The average harvest size depends mostly on the initial size of the fry and the total rearing period, but also on water temperature, food, and water quality. None of these variables has been standardized between the different experimental laboratories, thus exact quantitative comparisons are complicated. The average size of first-year stock, however, can be estimated by back-calculating initial fry sizes to a common weight and projecting the growth curve to one year. Based on this model—and assuming water temperatures of 26–28°C, daily feeding rates of 3% of the fish's biomass, and pellets of 18–30% crude protein—we predict that stocking a pond with 2.5-g fry will yield an average tambaqui weight of 840 g at the end of a year. This value seems lower than what has been reported in the literature, but many experiments began with initial fry weighing 10–100 g, or fish two to four months older than the average age estimated here (Rey Navarro 1984; Silva and Gurgel 1989; Carneiro Sobrinho et al. 1989; Valencia and Puentes 1989; Eckmann 1987; Carneiro 1991; Roubach 1992; Graef 1995). Tambaqui raised in ponds grow 2.7 times faster than wild populations.

Marketable tambaqui may have to be larger than those obtained at the end of one year. In Brazil, for example, people prefer tambaqui larger than 2 kg. Projecting the growth curve from data now available for 1.0–1.5 years of age, we estimate that tambaqui in monoculture will reach 3.5 kg in 2 years. There are few experimental data for long-term rearing, but in farms in Venezuela and in northern, northeastern, and southeastern Brazil, tambaqui weighing 2 kg have been harvested in eighteen months. Fish farmers near Manaus reported to us that they harvested tambaqui as large as 3 kg in eighteen months and 5 kg in three years. These fish were kept at very low densities (0.004 ind./m^2) and fed twice weekly on agricultural byproducts or pellets. Small-scale fish farmers in the state of Acre have reported harvesting 2.5-kg tambaqui in two years; these fish were fed mostly manioc and corn (Rezende personal communication). Admittedly, most farmers do not keep accurate records of their procedures and harvests, but we mention these promising reports here because academics could play an important role in devising a simple system to record these important data so that other farmers could become aware of them.

MONOCULTURE IN CAGES

Rearing fish in cages is one of the most intense systems used for monoculture. This method has a long history in Asia. In Brazil and Venezuela it has been tested in reservoirs, large earthen ponds, and rivers (Darmont and Salaya 1983; Nuñez and Salaya 1984; Merola and Cantelmo 1987; Merola and Souza 1988; Bello et al. 1989; Andrade et al. 1993; Falabella 1994). In Venezuela, where cages have been used since the early 1980s, and especially in the El Pao reservoir, commercial production has been reported to be 15–20 tons/yr of 800-g fish (Hernández et al. 1992).

Fish density is one of the most important factors in cage culture. Merola and Souza (1988) have shown that tambaqui grow better when reared at 100 ind./m^3 than at 150 ind./m^3. On the other hand, little difference in growth rates was found between stocking rates of 100 ind./m^3 and 50 ind./m^3. Commercial operations raising tambaqui appear to be more conservative and keep densities as low as 15 ind./m^3 (Bello et al. 1989; Mendes and Vallejos 1988).

As in ponds, most experimental studies of tambaqui raised in cages have been for relatively short periods, usually six months or less. If we project average growth rates from six months to one year, then the average size attained thus far appears to be slightly lower than that reported for ponds. Stocking densities below 100 ind./m^3 seem to have a positive effect on growth rate, but more short- and long-duration studies are needed before proper conclusions can be made.

POLYCULTURE

Polyculture involves raising two or more species of fish or other organisms together. A polycultural system is based on the ecological concept that increasing biological complexity means better energy transfer and use of resources. Special care needs to be taken to choose species that do not compete for food. Several poly-culture experiments have used tambaqui with detritus- or leaf-eating fish and ducks (Silva et al. 1984; Silva et al. 1984, 1993; Oliveira et al. 1988; Peralta and Teichert-Coddington 1989; Hernández 1992; Pontes et al. 1992; Hancz 1993). The most common fish species that have been used in polyculture with tambaqui are curimatã (*Prochilodus* spp.), carp (*Cyprinus carpio*), and tilapia (*Tilapia* spp.) (Araripe et al. 1988; Silva 1984; Silva et al. 1986). All of these experiments reported tambaqui growth rates similar to those found in monoculture, but a higher total fish production per unit of feed was achieved. Polyculture conversion efficiency is 30% higher than that of monoculture for 1.0–1.2-kg tambaqui fed with nutrient-balanced pellets. It should also be noted here that polycultures of tambaqui with morocotó (*Piaractus brachypomus*) and/or *Brycon* sp. lead to poor growth rates (Valencia and Puentes 1989), probably because of competition for the same food by the various species.

Another type of association is that of linking tambaqui culture with mammals and birds, such as pigs, ducks, and chickens. Only the pigs, ducks, and chickens are fed new pellets. Leftover pellets and feces are transferred to fish ponds (Alcántara et al. 1983; Melo et al. 1987; Pontes et al. 1992; Hernández et al. 1992). Fish-to-pig ratios range from 1:30 to 1:50, starting with 20-kg pigs. At densities of 0.25 ind./m^2, the tambaqui grows well in this type of system. The conversion efficiency of feed was 30% higher than when pigs were used alone. Because both animals have good market prices, the association seems promising for the Amazon region (Melo et al. 1987; Hernández et al. 1992). The addition of detritus-feeding fish with the tambaqui-pig system might increase stocking densities of tambaqui to 1.0 ind./m^2. As a final note, bacteriological tests thus far have not revealed contaminated fish or health problems from the use of pig feces (Silva et al. 1991). Human feces, however, should be avoided.

MORTALITY AND PRODUCTION

Under normal conditions the mortality rates for tambaqui in ponds and cages are similar (figure 12.3). Survival rates are usually greater than 90% in both systems; values below 75% are rarely reported. A high mortality of juveniles has been reported for individuals less than 160 g kept at water temperatures below 19°C. For most of the Amazon Basin, however, low temperatures will not be a problem. Excessive population densities can lead to stress and disease, especially when steps are not taken to prevent infestation (see chapter 11). Tambaqui larger than 500 g are more resistant to sharp environmental fluctuations (Ferrari et al. 1991)

Based on the mortality and growth-rate data available, the average production of tambaqui in monoculture ponds is 8.6 tons/ha/yr; in cages it is 376 tons/ha/yr (figure 12.4). In polyculture, tambaqui production per area is slightly lower than in monoculture, or 7.5 tons/ha/yr, but total fish production is at least 50% higher due

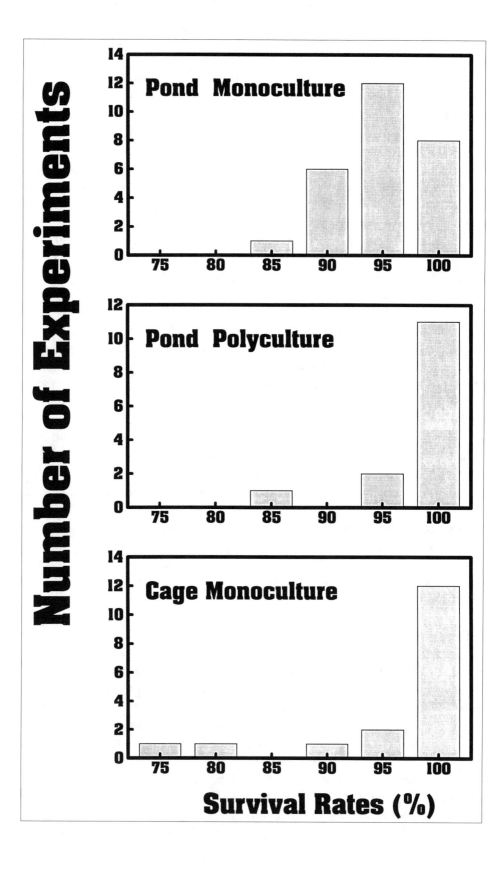

FIGURE 12.3
Survival rates of farmed tambaqui (>400 g) in fifty-eight experiments.

to the production of the other species. Rolim (1995) estimated a slightly lower production of 7.3 tons/ha/yr for fish farms in the state of Amazonas, Brazil, where pellets were being used and ponds were managed adequately. These data suggest that local fish farmers are efficient and that their yields are approaching those reported in scientific experiments. The above values do not take production costs into consideration.

HYBRIDS

Both tambaqui females and males have been crossed with other species of the pacu lineage with the same number of chromosomes, or 2n=54 (Silva et al. 1986; Almeida Toledo et al. 1987, 1988; Porto et al. 1992; Castangnolli et al. 1988; Pinheiro et al. 1991) (table 12.2). Hybrids have been produced in attempts to achieve disease resistance, faster growth rates, and tolerance to lower temperatures. Another reason for these breeding programs also appears to have been scientific curiosity (Senhorini et al. 1988; Fontes et al. 1990). The morphological characteristics of hybrids are the average of those of the parental genotypes. A hybrid of a female tambaqui and a Pantanal pacu male has more gill rakers than a pacu but fewer than a tambaqui (Barbosa and Oliveira 1988). An increase in gill rakers enables the hybrid to prey on zooplankton. Theoretically, this capability might be an advantage if favorable characteristics are gained as well from the pacu gene pool.

Hybrid experiments have not been particularly encouraging. The larvae and young juveniles of hybridized tambaqui and Pantanal pacu did not grow faster than the parent species. Tambacu larvae, however, showed a slightly better survival rate than other hybrids and the parent species (Senhorini et al. 1988). Whether hybrids are more resistant to lower temperatures is still unclear. Most experiments done with large juveniles showed no difference in growth performance between tambaqui and its hybrids using *Piaractus brachypomus* and

TABLE 12.2

Hybrids Using Tambaqui

Hybrid name	Male breeding stock	Female breeding stock	Country
Paqui	Pacu (*Piaractus mesopotamicus*)	Gamitana (*Colossoma macropomum*)	Brazil
Tambacu	Tambaqui (*Colossoma macropomum*)	Pacu (*Piaractus mesopotamicus*)	Brazil
Gamipaco	Gamitana (*Colossoma macropomum*)	Pacu (*Piaractus mesopotamicus*)	Peru
Pacogama	Paco (*Piaractus brachypomus*)	Gamitana (*Colossoma macropomum*)	Peru
Cachameta	Gamitana (*Colossoma macropomum*)	Palometa (*Mylossoma duriventris*)	Venezuela

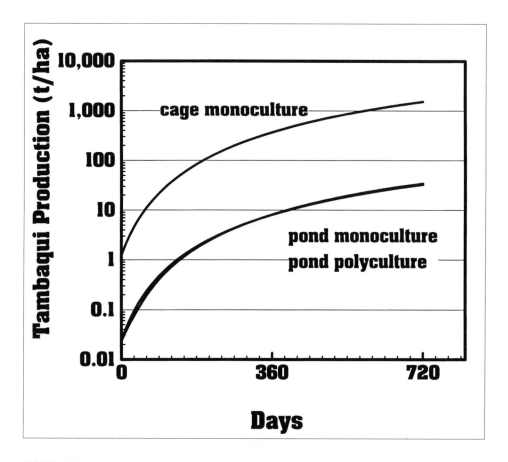

FIGURE 12.4

Tambaqui production in monoculture and polyculture ponds and monoculture cages.

Piaractus mesopotamicus. In some cases the tambaqui's growth was greater than that of the hybrid (Silva et al. 1986; Silva and Gurgel 1989; Pinheiro et al. 1991). Hybrids are now widely available and have been introduced into the Amazon.

COSTS

Production rates from intensive fish culture systems are often expressed in terms of kilograms of fish harvested per area. Although tambaqui can be raised in high densities in small spaces, such as in cages, the potential or actual profit is best expressed in production costs relative to gross revenue. Using the data available, we present a comparative analysis of the production costs of 10,000 tambaqui raised during a two-year period. This analysis considers investments, operational costs, and production (table 12.3).

The tambaqui production values used here are based on scientific experiments conducted in controlled environments; these values thus arise from nearly ideal

TABLE 12.3

Cost-benefit Analysis for Tambaqui at 1995 Prices in the Amazon

Variables and Profit	Unit	Monoculture			Polyculture	
		Pond: Intensive	Pond: Supplements	Cage	Pond Intensive	Pond Semi-intensive
Number of tambaqui	indiv.	10,000	10,000	10,000	10,000	10,000
Number of detritivores	indiv.	0	0	0	10,000	10,000
Number of pigs	indiv.	0	0	0	0	3,000
Tambaqui price	US$/kg	2.6	2.6	2.6	2.6	2.6
Detritivore price	US$/kg	na	na	na	0.7	0.7
Pig price	US$/kg	na	na	na	na	3
Production of tambaqui	kg	34,500	34,500	30,680	34,500	32,700
Production of detrivores	kg	0	0	0	3,000	3,000
Production of pigs	kg	0	0	0	0	240,000
Total production	kg	34,500	34,500	30,680	37,500	275,700
Feeding conversion efficiency		4	8	4	4	4
Production cycle for tambaqui	yrs.	2	2	2	2	2
Gross revenue	US$	89,700	89,700	79,768	91,800	567,120
Costs (2 ha)	US$	76,195	58,209	72,610	76,309	501,628
Net revenue	US$	13,504	31,490	7,157	15,491	65,491
Net revenue per year	US$	6,752	15,745	3,579	7,746	32,746
Ratio profit: operating cost	%	18%	54%	10%	20%	13%
Break even price	US$	2.2	1.69	2.4	2	1.81
Break even production	kg	29,306	22,388	27,927	23,123	
Investments	US$	23,597	26,457	11,245	23,597	33,023
Payback period	yrs.	3.8	1.7	4.7	3.4	1.3

conditions. Obviously, ideal conditions are not always available to fish culturalists but can be the basis for developing simple economic models. These are useful because fish culturalists rarely record exact cost data.

The principal factors used to model tambaqui fish culture were investments, operational costs, and profit. Investments were based on the construction of 2-ha ponds or 200-m^3 cages, either at a distance of about 70 km from Manaus. Investments included excavation, soil preparation, buildings, cages and basic equipment, and their depreciation. Operational costs included taxes, fuel, labor, equipment, building depreciation, fertilizer, and rations ($0.40/kg). It was assumed that a bank loan was needed to establish the operation, so interest and principal payments were also factored in. At present fish culturalists in the Amazon often use the FNO (Fundo para o Desenvolvimento do Norte), which is subsidized by the federal government, to obtain credit. Interest variables were based on the FNO's interest rates in 1995. All other values were based on average prices in the Manaus market in July 1995.

The cost analyses considered were intensive monoculture in earthen ponds or cages, intensive monoculture with added supplements, and polyculture of tambaqui with curimatã (*Prochilodus nigricans*) and pigs. In the case of intensive monoculture with locally acquired supplements (manioc, cacao, and floodplain seeds), food-to-fish conversion rates were assumed to be 8:1, of which 2 parts were commercial rations and 6 parts were agriculture products produced on 5 ha of land. In this case the cost of additional labor was also considered. Agricultural production was assumed to be 20 tons/ha based on data from the region (Silva 1991; Pereira 1992; Castro 1992). The polyculture stocking densities of tambaqui, curimatã, and pigs were based on recommendations given by Melo et al. (1987) and Hernández et al. (1992).

Given the economics and ecology of the Amazon region, the most efficient tambaqui production system appears to be intensive monoculture with supplements. This system can better use locally grown or harvested products for supplemental feed. It would yield $15,745/yr, and the ratio of profit to operations cost would be high (54%) (see table 12.3). Cage culture was the least lucrative because of high operational costs, especially the depreciation of equipment and the lower growth rates of tambaqui. Although cages are the least lucrative on an individual basis, they still yield $300/month. This figure may seem low, but in the Amazon it is more than twice the average income. Polyculture requires the highest investment, and it would have to be based largely on pigs. In this case fish culture would be a supplement to pig farming. Pigs would account for 85% of the total profit ($32,700/yr).

The payback period for investments is shortest in monoculture with feed supplements and polyculture with pigs (based on the average retail prices for tambaqui of at least $2.60/kg). These systems also offer greater financial protection (lower break-even price) against fluctuations in fish prices (see table 12.3). For adequate profit, producers would have to sell their fish directly to retailers.

CHAPTER THIRTEEN

EXTENSIVE FISH FARMING

Extensive fish-farming operations involve hatcheries or the collection of eggs, sperm, and fry in the wild (Piper et al. 1983). Fry are released into the wild, reservoirs, or flooded agricultural fields at appropriate times and places. Extensive aquaculture can replenish overexploited stocks. To what extent aquaculture can lead to greater production than occurs naturally is more questionable. At present no extensive fish-farming experiments are ongoing in the Amazon. Our discussion here is meant to alert readers to the problems and prospects of extensive aquaculture in the Amazon. Small-scale experiments will be needed to explore the possibilities further. We hasten to mention that no large-scale experiment should be allowed until adequate research has been done on the environmental impacts.

HATCHERIES

At least twenty countries in the world have hatcheries operated by state or federal governments. In South America, Brazil, Argentina, Colombia, and Venezuela all maintain fish hatcheries. The private sector, however, is more successful in rearing fish, though government operations are usually needed to restock the natural waters where entrepreneurs cannot make direct profits. Aquaculture plants in all of the above countries, and in the United States, are presently selling tambaqui fry. In Brazil nearly all of the production is in the northeastern or southern part of the country, though efforts have begun in the Amazon as well. Fry can be mass-produced to repopulate lakes, rivers, and dammed areas or to sell to farmers who will raise them.

In hatcheries, tambaqui fry need twenty to forty days to attain a common harvest size of 1–5 cm. During the early efforts to reproduce tambaqui, stations restricted production to a relatively short period each year in accordance with the natural spawning season of the species. The seasonal availability of fry needs to be reduced, and managers have approached this requirement from two perspectives. Researchers of CODEVASF, a government-financed institute concentrating on development in the São Francisco Valley in northeastern Brazil, have developed the technology to manage the spawning season of tambaqui so that fry are available year-round (Pinheiro et al. 1988). Venezuelans have taken a second approach by reducing the growth rates of young fish; thus fry of appropriate size are available for a longer period each year (Heredia and Gonzales 1990). Keeping larvae and juveniles at low densities (0.5 ind./m^2) in an extensive rearing system that depends only on foods produced naturally reduces growth rate. Once fish are transferred to proper rearing facilities, growth rate returns to normal.

We can make only a gross estimate of the total number of tambaqui fry now being produced. Most data are available in Brazil, which accounted for more than 85% of the 17 million tambaqui fry reported produced in the 1990–1991 period (CODEVASF and DNOCS personal communication; Burgos and Silva 1989; Hernández 1989; Hernández et al. 1992). By the mid-1990s tambaqui production from private aquaculture plants far surpassed government efforts. Amazonas state production, however, was still modest at approximately 2.5 million fry between 1992 and 1994. On the other hand, production from private hatcheries was at least 5 million fry (Rolim 1995).

Using the fry data available, we can estimate the total present potential production of tambaqui from aquaculture. Assuming a fry survival rate of 80% and an average production harvest size of 1 kg, the present total potential productivity of farm-raised tambaqui as food fish could be 16,000 tons/yr in the five countries mentioned above. Farmed tambaqui production, then, would be close to the annual mid-1980s total yield of fisheries based in Manaus, Iquitos, and the upper Orinoco system (Merona and Bittencourt 1988; Eckmann 1985; Novoa 1989). Given the general trend, we have every reason to believe that tambaqui hatcheries will eventually supply fry for production that could reach 100,000 tons or more by the year 2000. If the Amazon becomes a principal player in tambaqui production, as we suggest it should, then the total might be even greater.

REALITY OF INCREASING FLOODPLAIN PRODUCTION

The increased production of tambaqui in the wild can be seen from three perspectives. First, areas where overexploitation has occurred can be restocked. Second, absolute production, even in areas not overexploited, can probably be increased because natural mortality can be reduced by placing fry in appropriate nursery habitats. Third, in some cases floodplain habitats could be modified to increase fish production.

Bayley's (1983) biomass data for the Amazon River floodplain near Manaus strongly suggested that overfishing had reduced tambaqui populations by the late

1970s. At that time juvenile tambaqui were not being heavily fished; thus the reduction in the biomass was due to either overexploitation of adults, destruction of floodplain forest areas used by adults, or most likely both factors.

To date no extensive fish culture has been practiced in the Amazon Basin, although a few experiments have taken place in Venezuelan reservoirs (Bello et al. 1989). Extensive operations consist of releasing fry produced through the induced spawning of adults.

Under natural circumstances the tambaqui spawns in river channels. With such a fecund fish that does not protect its eggs, its spawning location is largely an adaptation to reduce predation. Both in terms of numbers and total mass, the tambaqui produces a huge quantity of eggs. Tambaqui eggs would almost certainly be easier prey in quiet floodplain waters than in the flowing channels that disperse them downstream. When fry are at least one week old and first enter floodplain waters, they have a much better chance of survival. In floodplains the fry can seek immediate refuge near floating plants and other vegetation. Spawning in river channels, however, might mean that a huge numbers of eggs do not get fertilized because of the relatively turbulent environment. Furthermore, many if not most eggs that do get fertilized may fail to find their way into a floodplain water body. Despite those limitations, the tambaqui evolved to spawn in river channels because egg mortality is less in that habitat than in floodplain water bodies.

Given the above ecology, extensive fish culture operations can intervene at the point where mortality is highest. Controlled conditions can ensure that most eggs are fertilized and that young fry are placed directly in floodplain nursery habitats without first having to run a predatory gauntlet where losses, under natural conditions, are extremely high. The biological result of the above intervention would be to increase production of this species on the floodplains.

Stock enhancement is one of the principal technologies used for extensive fish culture. This practice consists of releasing large numbers of farmed juveniles into the wild. In the wild, natural production sustains fish growth, reducing feeding costs to zero. This type of fish culture has been developed in Asia, especially Japan, but also in Norway and Canada (Welcomme 1994). Japan has been especially successful with Red Sea bream. Recapture rates of 30%, after fish have reached harvestable size, have been reported (Kotaki 1992). Similar results have been reported for Arctic char (*Salvelinus alpinus*), flounder, trout, and other species. Average recapture rates have been about 14–30% (Kitada et al. 1992; Finstad and Heggberget 1993; Ungson et al. 1993; Jonsson et al. 1995).

The only place in Brazil where young tambaqui have been stocked in the wild is in the Rio São Francisco in northeastern Brazil. CODEVASF has been stocking more than 20,000 fry per month. Local fishermen have captured few individuals. In contrast to the Amazon region, however, the Rio São Francisco has a limited floodplain, most of which has also been highly modified.

We might argue that the introduction of a large number of young tambaqui would only provide more food for predators. About 30–35% of the fish biomass and diversity of the Amazon River floodplains is made up of predators. In none of the studies done thus far have tambaqui been shown to be major prey. The second author has a large unpublished database on the feeding habits of piranhas in the same area of the Rio Madeira where the feeding habits of juvenile tambaqui were studied. These data suggest that piranhas rarely prey on tambaqui, though for reasons that are unclear. Piranhas and young tambaqui often swim together, though it is unknown whether mimicry is involved. Some of the predatory catfishes are known to prey on young tambaqui. In no case, however, have tambaqui been shown to be a major prey species of predatory catfishes. Boto (*Inia geoffrensis*) and tucuxi (*Sotalia fluviatilis*) dolphins can be common in floodplain waters, but Silva (1983) has shown that they rarely attack tambaqui. The giant pirarucu (*Arapaima gigas*) may have at one time been the major predator on tambaqui populations. Pirarucu feed heavily in both floating meadows and open waters. Pirarucu populations have been so diminished through overexploitation that they could no longer be a significant predator on tambaqui. Although more predation studies need to be made, the tambaqui apparently is relatively little preyed on compared with other species. Perhaps for this reason it is, or was, so abundant in floodplain lakes.

A second argument that could be levied against using the tambaqui for extensive fish culture in specific floodplain lakes is that the species is migratory. We can dismiss this concern because the species does not migrate until at least three years of age, or about 4.1 kg in size. Most harvesting could take place in discrete floodplain areas where the fry were introduced and before the fish reached migratory size. However, if any given floodplain were too intensively stocked, large numbers of young fish might possibly begin to move to adjacent areas.

As discussed in earlier chapters, adult tambaqui migrate seasonally to blackwater and clear-water tributaries to feed on fruits and seeds in flooded forests. This behavior probably evolved not only because huge flooded forest areas in the blackwater and clear-water tributaries exist, but also because migration reduces competition with the larger juveniles that are restricted to the floodplains of the muddy rivers. Also, the adults are possibly able to find more food in the tributaries because few fish there are able to feed on the larger fruits and seeds present. An extensive aquaculture for adult tambaqui would involve a minimum three- to four-year period, and most of the fish would have to be harvested in rivers relatively far from where fry were introduced into the muddy-river floodplains.

The question remains whether extensive operations based on juveniles in muddy-river floodplains would provide enough "escapees" to ensure the recruitment of adults into the tributaries. A much better approach exists, however: establishing fish reserves on the Amazon River floodplain and other muddy rivers where tambaqui would be allowed to reach adult sizes. These reserves would serve two purposes. First, they would protect the area's overall biodiversity. Second, they would provide a reproductive and recruitment population of adult tambaqui and many other migratory species for the lower reaches of the blackwater and clear-water tributaries of the central Amazon.

As early as 1947 the pioneering limnologist Harald Sioli suggested that the Amazon River floodplain could be modified for extensive fish culture (Sioli 1947). One of the principal factors that directly or indirectly controls fish production on the floodplains is water level. Floodplain lakes become shallow during the low-water period, and fish production undoubtedly decreases. Many lakes are fed by streams and drained by one small channel that cuts through the levee bordering the main channel. The outlet channel could be dammed at the end of the floods to retain both water and fish. These dams would be simple to construct as they would involve filling in only part of the channel with nearby earth. In many cases the water level could be maintained 2–3 m higher for up to six months than if no dam were present. When the water level began to rise rapidly again, the dam could be removed. This would allow fry born in the river channel to enter the floodplain area. Production would also be increased by stocking the "seminatural" lake with tambaqui fry.

ECONOMIC AND CULTURAL CONSIDERATIONS

The tambaqui appears to be a species for which stock enhancement in the Amazon could be successful. At present the Amazon region is producing more than 2.5 million tambaqui larvae, most of which come from Brazilian government ponds in the proximity of the Balbina Dam near Manaus. No fry are being released into the wild. Additional ponds would be needed to stock Amazon River floodplains, each of which would cost approximately $100,000. Logistically, these ponds should be distributed along the Amazon River at strategic points.

To increase present tambaqui production by 75%, 5 million juveniles per year with an average individual weight of 100 g would need to be stocked. Assuming a survival and/or recapture rate of 20%, tambaqui production would be increased by 1 million individuals weighing on average 3 kg in three years. The total potential harvest, then, would be increased by 3,000 tons.

Based on expenses in 1995, the total cost of the above stock enhancement, including harvesting, would be about $1.2 million (table 13.1). This investment would generate about $7.8 million in three years from the additional fish produced, or a profit of $6.65 million. These costs represent a first experiment that should be carried out before any additional stocking is allowed.

Intensive fish-culture operations can afford either to maintain a brood stock or purchase fry from aquaculture farms specializing in their production. Extensive operations entail high mortality, and thus much greater numbers of fry need to be introduced. A floodplain lake area of approximately 10 km^2 might require several thousand juveniles, but these would be too expensive to buy from brood farms, unless they were run or subsidized by the government.

Floodplain lakes are open systems, at least during the high-water season when most of them become connected. Theoretically, the federal government owns all

TABLE 13.1

Costs of Restocking Amazon Floodplains with Tambaqui

Economic indicators	Unit	Values
Recapture rate		20%
Fish released	individuals	5,000,000
Expected catch	individuals	1,000,000
Costs: 10 ha	US $	115,000
Costs: 100 ha	US $	1,150,000
Fish price (US$/kg)	US $	2.6
Gross revenue (100 ha)	US $	7,800,000
Net revenue (expected)	US $	6,650,000
Ratio of profit to operating costs	%	578
Break even price	US $	0.38
Break-even production	kg	441,402
Net return on capital	ratio	6.49
Payback period	years	0.57

floodplain waters and the resources in them. Each Amazon River floodplain area—usually based around a lake—has one to several villages or communities, and this is true in both Brazil and Peru. Historically, these groupings evolved as focal points for local feasts and religious celebrations. Interwoven into this system, and often dominating it, are absentee landowners who make large claims to floodplain areas.

Within the last decade or two, many local communities have assumed de facto control over fish and other resources. Urban fishermen are either forbidden from exploiting these areas or pay fees for their catches. The question is, if a floodplain lake area is stocked, who exactly has rights to the resulting fish production? We cannot provide the answer here since it will in large part be based on who supplies the capital for stocking these areas. Most likely, various types of agreements will have to be worked out between government officials, entrepreneurs, local communities, floodplain landlords, and commercial fishermen. Several projects in Brazil and Peru are now studying floodplain communities and searching for ways to manage the local resources (McGrath et al. 1994; Ayres 1993). Fish culture might possibly be integrated into these projects. Since cattle and water buffalo are the main preoccupation of most absentee landlords, the government may need to offer tax breaks for entrepreneurs who experiment with fish culture on or near the floodplains. An essential part of any such incentive would be the protection of floodplain habitats—especially flooded forests and floating meadows.

CHAPTER FOURTEEN

CONCLUSION

Six main features summarize the life strategy of the tambaqui: the use of various habitats over large regions; high fecundity; despite high fecundity relatively low investment in reproduction; high investment in growth; late maturity; and the ability to tap plankton and rainforest food chains. All of these have important implications for both the conservation of wild populations and the development of fish culture in the Amazon.

EVOLUTIONARY ECOLOGY

The tambaqui evolved to use all four of the major habitats associated with large rivers in northern South America. The three principal floodplain habitats are lakes, floodplain forests, and floating meadows, and all are important sources of food for the tambaqui. The river-channel habitat is used for migration and as a low-water refuge for adults. At the beginning of the annual floods in the Amazon, large populations of adults migrate to the lower reaches of clear-water and black-water tributaries. Although the black-water and clear-water tributaries are nutrient poor, they nevertheless have huge flooded forests where tambaqui can find abundant fruits and seeds.

Tambaqui will have to be tagged to determine exact migratory distances. Our general impression from field studies is that the annual ranges are less than those reported for South American migratory characins outside the Amazon Basin (see Lowe-McConnell 1977, 1979; 1987; Petrere Jr 1985b). In contrast to the 800–1,600 km that migratory characins cover in the Paraná system, Amazonian tambaqui may be moving no more than an average of 300–500 km annually. Too few data exist to make comparisons with the Orinoco system.

Most South American migratory characin fishes that spawn in river channels have high fecundity (Menezes and Vazzoler 1992; Vazzoler and Menezes 1992). Larvae are at greatest risk from dying of starvation when they are in the river channels, so large numbers of them are necessary if many are to survive until reaching the floodplains. Once fry reach floodplain waters, predation is the main cause of mortality.

The fecundity of most food fish species that spawn in the Amazon River channel is less than 30% of that of the tambaqui. Given present environmental conditions and fish communities, this average suggests that the tambaqui might be "overspending" in fecundity. The same survival success might be achieved if less energy were spent on reproduction or larger eggs were produced. Experimental studies, however, suggest that increased egg size does not enhance resistance to starvation (Araujo-Lima 1994). Likewise, for pelagic (open-water) larvae in general, increased egg size does not seem to lead to decreased predation on young fish (Wootton 1992). For these reasons, the tambaqui may have felt little selection pressure for increase in egg size and reduction in fecundity.

The tambaqui seems to spend less energy for reproduction when compared to other species with high fecundity (Wootton 1992). Only 40–50% of fat reserves accumulated during the growing season are used to produce eggs. The fish probably use the remaining energy to pay heavy metabolic demands. To invest more in reproduction, the species would have to reduce its growth rate and produce more fat reserves. Any greatly increased expenditure of body energy would most likely weaken the female and therefore compromise her life expectancy.

Large species that spawn in river channels have at least two evolutionary options. First, they can spawn numerous times with relatively moderate investment per reproductive cycle. Second, they can spawn fewer times but with a relatively larger investment of energy per reproductive cycle. The tambaqui follows the first option. Because more energy is invested in growth than in annual reproduction, larger females will produce more eggs in the long run. This strategy makes sense for a large herbivorous fish in a system such as the Amazon where periodic low flood levels, thus decreased food availability, can produce stressful years and presumably decreased fecundity.

The tambaqui matures relatively late in life compared with other Amazonian fish species. By the time the tambaqui reaches maturity at three to four years of age, it is already much larger than the maximum size of most other fish species found in the Amazon Basin. In general, life-history models predict that large organisms that do not practice parental care take longer to develop, but in return have higher fecundity (Calow 1985). Delayed maturity is also correlated with low adult mortality (Wootton 1992; Hutchings 1993). Even before tambaqui reach maturity they probably have no significant predators because of their large size.

Large bodies can store more energy than small bodies. This capacity is not only adaptive for reducing reproductive costs to females but also acts as a buffer to fluctuations in food availability. The flood cycle in the Amazon is fairly predictable, but aberrant years can lead to highly stressful conditions. Extended dry seasons can limit access to floodplain forests, and hence to fruits and seeds. In years when the floods are delayed, fat reserves somewhat protect a species such as the tambaqui that depends so heavily on flooded forests. Furthermore, large fish have lower metabolic rates per unit of body biomass than small species and are thus more resistant to food stress (Calder 1984).

The tambaqui is the only large fish in the world that possesses both highly developed gill rakers and huge molarlike teeth. This unique anatomical combination allows the fish to feed on the zooplankton "soup" found in open waters, especially those of the muddy-river floodplains, and the wealth of fruits and seeds produced in the seasonally flooded forests. After about two years of age tambaqui are able to crush hard nuts and swallow relatively large fleshy fruits. The fleshy fruits are shared with many fish species, but the tambaqui has few competitors for large nuts, such as those of rubber trees. Dominating the big end of the "nut-niche" linked to floodplain rainforests, the tambaqui is as much an evolutionary product of the rainforest as a fruit-eating monkey or bird.

TAMBAQUI FOR FISH CULTURE

The Amazon Basin has at least 2,500 fish species. The tambaqui is by far the best known. The tambaqui has been the single most important commercial fish species in the central Amazon for the past several decades, but a combination of floodplain deforestation and overexploitation now threatens wild stocks in the long run. The evidence presented in this book strongly suggests that the tambaqui could serve as an economic incentive for both the rapid development of fish culture in the Amazon and the protection of floodplain forests.

The tambaqui is now recognized as a first-class food species with high promise for national and international markets. As a highly flavorful and vegetarian rainforest species, the tambaqui also has great culinary charisma. Especially noteworthy are its large ribs surrounded with tender, moist flesh. Professional chefs feel that tambaqui ribs could become a food wave of the future, much as kiwi fruit did in the 1980s. Just as with kiwi, however, there must be a large and steady supply if a large-scale market is to be developed. At present that supply does not exist.

From the viewpoint of induced reproduction, tambaqui fish culture has progressed rapidly in the last decade. Overall research efforts, however, have been too far removed from the natural ecology of the species. Fish culturalists have seen the fish but not the forest. A strong export market will demand that the tambaqui's unique fruity flavor be retained. We believe that fish orchards offer the greatest hope for the development of tambaqui fish culture in the Amazon. Fruit- and seed-fed tambaqui from the Amazon would be more delicious, thus more competitive, than the pellet-fed fish now being raised on most farms outside the region. Fruit and seed trees for tambaqui could and should be planted on the floodplains and uplands. They would lead to a far more productive system than livestock ranching and also offer a realistic economic alternative to large-scale deforestation for cattle and water buffalo pastures. Floodplain fruit trees could be planted—or protected where they still remain—for both intensive and extensive fish farming. Amazon fish farmers will have to become agroforesters as well if they are to compete in world markets.

At present most fish-culture farms in the Amazon are found near Manaus and in the southern state of Acre, and the tambaqui is the principal species raised. Acre is in the headwater region of the southwestern Amazon, and the rivers there are too small to support large-scale fisheries. Fish culture in Acre faces little competition from fisheries.

The Brazilian Institute of the Environment (IBAMA) has registered more than seven hundred farms practicing fish culture in Acre. Most aquaculture is based in ponds of about 1 ha in average size. Production in the mid-1990s is estimated to be about 1,000 tons/yr. Acre fish farms already produce more tambaqui than is landed in all Amazonian cities except Manaus.

HABITAT PROTECTION

Although adult tambaqui have been overexploited in the last decade, the greatest danger that wild populations face in the long run is floodplain deforestation. Flooded forests provide both food and shelter for the tambaqui, and for most other fish species as well. Floodplain deforestation is concentrated along the Amazon River.

Pesticides are now being used for vegetable and grain farming on parts of the Amazon River floodplain, but to date this farming is relatively restricted because of the dominance of cattle and water buffalo ranching. Any sharp increase in pesticide use on the floodplain must be carefully monitored, as the water bodies shrink greatly during the low-water period and concentrate pollutants.

Young tambaqui and many other fish species use floating meadows as nursery habitats. The large-scale introduction of cattle and water buffalo results in the destruction of these habitats one to three months before their natural seasonal reduction during the low-water period. In the absence of livestock, during the low-water period relatively large remnants of floating meadows survive in floodplain lakes and along the levees of the river channels. Fish become concentrated in these habitats. When livestock are present, however, the floating meadow remnants are eaten. There may be a million head of livestock on the Amazon River floodplain, and the herd size is increasing annually. A single cow or water buffalo grazes at least a hectare of floating meadow in the two- to three-month period after the livestock are introduced onto the floodplains subsequent to the annual floods. At least a million hectares of floodplain floating meadows are presently being destroyed each year along the Amazon River, and we have very little idea of how this is affecting fish populations, though its potential threat is devastating.

GENETIC CONSIDERATIONS

The unfortunate, but usually necessary, tendency of most fish-culture operations is to limit the size of the gene pool so that certain characteristics—such as faster growth rate and greater disease resistance—can be selected. To date, tambaqui brood stock have not been selected for particular genetic characteristics, though experimentation has begun, especially with hybrids. Most of the fry now being sold appear to be derived from no more than a few dozen adults. If such a limited gene pool were used for extensive operations, it is possible that introduced populations could eventually "taint" the genetics of wild stocks. Also of special concern is the introduction of fertile hybrids that might completely change the genetics of wild tambaqui populations if they crossed with them. Biologists should thoroughly study any hybrids, sterile or fertile, before they are allowed to be turned loose in the wild to determine what the negative consequences might be on the local fish populations.

MINIMUM AREA FOR WILD POPULATIONS

No matter how successful fish-culture operations hopefully turn out to be, wild populations should also be managed. The tambaqui's life history embraces huge geographical areas. Recognition of this fact is essential if the species is to be managed and protected for long-term fisheries and genetic diversity for future brood stock. Wild populations of tambaqui cannot be protected by "managing" a few or even dozens of floodplain lakes through restocking or controlled fishing. The species is widespread in the Amazon Basin and migratory, and under natural circumstances larvae come from upstream populations of adults.

Probably only a single tambaqui population exists along the Amazon River. Currents carry newborn larvae downstream, leaving little opportunity for the genetic isolation of populations. Although tambaqui have not been tagged, the rarity of adults, but abundance of juveniles, in the eastern Amazon region near Santarém further bolsters the single-population hypothesis.

The largest tambaqui fisheries for adults are found west of the Rio Madeira, the region where most of the Amazon's flooded forests are found. However, the Amazon River floodplain area east of the Rio Negro is perhaps the main nursery region from which western populations are recruited. The implications are profound. If the floodplain lakes of the eastern region are overexploited for young tambaqui, as now appears to be happening, the western Amazonian tambaqui fisheries could be destroyed as well. The opposite could also be true. If adult populations are decimated in the western Amazon, the numbers of larvae produced annually might be insufficient for recruitment to the downstream floodplains.

Agassiz, L. 1829. *Selecta Genera et Species Piscium quos in Itinere per Brasiliam.* Munich: Typis C. Wolf.

Alcántara, B. F. 1986. "Avances en el cultivo de gamitana, *Colossoma macropomum* Cuvier 1818, en el laboratório de Iquitos del Imarpe." *Revista Latinoamericana de Acuicultura* 27:27–29.

———. 1989. "Situación del cultivo de *Colossoma* en el Peru." In Hernández, R. A., ed. *Cultivo de Colossoma.* Bogotá: Editora Guadalupe.

Alcántara, B. F., and F. H. Gerra. 1986. "Avances en la producción de alevinos de gamitana, *Colossoma macropomum*, y paco, *C. brachypomum*, por reproducción inducida." *Revista Latinoamericana de Acuicultura* 30:23–32.

———. 1988. "Avances en la producción de alevinos de gamitana, *Colossoma macropomum*, y paco, *C. brachypomum*, por reproducción inducida." *Folia Amazonica* 1:1–12.

Alcántara, B. F., F. H. Gerra, and E. W. Mori. 1983. "Ensayo preliminar de cultivo de gamitama, *Colossoma macropomum* Cuvier 1818, asociado a la cria de cerdos." *Revista Latinoamericana de Acuicultura* 18:39–46.

Almeida, R. G. 1980. "Aspectos taxonômicos e hábitos alimentares de três espécies de *Triportheus* (Pisces: Characoidei, Characidae) do Lago do Castanho, Amazonas." Master's thesis, INPA/UFAM, Manaus.

Almeida-Toledo, L. F., F. Foresti, S. M. Ramos, R. Ormanezi, V. J. S. Carosfeld, and S. A. Toledo Filho. 1988. "Estudos citogenéticos de híbridos entre fêmeas de pacu (*Piaractus mesopotamicus*) e machos de tambaqui (*Colossoma macropomum*)." *Boletim Técnico do CEPTA* 1:11–17.

Almeida-Toledo, L. F., F. Foresti, S. A. Toledo, G. Bernardino, W. Ferrari, and R. C. G. Alcántara. 1987. "Cytogenetic studies in *Colossoma mitrei, C. macropomum,* and their interspecific hybrid." *Proceedings of the World Symposium on Selection, Hybridization, and Genetic Engineering in Aquaculture, Berlin* 1:189–95.

Almeida-Val, V. M. F., M. L. B. Schwantes, and A. L. Val. 1990. "LDH Isozymes in Amazon Fish—I. Electrophoretic Studies on Two Species from Serrasalmidae Family, *Mylossoma duriventris* and *Colossoma macropomum*." *Comparative Biochemistry and Physiology* 95B:77–84.

Alves, L. F. 1993. "The Fate of Stream Water Nitrate Entering Littoral Areas of an Amazonian Floodplain Lake: The Role of Plankton, Periphyton, Inundated Soils, and Sediment." Ph.D. dissertation, University of Maryland.

Anderson, A. 1990. "Extraction and Forest Management by Rural Inhabitants in the Amazon Estuary." In Anderson, A., ed. *Alternatives to Deforestation: Steps Toward Sustainable Use of the Amazon Rain Forest*. New York: Columbia University Press.

Anderson, A. B., P. H. May, and M. J. Balick. 1991. *The Subsidy from Nature: Palm Forests, Peasantry, and Development on an Amazon Frontier*. New York: Columbia University Press.

Andrade, P. C. M., A. S. Tolentino, and C. E. C. Freitas. 1993. "Desenvolvimento de juvenis de tambaqui (*Colossoma macropomum* Cuvier, 1818) em gaiolas." *Revista da Universidade do Amazonas, Série Ciências Agrárias* 2:21–30.

Araripe, M. A. E., M. C. S. Leão, M. A. Oliveira, and L. C. U. Saunders. 1988. "Estudo físico e químico da água e do solo em ensaio de consórcio arroz, *Oryza sativa* L., tambaqui, *Colossoma macropomum* Cuvier, tilápia do Nilo, *Oreochromis niloticus*, e marrecos de pequim, *Anas platyrhynchus*." *Ciências Agronômicas* 19:45–51.

Araujo-Lima, C. A. R. M. 1984. "Distribuição espacial e temporal de larvas de Characiformes em um setor do Rio Amazonas, próximo a Manaus." Master's thesis, INPA/UFAM, Manaus.

——. 1990. "Larval Development and Reproductive Strategies of Amazonian Fishes." Ph.D. dissertation, University of Stirling.

——. 1994. "Egg Size and Larval Development in Central Amazon Fish." *Journal of Fish Biology* 44:371–89.

Araujo-Lima, C. A. R. M., B. R. Forsberg, R. Victoria, and L. Martinelli. 1986. "Energy Sources for Detritivorous Fishes in the Amazon." *Science* 234:1256–58.

Araujo-Lima. C. A. R. M., M. Goulding, B. R. Forsberg, R. Victoria, and L. Martinelli. Forthcoming. "The Ecomomic Value of the Amazon Flooded Forest Under a Fisheries Perspective." *Verhandlungen Internationalis Verein. Limnologie*.

Axelrod, H. R., C. W. Emmens, and W. E. Burgess. 1979. *Exotic Tropical Fishes*. Neptune City: TFH Publications.

Axelrod, H. R., and W. Vorderwinkler. 1957. *Encyclopedia of Tropical Fishes*. New York: Sterling Publishing Co.

Ayres, D. L. 1994. "A implantação de uma unidade de conservação em área de várzea: A experiência de Mamirauá." In M. A. D'Inçao and I. M. Silveira, ed. *Amazônia e a Crise da Modernação*. Belém: Museu Paraense Emílio Goeldi.

Ayres, J. M. 1993. *As Matas de Várzea do Mamirauá*. Brasília: Sociedade Civil Mamirauá.

Barbosa, J. M., and M. R. Oliveira. 1988. "Estudo analítico do híbrido do pacu *Colossoma mitrei* (Berg, 1895) x tambaqui *Colossoma macropomum* (Cuvier, 1818)." *Anais do V Simpósio Brasileiro de Aquicultura, Florianópolis, S.C.* 5:534–35.

Bardach, J. E., J. H. Ryther, and W. O. McLarney. 1972. *Aquaculture: The Farming and Husbundry of Freshwater and Marine Organisms.* New York: John Wiley & Sons.

Barthem, R. B. 1984. "Pesca experimental e seletividade de redes de espera para espécies de peixes amazônicos." *Boletim do Museu Paraense Emílio Goeldi (Zoologia)* 1(1):57–88.

——. Forthcoming. "A pesca na várzea do médio Solimões." Manuscript.

Bauchot, M. L., J. Daget, and R. Buchot. 1990. "L'ichthyologie en France au debut du XIX siecle. L'histoire naturelle des poissons de Cuvier et Valenciennes." *Bulletin du Musée National Histoire Naturelle de Paris* 4(12):3–142.

Bayley, P. B. 1983. "Central Amazon Fish Production: Biomass, Production, and Some Dynamic Characteristics." Ph.D. dissertation, Dalhousie University.

——. 1988. "Factors Affecting Growth Rates of Young Floodplain Fishes: Seasonality and Density-Dependence." *Environmental Biology of Fishes* 21:127–42.

Bayley, P. B. and M. Petrere Jr. 1989. "Amazon Fisheries: Assessment Methods, Current Status and Management Options." *Proceedings of the International Large River Symposium. Canadian Special Publications, Fisheries and Aquatic Science* 106:385–98.

Bello, R., L. González, Y. La Grave, L. Pérez, N. Prada, J. J. Salaya, and J. Santacana. 1989. "Monografia sobre el cultivo de cachama *Colossoma macropomum* en Venezuela." In R. A. Hernández, ed. *Cultivo de Colossoma.* Bogotá: Editora Guadalupe.

Bermudez, D. 1980. "Preliminary Experiences in the Control of Fish Diseases in Warm Water Aquaculture Operations in Venezuela." *Journal of Fish Diseases* 3:355–57.

Bermudez, D., and P. N. Kossowski. 1979. "Ensayo sobre la reproducción de *Colossoma macropomum.*" *Acta Científica Venezoelana* 1:128–34.

Bernardino, G., and R. C. G. Alcântara. 1988. "Reprodução artificial da cachama (*Colossoma macropomum*) (Cuvier, 1818)." *Red Acuicultura Boletin* 1:10–12.

Bernardino, G., R. C. G. Alcântara, and J. A Senhorini. 1988. "Procedimentos para a reprodução induzida e alevinagem do tambaqui *Colossoma macropomum* e pacu *Piaractus brachypomus.*" *Anais do V Simpósio Brasileiro de Aquicultura, Florianópolis, S.C.* 2:274–79.

Bernardino, G., J. O. J. Mendonça, and L. P. Ribeiro. 1986. "Indução a desova do tambaqui (*Colossoma macropomum*) com extrato bruto de hipófises." *Anais do IV Simpósio Brasileiro de Aquicultura, Cuiabá-MT* 4:1.

Best, R. C. 1984. "The Aquatic Mammals and Reptiles of the Amazon." *The Amazon: Limnology and Landscape Ecology of a Mighty River and Its Basin.* In H. Sioli, ed. Dordrecht, Netherlands: W. Junk Publishers.

Betendorf, J. F. 1901. "Chrónica da missão dos padres da Companhia de Jesus no

Estado do Maranhão." *Revista do Instituto Histórico e Geográfico Brasileiro* 72(1):1 –682.

Bohlke, J. E., S. E. Weitman, and N. A. Menezes. 1978. "Estado atual da sistemática dos peixes de água doce da América do Sul." *Acta Amazonica* 8:657–77.

Boischio, A. M. P. 1992. "Produção pesqueira em Porto Velho, Rondônia (1984– 1989)—alguns aspectos ecológicos das espécies comercialmente relevantes." *Acta Amazonica* 22(1):163–72.

Borges, G. A. 1986. "Ecologia de três espécies do gênero *Brycon* Muller & Trochel, 1844 (Pisces, Characiformes) no Rio Negro-Amazonas, com ênfase na caracterização taxonômica e alimentação." Master's thesis, INPA/UFAM, Manaus.

Braum, E. 1983. "Beobachtungen über eine reversible Lippenextension und ihre Rollebei der Notatmung von *Brycon* sp. (Pisces, Characidae) und *Colossoma macropomum* (Pisces, Serrasalmidae)." *Amazoniana* VII:355–74.

Brett, J. R. 1979. "Environmental Factors and Growth." *Fish Physiology.* In W. S. Hoar and D. J. Randall, ed. London: Academic Press.

Brett, J. R., and T. D. Groves. 1979. "Physiological Energetics." *Fish Physiology.* In W. S. Hoar and D. J. Randall, ed. London: Academic Press.

Brinkmann, W. L., and U. M. Santos. 1973. "Heavy Fish-Kill in Unpolluted Floodplain Lakes of Central Amazonia, Brazil." *Biological Conservation* 5:147–49.

Britski, H. A. 1977. "Sobre o gênero *Colossoma* (Pisces, Characidae)." *Ciência e Cultura* 29:810.

——. 1992. "Taxonomia dos gêneros *Colossoma* e *Piaractus.*" Manuscript.

Brittan, M. R., and G. D. Grossman. 1978. "A Pacu (*Colossoma,* Family Characidae) Caught in the Sacramento River." *California Fish and Game* 23:171–73.

Buarque de Holanda Ferreira, A. 1975. *Novo Dicionário de Língua Portuguesa.* Rio de Janeiro: Editora Nova Fronteira.

Burgos, P. F. O., and J. W. B. Silva. 1989. *Diagnóstico da Aquicultura na Região Nordeste do Brasil.* Brasília: FAO.

Burns, B. 1965. "Manaus, 1910: Portrait of a Boom Town." *Journal of Inter-American Studies* VII(3):400–21.

Cala, P. 1977. "Los peces de la Orinoquia colombiana: Lista preliminar anotada." *Lozania (Acta Zoologia Colombiana)* 24:1–21.

Calder, W. A. 1984. *Size, Function, and Life History.* Cambridge: Harvard University Press.

Calow, P. 1985. "Adaptive Aspects of Energy Allocation." *Fish Energetics.* In P. Tytler and P. Calow, ed. London: Croom Helm.

Campbell, D. G., J. L. Store, and A. Rosa Jr. 1992. "A Comparison of the Phytosociology and Dynamics of Three Floodplain (Várzea) Forests of Known Ages, Rio Juruá, Western Brazilian Amazon." *Botanical Journal of the Linnean Society* 108:213–37.

Campos, A. A. 1944. "Peixes da sub-família Myleinae." *Papeis Avulos do Departamento de Zoologia da Secretaria da Agricultura* 4(15):210–12.

Campos Baca, L. 1994. "The Culture of Gamitana (*Colossoma macropomum*, Cuvier, 1818) in Latin America." Master's thesis, Southern Illinois University.

Campos Baca, L., and P. Padilla. 1985. "Effectos de 'kudzu' (*Pueraria phaseooloides*) y del 'cetico' (*Cecropia*) como fuentes de proteina en alimentación de gamitana *Colossoma macropomum*." *Boletim Técnico, Instituto de Investigaciónes de la Amazonia Peruana* 1:12.

Canestri, V. 1970. "Alimentación frutívora en *Colossoma brachypomus* (Osteichtyes —Cypriniformes—Characidae)." *Memoria Sociedad de Ciencias Naturales, La Salle* 30:196–205.

Cantelmo, O. A., and J. A. Senhorini. 1989. "Alimentação artificial de larvas e alevinos de peixes." *Red Acuicultura Boletin* 3:3–6.

Carneiro, A. R. X. 1991. "Elaboração e uso de ensilado biológico de pescado na alimentação de alevinos de tambaqui *Colossoma macropomum* (Cuvier, 1818)." Master's thesis, INPA/UFAM, Manaus.

Carneiro, D. J. 1981. "Digestibilidade protéica em dietas isocalóricas para tambaqui, *Colossoma macropomum* (Cuvier) (Pisces, Characidae)." *Anais do Simpósio Brasileiro de Aquacultura* II:78–80.

Carneiro Sobrinho, A., R. R. Melo, J. W. L. Silva, and M. I. S. Nobre. 1989. "Resultados de um experimento sobre o cultivo do tambaqui, *Colossoma macropomum* Cuvier, 1818, na densidade estocagem de 10,000 peixes/ha." *Ciências Agronônicas* 20:25–31.

Carosfeld, J. 1989. "Reproductive Physiology and Induced Breeding of Fish As Related to Culture of *Colossoma*." *Cultivo de Colossoma*. In R. A. Hernández, ed. Bogotá: Editora Guadalupe.

Carvalho, J. C. M. 1983. *Viagem Filosófica pelas Capitanias do Grão Pará, Rio Negro, Mato Grosso, e Cuiabá (1783–1793)*. Belém: Museu Paraense Emílio Geoldi/ CNPq.

Carvalho, M. L. 1981. "Alimentação do tambaqui jovem (*Colossoma macropomum* Cuvier, 1818) e sua relação com a comunidade zooplanctônica do Lago Grande—Manaquiri, Solimões—AM." Master's thesis, INPA/UFAM, Manaus.

Castagnolli, N., D. F. Brasil, M. V. Val Sella, M. L. G. Pinto, and A. A. M. Rosa. 1988. "Induced Breeding of the Pacu (*Piaractus mesopotamicus* = *Colossoma mitrei*) and Tambaqui (*Colossoma macropomum*) with LH-RHa and Crude or Partially Purified Fisg Gonadotropin." *Proccedings of Aquaculture International Congress, Vancouver, 1988* 74:1.

Castangnolli, N., and A. A. M. Rosa. 1988. "Produção de híbridos de tambaqui, *Colossoma macropomum*, e pacu, *Piaractus mesopotamicus*, através da reprodução induzida com LH-RHa." *Anais do VI Simpósio Latino-Americano de Aquicultura, Florianópolis, S.C.* VI:134–40.

Castelo, F. P., D. R. Amaya, and F. C. Strong. 1980. "Aproveitamento e características da gordura cavitária do tambaqui, *Colossoma macropomum* Cuvier 1818." *Acta Amazonica* 10:557–76.

Castillo, A. C. 1986. "Reprodución inducida de la cachama *Colossoma macropomum* en el centro Acuicola Zapatec, Mortelos, México." *Revista Latinoamericana de Acuicultura* 30:5–6.

Castro, A. 1992. "O extrativismo do açaí no Amazonas." Manuscript.

Castroviejo, S., and G. Lopez. 1985. "Estudio y descripción de las comunidades vegetales del 'Hato el Frio' los Llanos de Venezuela." *Memoria Sociedad de Ciencias Naturales, La Salle* XLV:79–149.

Caulton, M. S. 1982. "Feeding, Metabolism, and Growth of *Tilapias*: Some Quantitative Considerations." *The Biology and Culture of Tilapias. ICLARM Conference Proceedings*. In R. S. V. Pullin and R. H. Lowe-McConnell, ed. Manila: International Center for Living Aquatic Resources.

Ceccarelli, P. S. 1988. "Sucseptibilidade a infestção de *Learnaea* Copepoda, Learnaedia, Linnaeus em diferentes espécies de peixes cultivados no CEPTA e testes de infestação do pacu (*Piaractus mesopotamicus*)." *Boletim Técnico do CEPTA* 1:31–35.

Ceccarelli, P. S., L. B. Figueira, and C. Ferraz de Lima. 1990. "Observações sobre a ocorrência de parasitos no CEPTA entre 1983–1990." *Boletim Técnico do CEPTA* 3:43–54.

Ceccarelli, P. S., and C. A. Oliveira. 1986. "Testes com antibióticos e quimioterapicos no controle da colunariose em tambaqui." *Anais do IV Simpósio Brasileiro de Aquicultura, Cuiabá, MT* IV:56–57.

Chabalin, E., F. J. V. Palhares, J. A. Ferraz de Lima, and E. M. Neves. 1992. "Viabilidade econônica da utilização de resídios hortifrutigranjeiros na criação de pacu *Piaractus mesopotamicus* em gaiolas." *Boletim Técnico do CEPTA* 5:23–29.

Chabalin, E., J. A. Senhorini, and J. A. Ferraz de Lima. 1989. "Estimativa do custo de produção de larvas e alevinos." *Boletim Técnico do CEPTA* 2:61–74.

Choudhury, A., and T. A. Dick. 1993. "Parasites of Lake Sturgeon, *Ascipenser fulvescens* (Chondrostei: Ascipenseridae), from Central Canada." *Journal of Fish Biology* 42:571–84.

Colonnello, G., S. Castroviejo, and G. Lopez. 1986. "Comunidades vegetales asociadas al Rio Orinoco en el sur de Monagas y Sinzoategui." *Memoria Sociedad de Ciencias Naturales, La Salle* XLVI:127–66.

Conroy, D. A. 1989. "Reseña sobre las principales enfermedades infecto contagiosas y parasitosis de peces del género *Colossoma*." *Cultivo de Colossoma*. In R. A. Hernández, ed. Bogotá: Editora Guadalupe.

Conroy, D. A., and M. E. Mujica. 1985. "Estudios sobre la prevención y control de enfermedads en larvas de cachamas, *Colossoma macropomum* (Cuvier 1818), producidas en cautiveiro por médio de la reprodución inducida." *Revista de La Facultad de Ciencias Veterinarias de la Universidad Central de Venezuela* 32:97–102.

Cope, E. D. 1871. "Fishes from the Amazon River Above the Mouth of the Rio Negro." *Proceedings of the Academy of Natural Sciences, Philadelphia* 12:55.

Cunha, A. G. 1987. *Dicionário Histórico das Palavras Portuguêsas de Origem Tupi*. São Paulo: Edições Melhoramentos.

Cuvier, G. 1818. "Sur les poissons du sous-genre Myletes." *Mémoires du Musée de L'Histoire Naturelle, Paris* 4:444–56.

Dabrowski, K. R. 1985. "Energy Budget of Coregonid (*Coregonus* spp.) Fish Growth, Metabolism, and Reproduction." *Oikos* 45:358–64.

Daget, J., and L. Saldanha. 1989. *Histoires Naturelles Franco-Portugaises du XIX Siecle.* Lisboa: Instituto Nacional de Investigações das Pescas.

Dahl, G. 1971. *Los Peces del Norte de Colombia.* Bogotá: INDERENA.

Darmont, M., and J. J. Salaya. 1983. "Ensayo de cultivo de la cachama, *Colossoma macropomum*, Cuvier 1818, en jaulas flotantes rígidas." *Memorias Asociación Latinoamericana de Acuicultura* 5:465–79.

Dias, J. C. R., N. Castangnoli, and D. J. Carneiro. 1988. "Alimentação de larvas de pacu (*Colossoma miteri*, Berg) com dietas naturais e artificais." *Anais do VI Simpósio Latino-Americano de Aquicultura, Florianópolis, S.C.* VI:500–504.

Díaz-Ungría, C. 1968. "Helmintos de peces de Venezuela con descripción de un género y tres espécies nuevas." *Boletin de la Sociedad Venezoelana de Ciencia Natural* 27:537–70.

DNAEE (Departamento Nacional de Aguas e Energia Elétrica). 1982. *Codificação da Rede Hidrográfica—Bacia do Rio Amazonas.* Rio de Janeiro: DNAEE.

D'Oliveira, M. V. N. 1989. "Regeneração natural de uma floresta de várzea explorada por método tradicional, no Paraná Abufari, no médio Rio Rurus." Master's thesis, INPA/UFAM, Manaus.

Eckmann, R. 1985. "The Fisheries Situation in the Peruvian Amazon." *Animal Research and Development* 21:59–86.

——. 1987. "Growth and Body Composition of Juvenile *Colossoma macropomum* Cuvier 1818 (Characoidei) Feeding on Artificial Diets." *Aquaculture* 64:293–303.

Eigenmann, C. H. 1903. "New Genera of South American Fresh-Water Fishes and New Names for Some Old Genera." *Smithsonian Micellaneous Collections* 45(1431):144–48.

——. 1915. "The Serrasalminae and Mylinae." *Annals of the Carnegie Museum* 9:226–71.

Eigenmann, C. H., and C. H. Kennedy. 1903. "On a Collection of Fishes from Paraguay with a Synopsis of the American Genera of Cichlids." *Proceedings of the Academy of Natural Sciences, Philadelphia* 55(2):497–537.

Eliott, J. M., U. H. Humpesch, and M. A. Henley. 1987. "A Comparative Study on Eight Mathematical Models for the Relationship Between Water Temperature and Hatching Time of Eggs of Freshwater Fish." *Archiv für Hydrobiologie* 109:257–77.

Esteves, F. A. 1988. *Fundamentos de Limnologia.* Rio de Janeiro: Interciência/FINEP.

Estevez, R. M. 1987. "La cachama." *Revista Latinoamericana de Acuicultura* 31:54.

Falabella, P. G. R. 1994. *A Pesca no Amazonas: Problemas e Soluções.* Manaus: Imprensa Oficial.

Fange, R., and D. Grove. 1979. "Digestion." In W. J. Hoar, D. J. Randall, and J. R. Brett, ed. *Fish Physiology.* New York: Academic Press.

FAO (Food and Agricultural Organization). 1992. "FAO/Japan Expert Consultation on the Development of Community-Based Coastal Fishery Management Systems for Asia and the Pacific." *Fisheries Report* 1:197–204.

Ferrari, V. A., A. F. B. Lucas, and L. A. Gaspar. 1991. "Desempenho do tambaqui *Colossoma macropomum* Cuvier, 1818, em monocultura experimental sob condições de viveiro-estufa e viveiro convencial (1 fase) e em viveiro convencional (2 fase) no Sudeste." *Boletim Técnico do CEPTA* 4:23–37.

Ferraz de Lima, J. A. 1989. "Atuações do CEPTA para a expanção do cultivo dos *Colossoma* e *Piaractus*." *Cultivo de Colossoma.* In R. A. Hernández, ed. Bogotá: Editora Guadalupe.

Ferraz de Lima, J. A., A. Bustamante, E. Chabalin, F. J. V. Palhares, J. H. Souza, and L. A. Gaspar. 1992. "Utilização de resíduos de produtos hortigranjeiros para criação de pacu *Piaractus mesopotamicus* Holmberg, 1887 em gaiolas." *Boletim Técnico do CEPTA* 5:1–19.

Ferreira, A. R. 1972. *Viagem Filosófica pelas Capitanias do Grão Pará, Rio Negro, Mato Grosso, e Cuiabá.* Rio de Janeiro: Conselho Nacional de Cultura.

Ferreira, E. J. G. 1984. "A ictiofauna da represa hidrelétrica de Curuá-una, Santarém, Pará. I - Lista e distribuição das espécies." *Amazoniana* 8(3):351–63.

———. 1992. "A ictiofauna do Rio Trombetas na área de influência da futura usina hidrelétrica de Cachoeira Porteira, Pará." Ph.D. dissertation, INPA/UFAM, Manaus.

Ferreira, E. J. G., G. M. Santos, and M. Jegu. 1988. "Aspectos ecológicos da ictiofauna do Rio Mucajaí, na área da Ilha Paredão, Roraima, Brasil." *Amazoniana* 10(3):339–52.

Ferreira, L. V. 1991. "O efeito do período de inundação na zonação de comunidade, fenologia e regeneração em uma floresta de igapó na Amazônia Central." Master's thesis, INPA/UFAM, Manaus.

Fex de Santis, R. 1991. "Crescimiento y sobrevivencia de larvas de cachama (*Colossoma macropomum*) con alimento vivo y no vivo." *Red Acuicultura Boletin* 5:9–12.

Fim, J. D. I. 1992. "Influência da alimentação no ciclo de vida da *Moina micrura* (Crustacea: Cladocera) en viveiros de peixes." Master's thesis, INPA/UFAM, Manaus.

Finkers, J. 1986. *Los Yanomami y Su Sistema Alimenticio.* Caracas: Vicariato Apostólico de Puerto Ayacucho.

Finstad, B., and T. G. Heggberget. 1993. "Migration, Growth, and Survival of Wild and Hatchery-Reared Anadromous Arctic Charr (*Salvelinus alpinus*) in Finnmark, Northern Norway." *Journal of Fish Biology* 43:303–12.

Fisher, T. 1978. "Plâncton e produção primária em sistemas aquáticos da Amazônia central." *Acta Amazonica* 8:43–55.

Fisher, T. R., J. M. Melack, B. Robertson, and L. F. Alves. 1983. "Vertical Distribution of Zooplakton and Physico-Chemical Conditions During a 24-Hour Period in an Amazon Floodplain Lake—Lago Calado, Brazil." *Acta Amazonica* 13:475–87.

Fontes, N. A., J. A. Senhorini, and A. F. B. Lucas. 1990. "Efeito de duas densidades de estocagem no desempenho larval do paqui, *Piaractus mesopotamicus* (fêmea) x *Colossoma macropomum* (macho) em viveiros." *Boletim Técnico do CEPTA* 3:23–32.

Forsberg, B., C. A. R. M. Araujo-Lima, L. A. Martinelli, R. L. Victoria, and J. A. Bonassi. 1993. "Autotrophic Carbon Sources for Fish of the Central Amazon." *Ecology* 74:643–52.

Forsberg, B. R., A. H. Devol, J. E. Richey, L. A. Martinelli, R. L. Victoria, and H. Santos. 1988. "Factors Controlling Nutrient Concentrations in Amazon Flood-plain Lakes." *Limnology and Oceanography* 33:41–56.

Forte, A. G. 1982. "Resultados da aclimatação do tambaqui *Colossoma macropomum* (Cuvier 1818) para piscicultura do Nordeste brasileiro." Fortaleza, Ceará: DNOCS (internal document).

Foster, R. 1990. "The Floristic Composition of the Rio Manu Floodplain Forest." *Four Neotropical Rainforests*. In A. Gentry, ed. New Haven: Yale University Press.

Fowler, H. W. 1954. *Os Peixes de Água Doce do Brasil*. São Paulo: Departamento de Zoologia da Secretaria de Agricultura.

Freitas, J. W. F., and J. J. S. Gurgel. 1985. "Estudo de alguns parâmetros biométricos e da composição química do tambaqui *Colossoma macropomum* Cuvier, 1818 e da pirapitinga *Colossoma brachypomum* Cuvier 1818, criados en cativeiro." *Boletim Técnico do DNOCS* 43:47–66.

Fritz, S. 1922. *Journal of the Travels and Labours of Father Samuel Fritz in the River of the Amazons Between 1686 and 1723*. London: Hakluyt Society.

Fuller, P., L. Nico, C. Boydstun, A. Benson, and J. D. Williams. 1995. "Preliminary Report on Non-Indigenous Fishes in Inland Waters of the United States (South-eastern Biological Science Center, National Biological Service, Gainesville, Florida)." Manuscript.

Furch, B. 1984. "Untersuchungen zur Überschwemmungs-Toleranz von Baumen der Várzea und des Igapó. Blattpigmente." *Biogeographica* 19:77–83.

Gery, J. 1977. *Characoids of the World*. Neptune City, N.J.: TFH Publications.

——. 1986. "Notes de characologie neotropicale. I. Progrès dan la systematique des genres *Colossoma* et *Piaractus*." *Revue Française de Aquariologie* 12:97–102.

Gibson, R. N., and I. A. Ezzi. 1985. "Effect of Particle Concentration on Filter- and Particulate-Feeding in the Herring *Clupea harengus*." *Marine Biology* 88:109–16.

Gibson, R. N., and I. A. Ezzi. 1992. "The Relative Profitability of Particulate- and Filter-Feeding in the Herring *Clupea harengus* L." *Journal of Fish Biology* 40:577–90.

Giugliano, R., R. Shrimpton, D. B. Arkcoll, L. G. Giugliano, and M. Petrere Jr. 1978. "Diagnóstico da realidade alimentar e nutricional do Estado do Amazonas." *Acta Amazonica (Supplemento)* 8:5–54.

Golvan, Y. J. 1956. "Acanthocephala d'Amazonie. Redescription *Oligacanthor-rhynchus inheringi* Travassos, 1916 et *Neoechinorhynchus buttnerae* n. sp. (Neoacanthocephala, Neoechinorhynidae)." *Ann. Parasit. Hum. Comp.* 31:500–524.

Gottsberger, G. 1978. "Seed Dispersal by Fish in the Inundated Regions of Humaitá, Amazonia." *Biotropica* 10(3):170–83.

Goulding, M. 1979. *Ecologia da Pesca do Rio Madeira*. Manaus: CNPq/INPA.

——. 1980. *The Fishes and the Forest: Explorations in Amazonian Natural History*. Berkeley: University of California Press.

——. 1981. *Man and Fisheries on an Amazon Frontier*. The Hague: Dr. W. Junk Publishers.

——. 1983. "Amazonian Fisheries." *The Dilemma of Amazonian Development*. In E. F. Moran, ed. Boulder, Colo.: Westview Press.

——. 1988. "Ecology and Management of Migratory Food Fishes of the Amazon Basin." *Tropical Rainforests: Diversity and Conservation*. In F. Almeda and C. M. Pringle, ed. San Francisco: California Academy of Sciences.

——. 1989. *Amazon: The Flooded Forest*. London: The BBC.

——. 1993. "Flooded Forests of the Amazon." *Scientific American* 266(3):114–20.

Goulding, M., and M. L. Carvalho. 1982. "Life History and Management of the Tambaqui (*Colossoma macropomum*, Characidae): An Important Amazonian Food Fish." *Revista Brasileira de Zoologia* 1(2):107–33.

Goulding, M., M. L. Carvalho, and E. G. Ferreira. 1988. *Rio Negro: Rich Life in Poor Water: Amazonian Diversity and Foodchain Ecology As Seen Through Fish Communities*. The Hague: SPB Academic Publishing.

Goulding, M., N. J. H. Smith, and D. Mahar. 1996. *Floods of Fortune: Ecology and Economy Along the Amazon*. New York: Columbia Unversity Press.

Graef, E. 1995. "As espécies de peixes com potencial para criação no Amazonas." *Criando Peixes na Amazônia*. In A. L. Val. and A. Honczarik, ed. Manaus: INPA.

Gray, I. E. 1954. "Comparative Study of the Gill Area of Marine Fishes." *Biological Bulletin* 107:219–25.

Greenwood, P. H., and G. Howes. 1975. "Neogene Fossil Fishes from the L. Albert and L. Edward Rift (Zaire)." *Bulletin of British Museum of Natural History (Geology)* 26:71–127.

Groombridge, B., ed. 1992. *Global Biodiversity: Status of the Earth's Living Resources*. New York: Chapman and Hall.

Guerra Flores, H., B. F. Alcántara, J. Maco Garcia, and H. Sanchez Riveiro. 1990. "La pesqueria en el Amazonas peruano." *Interciência* 15(6):469–75.

Guyot, J. L., D. Corbin, J. Quintanilla, and H. Calle. 1991. "Hydrochemie de lacs dans la region de Trinidad (Amazonie bolivienne). Influence d'un fleuve andin: le Rio Mamoré." *Revue de Hydrobiologie Tropical* 24:3–12.

Halver, J. E. 1989. *Fish Nutrition*. San Diego: Academic Press.

Hamilton, S. K., and L. W. Lewis Jr. 1987. "Causes of Seasonality in the Chemistry of a Lake on the Orinoco River Floodplain, Venezuela." *Limnology and Oceanography* 32:1277–90.

Hancz, C. 1993. "Performance of the Amazonian Tambaqui, *Colossoma macropomum*, in Pond Polyculture." *Aquacultural Engineering* 12:245–54.

Hanek, G. 1982. "La pesqueria en la Amazonia peruana: Presente y futuro." *Documento Técnico de Pesca, FAO, Rome* 14:1–150.

Hardy, E. R. 1992. "Changes in Species Composition of Cladocera and Food Availability in a Floodplain Lake, Lago Jacaretinga, Central Amazon." *Amazoniana* 12:155–68.

Hasler, A. D., and A. T. Scholz. 1983. *Olfactory Imprinting and Homing in Salmon.* Berlin: Springer-Verlag.

Hayashi, C., and S. M. F. Zuim. 1981. "Metabolismo respiratório do peixe tambaqui (*Colossoma macropomum* Cuvier, 1818) sob influência de diferentes níveis de proteína." *Anais do II Simpósio Brasileiro de Aquicultura, Jaboticabal* 2:114–16.

Hecht, S., and A. Cockburn. 1990. *The Fate of the Forest: Developers, Destroyers, and Defenders of the Amazon.* New York: Harper-Perennial.

Heming, T. A., and R. K. Buddington. 1988. "Yolk Absorption in Embryonic and Larval Fishes." *Fish Physiology.* In W. S. Hoar and D. Randall, ed. New York: Academic Press.

Hemming, J. 1978. *Red Gold; The Conquest of the Brazilian Indians.* Cambridge: Harvard University Press.

Herculano, L. 1987. "Cultivo experimental de tambaqui, *Colossoma macropomum* Cuvier 1818, usando 4 tipos de dietas." *Proccedings of the Latin American Seminar on Aquaculture.* In J. A. J. Verreth, M. Carrilo, and S. Zauny, ed. Wageningen, Germany: IFS.

Heredia, B., and J. Gonzalez. 1990. "Ganancia compensatoria en *Colossoma macropomum,* (Cuvier 1818)." *Red Acuicultura Boletin* 4:5–7.

Hernández, R., ed. 1989. *Cultivo de Colossoma.* Bogotá: Editora Guadalupe.

Hernández, R., D. Muñoz, J. A. Ferraz de Lima, R. Fex, W. Vasquez, R. Gonzalez, R. Morales, F. Alcántara, T. M. Luna, C. Kossowki, J. Pérez, J. A. Mora, P. J. Contreras, F. Diáz, E. M. Fadul, and P. Montoya. 1992. "Estado atual del cultivo de *Colossoma* y *Piaractus* en Brasil, Colombia, Panamá, Peru, y Venezuela." *Red Acuicultura Boletin* 6:3–28.

Hernao, A. R., and Q. A. Grajares. 1989. "Nutrición de la cachama negra (*Colossoma macropomum*). I. Niveles proteinicos e importancia relativa de la proteina animal." *Memorias de la Segunda Reunión de Red Nacional de Acuicultura.* In R. A. Hernández and R. Puentes, ed. Bogotá: Red Nacional de Acuicultura.

Holeton, G. F., and E. D. Stevens. 1978. "Swimming Energetics of an Amazonian Characin in Black and White Water." *Canadian Journal of Zoology* 56:983–87.

Honda, E. M. S. 1974. "Contribuição ao conhecimento da biologia de peixes do Amazonas. II. Alimentação do tambaqui (*Colossoma macropomum*)." *Acta Amazonica* 4:47–53.

Howells, R. G., R. L. Benefield, and J. M. Mambretti. 1991. "Records of Pacus (*Colossoma* spp.) and Piranhas (*Serrasalmus* spp.) in Texas." *Management Data Series—Texas Parks and Wildlife Department* 70:1–4.

Hutchings, J. A. 1993. "Adaptive Life Histories Affected by Age-Specific Survival and Growth Rate." *Ecology* 74:673–84.

Hyatt, K. D. 1979. "Feeding Strategy." *Fish Physiology.* In W. S. Hoar, D. J. Randall, and J. R. Brett, ed. New York: Academic Press.

Ibarra, M., and D. J. Stewart. 1989. "Longitudinal Zonation of Sandy Beach Fishes in the Napo River Basin, Eastern Equador." *Copeia* 1989:364–81.

IBGE (Instituto Brasileiro de Geografia e Estatística). 1992. *Anuário Estatístico do Brasil*. Rio de Janeiro: IBGE.

Irish, F. J. 1986. "Stucture and Function of the Feeding Apparatus of the Serrasalmine Fishes *Colossoma* and *Piaractus* (Teleostei, Characidae)." *American Society of Ichthyology and Herpetology. Progam Abstracts* 1986:57.

Isaac, V. U., and M. L. Ruffino. 1996. "Population Dynamics of Tambaqui *Colossoma macropomum* Cuvier 1818, in the Lower Amazon, Brazil." *Fisheries Management* 3:315-333.

Jobling, M. 1986. "Mythical Models of Gastric Emptying and Implications for Food Consumption Studies." *Environmental Biology of Fishes* 16:35–50.

——. 1994. *Fish Bioenergetics*. London: Chapman & Hall.

Jonsson, N., B. Jonsson, P. Aass, and L. P. Hansen. 1995. "Brown Trout *Salmo trutta* Released to Support Recreational Fishing in a Norwegion Fjord." *Journal of Fish Biology* 46:70–84.

Junk, W. J. 1970. "Investigations on the Ecology and Production-Biology of the 'Floating Meadows' (Paspalo-Echinochloetum) on the Middle Amazon. Part I: The Floating Vegetation and Its Ecology." *Amazoniana* II:449–95.

——. 1973. "Investigations on the Ecology and Production-Biology of the 'Floating Meadows' (Paspalo-Echinochloetum) on the Middle Amazon. II. The Aquatic Fauna in the Root Zone of Floating Vegetation." *Amazoniana* 4:9–102.

——. 1985a. "Temporary Fat Storage, an Adaptation of Some Fish Species to the Water Level Fluctuations and Related Environmental Changes of the Amazon River." *Amazoniana* 9(3):315–52.

——. 1985b. "Amazon Floodplain: A Sink or Source of Organic Carbon?" *Major World Rivers, Part 3*. In E. T. Degens, S. Kempe, and R. Herrera, ed. Hamburg: Institut Universitat Hamburg, Sonderb.

Junk, W. J., and M. T. F. Piedade. 1993. "Biomass and Primary-Production of Herbaceous Plant Communities in the Amazon Floodplain." *Hydrobiologia* 263:155–62.

Junk, W. J., G. M. Soares, and F. M. Carvalho. 1983. "Distribution of Fish Species in a Lake of the Amazon River Floodplain near Manaus (Lago Camaleão) with Special Reference to Extreme Oxygen Conditions." *Amazoniana* VII:397–431.

Kahn, F. 1988. "Ecology of Economically Promising Palms in Peruvian Amazonia." *Advances in Economic Botany* 6:42–49.

——. 1991. "Las palmeiras de los bosques tropicales." *Bulletin de L'Institut Français D'Etudes Andines* 21(2):415–796.

Kitada, S., Y. Taga, and H. Kishino. 1992. "Effectiveness of a Stock Enhancement Program Evaluated by a Two-Stage Sampling Survey of Commercial Landings." *Canadian Journal Fisheries and Aquatic Sciences* 49:1573–82.

Kohla, U., U. Saint-Paul, J. Friebe, D. Wernicke, V. Hilbe, E. Braum, and J. Gropp. 1992. "Growth, Digestive Enzyme Activities, and Haepatic Glycogen Levels in

Juvenile *Colossoma macropomum* Cuvier from South America During Feeding, Starvation. and Refeeding." *Aquaculture and Fisheries Managment* 23:189–208.

Kossowski, C., N. Prada, D. Bermudez, and F. Madrid. 1986. "Reporte sobre reproduciónes espontaneas en cautiveiro de cachama *Colossoma macropomum* en la estación de piscicultura de la Universidad Centro Occidental Lisandro Alvarado." *Revista Latinoamericana de Acuicultura* 29:4.

Koste, W., and B. Robertson. 1983. "Taxonomic Studies of the Rotifera (Phylum Aschelminthes) from a Central Amazonian Várzea Lake, Lago Camaleão (Ilha da Marchantaria, Rio Solimões, Amazonas, Brazil)." *Amazoniana* VIII:225–54.

Kotaki, K. 1992. "The State and Prospects of Stock Enchancement ('Sabai Gyogyo') Projects in Japan." *FAO Fisheries Report* 474:197–204.

Kritsky, D. C., V. E. Thatcher, and R. J. Kayton. 1980. "Neotropical Monogenoidea. 15. The Anacanthorinae Price, 1967, with Proposal of Four New Species of *Anacanthorus* Mmizelle & Price, 1965, from Amazon Fishes." *Acta Amazonica* 10:411–17.

Kubitzki, K., and A. Ziburski. 1993. "Seed Dispersal in Floodplain Forests of Amazonia." *Biotropica* 26(1):30–43.

Landau, M. 1992. *Introduction to Aquaculture*. New York: John Wiley & Sons.

LaNoue, J., and G. Choubert. 1983. "Digestibility in Rainbow Trout: Comparison of the Direct and Indirect Methods of Mearurement." *Progressive Fish Culturist* 48:190–95.

Lauzanne, L., G. Loubens, and B. Le Guennec. 1991. "Liste commentée des poissons de l'Amazonie bolivienne." *Revue de Hydrobiologie Tropical* 24:61–76.

Lazzaro, X. 1987. "A Review of Planktivorous Fishes: Their Evolution, Feeding Behaviour, Selectivities, and Impacts." *Hydrobiologia* 146:97–167.

Lewis Jr, W., and F. Weibezahn. 1981. "The Chemistry and Phytoplankton of the Orinoco and Caroni Rivers, Venezuela." *Archives Fur Hydrobiologie* 91:521–28.

Lopes, J. P., and O. Fontenele. 1982. "Produção de alevinos de tambaqui *Colossoma macropomum* Cuvier, 1818, para peixamento de açudes e estocagem de viveiros no nordeste do Brasil." Fortaleza: DNOCS, internal document.

Loubens, G., and J. L. Aquim. 1986. "Sexualidad y reproducción de los principales peces de la cuenca del Rio Mamoré, Beni, Bolivia." *Informe Científico (ORSTOM, CORDEBENI, UTB, Trinidad, Bolivia)* 5:1–20.

Loubens, G., L. Lauzanne, and B. Le Guennec. 1992. "Les millieux aquatiques de la région de Trinidad (Béni, Amazonie boliviénne)." *Revue de Hydrobiologie Tropical* 25:3–21.

Lovshin, L. L. Forthcoming. "Colosomids." *Production of Aquatic Animals—Fishes*. Amsterdam: Elsevier Science Publishing.

Lovshin, L.L., A.B. Fernandes, J.A. Silva and A. Carneiro-Sobrinho. 1974. "Preliminary pond culture test of pirapitinga (*Colossoma bidens*) and tambaqui (*Colossoma macropomum*) from the Amazon Basin." *FAO Fisheries Report* 159 (1) 185–193.

Lowe-McConnell, R. H. 1977. *Ecology of Fishes in Tropical Waters*. London: Edward Arnold.

——. 1979. "Ecological Aspects of Seasonality in Fishes of Tropical Waters." *Symposia of the Zoological Society of London* 44:219–41.

——. 1987. *Ecological Studies in Tropical Fish Communities*. Cambridge: Cambridge University Press.

Luna, M. T. 1987. "El efecto del contenido proteico y energético en la alimentación artificial sobre el crescimento de *Colossoma macropomum*." *Ivestigación Acuicola en America Latina*. J. A. J. Verreth, M. Carrilo, S. Zauny, and E. A. Huisman, ed. Lima: Wageningen.

Luna, M. T., and H. C. Suarez. 1988. "Utilización de alimentos de complemento en el cultivo semi-intensivo de alevinos de *Colossoma macropomum*." *Anais do V Simpósio Brasileiro de Acuicultura, Florianópolis, S.C.* 5:520–25.

Lundberg, J. G., A. Machado-Allison, and R. F. Kay. 1986. "Miocene Characid Fishes from Colombia: Evolutionary Stasis and Extirpation." *Science* 234:208–9.

Macedo, E. M. 1979. "Necessidades proteicas na nutrição do tambaqui, *Colossoma macropomum* Cuvier 1818 (Pisces, Characidae)." Master's thesis, UNESP, Jaboticabal.

McGrath, D. G., F. Castro, and C. Fitemma. 1994. "Reservas de lago e o manejo comunitário da pesca no baixo Amazonas: Uma avaliação preliminar." *Amazônia e a Crise da Modernação*. In M. A. D'Incao and I. M. Silveira, ed. Belém: Museu Paraense Emílio Goeldi.

Machado-Allison, A. 1982a. "Estudios sobre la subfamilia Serrasalminae (Teleostei, Characidae). Parte I. Estudio comparado de los juveniles de las cachamas de Venezuela." *Acta Biológica Venezuelica* 11:1–101.

——. 1982b. "Studies on the Systematics of the Subfamily Serrasalminae (Pisces: Characidae)." Ph.D. dissertation, The George Washington University.

——. 1987. *Los Peces de Los Llanos de Venezuela*. Caracas: Universidad Central de Venezuela.

Machado-Allison, A., C. Lasso, and R. Royero. 1993. "Inventario preliminar y aspectos ecológicos de los peces de los rios Aguaro e Guariquito (Parque Nacional), estado Guarico, Venezuela." *Memoria Sociedad de Ciencias Naturales, La Salle* LIII:55–80.

Magalhães, A. C. 1931. *Monographia Brazileira de Peixes Fluviães*. São Paulo: Graphicars Romiti, Lanzara & Zanin.

Mahar, D. J. 1976. "Fiscal Incentives for Regional Development: A Case Study of the Western Amazon Basin." *Journal of Inter-American Studies and World Affairs* 18(3):357–79.

Maia, E. 1992. "Otimização da metodologia para a caracterização de constituintes lipídicos e determinação da composição de ácidos graxos e amino ácidos de peixes de água doce." Ph.D. dissertation, UNICAMP, Campinas, SP.

Malca, R. P. 1989. "Situación del cultivo de *Colossoma* en Panamá." *Cultivo de Colossoma*. In R. Hernández, ed. Bogotá: Editora Guadalupe.

Malta, J. C. O. 1983. "Os argulídeos (Crustacea, Branchiura) da Amazônia brasileira. 4. Aspectos da ecologia de *Argulus multicolor* Stekhoven, 1937, e *Argulus pestifer* Ringuelet, 1948." *Acta Amazonica* 13:489–95.

———. 1984. "Os peixes de um lago de várzea da Amazônia Central (Lago Janauacá, Rio Solimões) e suas relações com os crustáceos ectoparasitas (Branchiura: Argulidae)." *Acta Amazonica* 14(3–4):355–72.

Malta, J. C. O., and A. Varella. 1983. "Os argulídeos (Crustacea: Branchiura) da Amazônia brasileira. 3. Aspectos da ecologia de *Dolops striata* Bouvier, 1899 e *Dolops carvalhoi* Castro, 1949." *Acta Amazonica* 13(2):299–306.

Mansutti, A. 1988. "La pesca entre los Piaroas (Uwotjuja) del Orinoco y la cuenca del Sipapo." *Memoria Sociedad de Ciencias Naturales, La Salle* XLVIII:3–39.

Marlier, G. 1967. "Ecological Studies on Some Lakes of the Amazon Valley." *Amazoniana* I(2):91–116.

Marx, F., and J. G. S. Maia. 1985. "Determination of Fat Soluble Vitamins from Amazonian Fresh-Water Fishes." *Acta Amazonica* 15:185–91.

Meade, R. H., C. F. Nordin Jr, D. P. Hernández, A. Mejia, and J. M. P. Godoy. 1983. "Sediment and Water Discharge in Rio Orinoco, Venezuela, and Colombia." *Proceedings of the Second International Symposium on River Sedimentation* 2:1134–44.

Meade, R., J. M. Rayol, S. C. Conceição, and J. R. G. Natividade. 1991. "Backwater Effects in the Amazon River Basin of Brazil." *Environmental Geology and Water Science* 18(2):105–14.

Medina, J. T., and H. C. Heaton. 1934. *The Discovery of the Amazon, According to the Account of Friar Gaspar de Carvajal and Other Documents*. New York: American Geographical Society.

Melack, J. M., and T. R. Fisher. 1983. "Diel Oxygen Variations and Their Ecological Implications in Amazon Floodplain Lakes." *Hydrobiologie* 98:422–42.

———. 1990. "Comparative Limnology of Tropical Floodplain Lakes with an Emphasis on the Central Amazon." *Acta Limnológica Brasiliensia* III:1–48.

Melo, F. R., A. Carneiro Sobrinho, J. W. B. Silva, and F. M. Barros Filho. 1987. "Resultados de um policultivo de tambaqui, *Colossoma macropomum* Cuvier, 1818; híbrido de tilapias, *Oreochromis hornorum* Trew. x *O. niloticus* L. 1766; e carpa espelho, *Cyprinus carpia* l. 1758 vr. *specularis* consorciado com suinos." *Ciência e Cultura* 39:379–86.

Mendes, P. P., and R. O. Vallejos. 1988. "Efeito da densidade de estocagem no crescimento de *Colossoma macropomum* (Cuvier, 1818) em gaiolas." *Anais do V Congresso Brasileiro de Engenharia de Pesca* 5:223–42.

Mendonça, J. O. J. 1984. "A reprodução induzida em *Colossoma macropomum*." *Anais do III Simpósio Brasileiro de Aquicultura, São Carlos* 3:87–90.

Menezes, N. A., and A. E. Vazzoler. 1992. "Reproductive Characteristics of Characiformes." *Reproductive Biology of South American Vertebrates*. In W. C. Hamlett, ed. New York: Springer-Verlag.

Merola, J., and F. Pagan-Font. 1988. "Pond Culture of the Amazon Fish Tambaqui, *Colossoma macropomum*: A Pilot Study." *Aquacultural Engineering* 7:113–25.

Merola, N., and A. Andreotti. 1988. "Estudo preliminar sobre a acetptación y preferencia del tambaqui *Colossoma macropomum*, cultivado en dos comunidades del estado de São Paulo." *Anais do VI Simpósio Latinoamericano de Aquicultura, Florianópolis, S.C.* 6:226.

Merola, N., and O. Cantelmo. 1987. "Growth, Feed Conversion, and Mortality of Cage-Reared Tambaqui, *Colossoma macropomum*, Fed Various Dietary Feeding Regimes and Protein Levels." *Aquaculture* 66:223–33.

Merola, N., and J. H. Souza. 1988. "Cage Culture of the Amazon Fish Tambaqui, *Colossoma macropomum*, at Two Stocking Densities." *Aquaculture* 71:15–21.

Merona, B. 1988. "Les poissons. Description et dynamique des peuplement du lac." *Condition Ecologiques et Economiques de la Production d'une île de Várzea—Rapporte Terminal.* Manaus: ORSTOM/INPA.

Merona, B. and M. M. Bittencourt. 1988. "A pesca na Amazônia através dos desembarques no mercado de Manaus: resultados preliminares." *Memoria Sociedad de Ciencias Naturales, La Salle* XLVIII:433–53.

Miles, C. 1971. *Los Peces del Rio Magdalena.* Ibaguie, Colombia: Universidad del Tolima.

Moats, Jeff. Kapok International. Cleveland. (Personal communications 1995, 1996).

Molnár, K., and A. B. Békési. 1993. "Description of a New *Myxobolus* Species, *M. colossomatis* n. sp. from the Teleost *Colossoma macropomum* of the Amazon River Basin." *Journal of Applied Ichthyology* 9:57–63.

Moncayo, L. M. A. E., C. Castaneda, E. Morelos, and A. Larios. 1988. "Resultados obtenidos sobre la reproducción de *Colossoma macropomum* Cuvier, 1818 (Pisces: Serrasalmidae) en México." *Simpósio Brasileiro de Aquicultura* 5:526–33.

Morais Filho, M. B., J. A. Senhorini, and J. J. Deleon. 1983. "Larvicultura: criação de larvas de tambaqui *Colossoma macropomum* (Cuvier) 1818." São Paulo: Centro Regional Latino Americano de Aquicultura, internal document.

Mori, L. A. 1993. "Estudo da possibilidade de substituição do fubá de milho (*Zea mays*) por farinha de pupunha (*Bactris gasipaes*), em rações de alevinos de tambaqui (*Colossoma macropomum*)." Master's thesis, INPA/UFAM, Manaus.

Mujica, M. E. 1982. "Estudios preliminares sobre enfermedades que afetan los peces de aguas cálidas aptos para el cultivo en la estación hidrobilógica de Guanapito, estado de Guárico, Venezuela." Manuscript.

Mujica, M. E., and G. Armas de Conroy. 1985. "Una trematodosis en *Colossoma macropomum* (Cuvier, 1818) bajo condiciónes de cultivo." *Revista de La Facultad de Ciencias Veterinarias, Universidad Central de Venezuela* 32:103–11.

NEODAT. The Inter-Institutional Database of Fish Biodiversity in the Neotropics. http://fowler.acnatsci.org

Ney Navarro, F. 1984. "Informe sobre el cultivo de *Colossoma macropomum*." *Série Memorias. Eventos Científicos Colombianos* 9:35–39.

Novoa, D. F, 1982. *Los Recursos Pesqueros del Rio Orinoco y Su Explotación.* Caracas: Corporación Venezolana de Guayana.

Novoa, D. F. 1989. "The Multispecies Fisheries of the Orinoco River: Development, Present Status, and Management Strategies." *Proceedings of the International Large River Symposium* 106:345–56.

Novoa, D., F. Ramos, and E. Cartaya. 1984. "Las pesquerias artesanales del Rio Orinoco, sector Caicara-Cabruta, Parte I." *Memoria Sociedad de Ciencias Naturales, La Salle* XLIV:163–215.

Nuñez, J. M., and J. J. Salaya. 1984. "Cultivo de cachama *Colossoma macropomum* Cuvier 1818, en jaulas flotantes no rígidas en la reprensa de Guanapito, Estado Guarico, Venezuela." *Memorias Asociación Latinoamericana de Acuicultura* 5:481–94.

Odinetz-Collart, O., and L. C. Moreira. 1989. "Quelques caracteristiques physico-chimiques d'un lac de várzea en Amazonie centrale (Lago do Rei, île de Careiro)." *Revue de Hydrobiologie Tropical* 22:191–99.

Oliveira, M. A., M. C. S. Leão, M. A. E. Araripe, and L. C. U. Saunders. 1988. "Produção de tilapia do Nilo, *Oreochromis niloticus*, tambaqui, *Colossoma macropomum*, e marrecos de pequim, *Anas platyrhinchus*, em arroz irrigado em solo salino-sódico da fazenda experimental da UFC, no vale do Rio Curu-Ceará, Brasil." *Ciências Agronômicas* 19:53–58.

Oltman, R. E., H. O. Sternberg, F. C. Ames, and L. C. Davis Jr. 1964. "Amazon River Investigations Reconnaissance Measurements of July 1963." *Geological Survey Circular* 486:1–15.

Ortega, H., and F. Chang. 1992. "Ictiofauna del Santuário Nacional Pampas del Heath—Madre de Dios—Peru." *Memoria X Conabiologia* 2:215–21.

Ortega, H., and R. P. Vari. 1986. "Annotated Checklist of the FreshWater Fishes of Peru." *Smithsonian Contributions to Zoology* 437:1–25.

Orti, G., P. Petry, J. I. Porto, M. Jegú, and A. Meyer. 1996. "Patterns of Nucleotide Change in Mitochondrial Ribosomal RNA Genes and Phylogeny of Piranhas." *Journal of Molecular Evolution* 42: 169–82.

Paixão, I. M. P. 1980. "Estudo da alimentação e reprodução de *Mylossoma duriventris* Cuvier, 1818 (Pisces, Characoidei), do Lago Janauacá, AM, Brasil." Master's thesis, INPA/UFAM, Manaus.

Paredes, V. 1984. "Enfermedades parasitarias de peces tropicales en las zonas de Iquitos y Pucallpa en el Perú." *Memórias do Simpósio Latinoamericano de Acuicultura* 5:715–23.

Pauly, D., and R. S. V. Pullin. 1988. "Hatching Time in Spherical, Pelagic, Marine Fish Eggs in Response to Temperature and Egg Size." *Environmental Biology of Fishes* 22:261–71.

Peralta, M., and D. R. Teichert-Coddington. 1989. "Comparative Production of *Colossoma macropomum* and *Tilapia nilotica* in Panama." *Journal of the World Aquaculture Society* 20:236–39.

Pereira, E. J. F., and M. Lubin. 1980. "El morocoto *Colossoma macropomum*: una posible solución para la piscicultura em regiones semiaridas cercanas al mar." *Memórias do II Simpósio Latino-Americano de Aquicultura* 1:1685–1705.

Pereira Filho, M. 1995. "Alternativas para a alimentação de peixes em cativeiro." *Criando Peixes na Amazônia*. In A. L. Val and A. Honczarik, ed. Manaus: INPA.

Pereira, H. S. 1992. "Extrativismo e agricultura: as escolhas de uma comunidade riberinha do médio Solimões." Master's thesis, INPA/UFAM, Manaus.

Peters, R. H. 1987. "Metabolism of *Daphnia*." *Daphnia*. In R. H. Peters and R. Bernardi, ed. Rome: Instituto Italiano Idrobiologia.

Petrere Jr, M. 1978a. "Pesca e esforço de pesca no Estado do Amazonas. I. Esforço e captura por unidade de esforço." *Acta Amazonica* 8(3):439–54.

——. 1978b. "Pesca e esforço de pesca no Estado do Amazonas. II. Locais, aparelhos de captura, e estatística de desembarque." *Acta Amazonica* 8(2/3):1–54.

——. 1983a. "Relationships Among Catches, Fishing Effort, and River Morphology for Eight Rivers in Amazonas State (Brazil), During 1976–1978." *Amazoniana* 8:281–96.

——. 1983b. "Yield per Recruit of the Tambaqui, *Colossoma macropomum* Cuvier, in the Amazonas State, Brazil." *Journal of Fish Biology* 22:133–44.

——. 1985a. "A pesca comercial no Rio Solimões-Amazonas e seus afluentes: Análise dos informes do pescado desembarcado no mercado municipal de Manaus (1976–78)." *Ciência e Cultura* 37:1987–99.

——. 1985b. "Migraciónes de peces de água dulce en America Latina: Algunos comentários." *Copescal Documento Ocasional* 1:1–31.

——. 1986. "Amazon Fisheries. I. Variation in the Relative Abundance of Tambaqui (*Colossoma macropomum* Cuvier, 1818) Based on Catch and Effort Data of the Gill-Net Fisheries." *Amazoniana* IX:527–47.

Piedade, M. T. F. 1985. "Ecologia e biologia reprodutiva de *Astrocaryum jauari* Mart como exemplo de população adaptada as áreas inundáveis do Rio Negro (igapós)." Master's thesis, INPA/UFAM, Manaus.

Pietro, A., and E. Fajer, M. Vinjoy, and R. Cartaya. 1986. "Monogeneas parasitos de las espécies de peces exóticas." *Acuicultura: Boletim Técnico* 22:11.

Pinheiro, A. R. C. 1985. "Biologia pesqueira do tambaqui, *Colossoma macropomum* (Cuvier, 1818), capturado no município de Tefé, Estado do Amazonas." Master's thesis, Universidade Federal do Ceará, Fortaleza.

Pinheiro, J. L. P., and M. C. N. Silva. 1988. "Tambaqui (*Colossoma macropomum*—Cuvier, 1818). Ampliação do período de desova." Brasília: CODEVASF, internal document.

Pinheiro, J. L. P., M. C. N. Silva, M. A. A. Soares, N. H. Souza, and A. Woynarovich. 1988. "Tambaqui, produção intensiva de larvas no baixo São Francisco." Brasília: CODEVASF, internal document.

Pinheiro, M. H. P., J. W. B. Silva, M. I. S. Nobre, and F. A. Pinheiro. 1991. "Cultivo do híbrido tambaqui, *Colossoma macropomum* Cuvier, 1818, com a pirapitinga (*C. brachypomum*) Cuvier, 1818, na densidade de 5,000 peixes/ha." *Ciências Agronômicas* 22:77–87.

Pinto, A. M. 1894. *Apontamentos para o Diccionário Geográphico do Brazil*. Rio de Janeiro: Imprensa Nacional.

Piper, R. G., I. B. McElwain, L. E. Orme, J. P. McCraren, L. G. Fowler, and J. R. Leonard. 1983. *Fish Hatchery Management*. Washington, D.C.: U.S. Department of the Interior, Fish and Wildlife Service.

Pontes, F. C. A., J. W. B. Silva, A. Carneiro Sobrinho, and A. T. Bezerra. 1992. "Policultivo de tambaqui *Colossoma macropomum* Cuvier, 1818; carpa espelho *Cyprinus carpio* L. 1758 vr. *specularis* e macho de tilapia do nilo *Oreochromis niloticus* (l. 1766) consorciado com marreco de pequim, *Anas platyrhynchus* L." *Ciências Agronômicas* 23:93–102.

Porto, J. I. R., E. Feldberg, C. M. Nakayama, and J. N. Falcao. 1992. "A Checklist of Chromosome Numbers and Karyotypes of Amazonian Freshwater Fishes." *Revue de Hydrobiologie Tropical* 25:287–99.

Prance, G. T. 1978. "The Origin and Evolution of the Amazonian Flora." *Interciencia* 3(4):207–22.

Priede, I. G. 1985. "Metabolic Scope in Fishes." *Fish Energetics: New Pespectives*. In P. Tytler and P. Calow, ed. London: P. Croom Helm.

Prus, T. 1970. "Calorific Content of Animals As an Element of Bioenergetical Investigations." *Polskie Archiwum Hydrobiologii* 17(1/2):183–99.

Rankin-De-Merona, J. 1988. "Relations poissons forêt." *Conditions écologiques et économiques de la production d'une île de Varzea: Ile du Careiro*: Rapporte Terminale. Manaus: ORSTOM/INPA.

Rey Navarro, F. 1984. "Informe sobre el cultivo de *Colossoma macropomum*." *Série Memorias Eventos Científicos Colombianos* 9:35–39.

Richey, J. E., R. H. Meade, E. Salati, A. H. Devol, C. F. Nordin Jr, and U. Santos. 1986. "Water Discharge and Suspended Sediment Concentrations in the Amazon River: 1982–1984." *Water Resources Research* 22:756–64.

Ricker, W. E. 1979. "Growth Rates and Models." *Fish Physiology*. In W. S. Hoar, D. J. Randall, and J. R. Brett, ed. New York: Academic Press.

Robertson, B. A., and E. R. Hardy. 1984. "Zooplankton of Amazonian Lakes and Rivers." *The Amazon: Limnology and Landscape Ecology of a Mighty Tropical River and Its Basin*. In H. Sioli, ed. Dordrecht, Netherlands: Dr. Junk Publishers.

Robinson, J. G., and K. H. Redford. 1991. *Neotropical Wildlife Use and Conservation*. Chicago: University of Chicago Press.

Rojas, G. B. S., and G. Ascon-Dionisio. 1988. "Ensayo sobre reproducción inducida de gamitama, *Colossoma macropomum* (Cuvier 1818) com gonadotropina coriónica humana." *Revista Latinoamericana de Acuicultura* 35:34–43.

Rolim, P. P. 1995. "Infraestrutura básica para a criação de peixes no Amazonas." *Criando Peixes na Amazônia*. In A. L. Val and A. Honczarik, ed. Manaus: INPA.

Roman, B. 1983. *Las Pirañas y Demas Characidios*. Caracas: Fundación Científica Fluvial de Los Llanos.

Ross, L. G., and B. Ross. 1984. *Anaesthetic and Sedative Techniques for Fish*. Stirling: Universty of Stirling.

Roubach, R. 1992. "Uso de frutos e sementes de florestas inundáveis na alimentação de *Colossoma macropomum* (Cuvier, 1818) (Pisces, Characidae)." Master's thesis, INPA/UFAM, Manaus.

Roubach, R., and U. Saint-Paul. 1994. "Use of Fruits and Seeds from Amazonian Inundated Forests in Feeding Trials with *Colossoma macropomum* (Cuvier, 1818) (Pisces, Characidae)." *Journal of Applied Ichthyology* 10:134–40.

Rubim, M. A. L. 1993. "A Case Study on Life-History of Wild Rice—From Germination to Emergence of Inflorescence." *Investigations of Plant Genetic Resources in the Amazon Basin with Emphasis on the Genes Oryza.* In H. Morishima and P. S. Martins, ed. São Paulo: MISRP/FAPESP.

Ruffino, M. L., and V. J. Isaac. 1994. "The Fisheries of the Lower Amazon: Questions of Management and Development." *Acta Biológica Venezuelica* 15(2):37–46.

Saint-Paul, U. 1983. "Investigations on the Respiration of the Neotropical Fish *Colossoma macropomum* (Serrasalmidae). The Influence of Weight and Temperature on the Routine Oxygen Consumption." *Amazoniana* 7:433–43.

———. 1984a. "Ecological and Physiological Investigations of *Colossoma macropomum*, a New Species for Fish Culture in Amazonia." *Memorias de La Asociación Latinoamericana de Acuicultura* 5:510–18.

———. 1984b. "Investigations on the Seasonal Changes in the Chemical Composition of Liver and Condition from a Neotropical Characoid Fish *Colossoma macropomum* (Serrasalmidae)." *Amazoniana* IX:147–58.

———. 1984c. "Physiological Adaptation to Hypoxia of a Neotropical Characoid Fish *Colossoma macropomum*, Serrasalmidae." *Environmental Biology of Fishes* 11:52–62.

———. 1988. "Diurnal Routine O_2 Consumption at Different O_2 Concentrations by *Colossoma macropomum* and *Colossoma brachypomum* (Teleostei: Serrasalmidae)." *Comparative Biochemistry and Physiology* 89A:675–82.

———. 1990. "Aquaculture in Latin America." *European Aquaculture Society Special Publication* 13:434.

———. 1991. "Advantages of Neotropical Fish Species for Aquaculture Development in Amazonia." *Bulletin of Ecological Society of America* 21:23–26.

———. 1991. "The Potential for *Colossoma* in Latin America." *Inofish International* 2/91:49–53.

Saint-Paul, U., and U. Werder. 1978. "Aspectos generales sobre la piscicultura en Amazonas y resultados preliminares de experimentos de alimentación de *Brycon melanopterum* con raciónes peletizadas con diferentes composiciónes." *I Simpósio de La Associación Latinoamericana de Aquacultura, Venezuela* I:1–22.

———. 1981. "The Potential of Some Amazonian Fishes for Warm Water Aquaculture." *Proceedings World Symposium on Aquaculture In Heated Effluents and Recirculation Systems (Stavanger, 28–30 May 1980)* 2:275–87.

Saint-Paul, U., U. Werder, and A. S. Teixeira. 1981. "Use of Water Hyacinth in Feeding Trials with Matrinchã (*Brycon* sp.)." *Journal of Aquatic Plant Management* 19:18–22.

Salati, E., and J. Marques. 1984. "Climatology of the Amazon Region." *The Amazon: Limnology and Landscape Ecology of a Mighty River.* In H. Sioli, ed. Dordrecht, Netherlands: Dr. W. Junk.

Saldaña, J., and B. Venables. 1983. "Energy Compartimentalization in a Migratory Fish *Prochilodus mariae* (Prochilodontidae) of the Orinoco River." *Copeia* 1893(3):617–23.

Saldaña, R. G. B., and D. G. Acori. 1986. "Ensayo sobre la reproducción de gamitana *Colossoma macropomum* (Cuvier) con gonadotropina corioncia humana." *Hidrobios* 10:1–12.

Saldaña, R. G. B., and D. G. Acori. 1988. "Ensayo sobre reproducción inducida de gamitana, *Colossoma macropomum* (Cuvier, 1818) con gonadotropina corionica humana." *Revista Latinoamericana de Acuicultura* 35:35–44.

Sanchez, L., and E. Vasquez. 1986. "Notas sobre las macrofitas acuáticas de la sección baja del Rio Orinoco." *Memoria Sociedad de Ciencias Naturales, La Salle* XLVI:107–25.

———. 1988. "Estudio estacional y longitudinal de la hidroquímica de fitoplacton en una sección del bajo Orinoco (Venezuela)." *Memoria Sociedad de Ciencias Naturales, La Salle* XLVI:69–83.

Sanchez, V. P. 1981. "Enfermedads parasitarias del sabalo cola roja *Brycon erytropterum* y gamitana *Colossoma macropomum* de la zona de Iquitos." *IFS Informe Provisionalo* 10 *Acuicultura* III:261–69.

Santos, G. M. 1986. "Composição do pescado e situação da pesca no Estado de Rondônia." *Acta Amazonia* 16(17):43–84.

———. 1991. "Pesca e ecologia dos peixes de Rondônia." Ph.D. dissertation, INPA/UFAM, Manaus.

Santos, G. M., and F. M. Carvalho. 1982. "Levantamento preliminar da ictiofauna na área de influência da UHE de Santa Izabel." Manuscript.

Santos Silva, E. N. 1991. "Composição, abundância, e reprodução de Calanoida (Copepoda) do Lago Calado, Amazônia Central." Master's thesis, INPA/UFAM, Manaus.

Schmidt, G. W. 1973. "Primary Production of Phytoplankton in the Three Types of Amazonian Waters. II. The Limnology of a Tropical Floodplain Lake in Central Amazonia (Lago Castanho)." *Amazoniana* IV:135–38.

Schmidt, G. W. 1976. "Primary Productivity of Phytoplankton in a Bay of the Lower Rio Negro (Amazonas, Brazil)." *Amazoniana* V:517–28.

Senhorini, J. A., G. M. Figueiredo, N. A. Fontes, and J. Carlosfeld. 1988. "Larvicultura e alevinagem do pacu *Piaractus mesopotamicus* (Holmberg, 1887), tambaqui *Colossoma macropomum* (Cuvier, 1818), e seus respectivos híbridos." *Boletim Técnico do CEPTA* 1:19–30.

Shang, Y. C. 1990. *Aquaculture Economic Analysis: An Introduction.* Baton Rouge: The World Aquaculture Society.

Silva, A. B., A. Carneiro Sobrinho, and F. R. Mello. 1977. "Desova induzida de tambaqui *Colossoma macropomum* Cuvier, 1818, com uso de hipófise de curimatá comum, *Prochilodus cearensis* Steindachner." *I Simpósio de La Asociación Latino-Americana de Acuicultura, Maracay, Venezuela* 1:1.

———. 1981. "Desova induzida de tambaqui, *Colossoma macropomum* (Cuvier, 1818), com uso de hipófise de curimatá comum, *Prochilodus cearensis* Steindachner." *Coletânea de Trabalhos Técnicos do DNOCS.* In DNOCS, ed. Fortaleza: DNOCS.

———. 1983. "Contribuição ao estudo do cultivo intensivo do tambaqui, *Colossoma macropomum,* alimentado com torta de babaçu, *Orbignya martiana.*" *Anais do III Simpósio Brasileiro de Aquicultura, São Carlos* :147–55.

Silva, A. B., J. A. Fernandez, A. Carneiro Sobrinho, and L. L. Lovshin. 1974. "Testes preliminares em viveiros com tambaqui, *Colossoma bidens.* Observações preliminares em viveiro com pirapitinga, *Mylossoma bidens.*" Manuscript.

Silva, A. B., E. P. Santos, J. C. T. Mello, A. Carneiro Sobrinho, and F. R. Mello. 1984. "Análise quantitativa de um ensaio em piscicultura intensiva de tambaqui, *Colossoma macropomum.*" *Ciência e Cultura* 36:82–86.

Silva, J. W. B. 1984. "Resultado de um experimento de policultivo de tambaqui, *Colossoma macropomum* Cuvier, 1818, híbrido de tilapias (*Oreochromis hornorum* Trew. x *O. niloticus* L. 1776) e carpa espelho (*Cyprinus carpio* L. 1758 vr. *specularis.*" *Boletim Técnico do DNOCS* 42:63–89.

Silva, J. W. B., P. F. Alencar, J. O. Farias, and M. I. S. Nobre. 1984. "Resultados de um experimento sobre policultivo de carpa espelho, *Cyprinus carpio* L. 1758 vr. *specularis,* e tambaqui, *Colossoma macropomum* Cuvier, 1818." *Boletim Técnico do DNOCS* 42:121–52.

Silva, J. W. B., M. I. O. Caminha, M. I. S. Nobre, and F. M. Barros Filho. 1986. "Resultados de um ensaio sobre o cultivo do híbrido do tambaqui, *Colossoma macropomum* Cuvier, 1818; com a pirapitinga, *Colossoma brachypomum* Cuvier, 1818 realizado no Centro de Pesquisas Ictiológicos 'Rodolpho von Ihering,' Petencostes, Ceará, Brasil." *Ciências Agronômicas* 17:7–18.

Silva, J. W. B., A. Carneiro Sobrinho, F. R. Melo, and L. S. Souza. 1987. "Resultados de um policultivo de tambaqui, *Colossoma macropomum* Cuvier 1818; carpa espelho *Cyprinus carpio* L., 1758 vr. *specularis* e macho da tilapia do Nilo, *Oreochromis niloticus* L., 1766, alimentados com milho, *Zea mays* L." *Boletim Técnico do DNOCS* 45:5–26.

Silva, J. W. B., and J. J. S. Gurgel. 1989. "Situação do cultivo de *Colossoma macropomum* no ambito do Departamento Nacional de Obras contra as Secas (DNOCS)." *Cultivo de Colossoma.* In R. Hernández, ed. Bogotá: Editora Guadalupe.

Silva, J. W. B., A. J. T. Martins, M. I. S. Nobre, and J. W. C. Freitas. 1993. "Policultivo de carpa espelho *Cyprinus carpio* L., 1758 vr. *specularis* e tambaqui, *Colossoma macropomum* Cuvier, 1818, alimentados com milho *Zea mays* L." *Ciências Agronômicas* 24:87–90.

Silva, J. W. B., F. A. Pinheiro, A. Carneiro Sobrinho, and M. E. Nobre. 1985. "Resultados de um experimento sobre policultivo de tambaqui, *Colossoma macropomum* Cuvier, 1818, com machos de tilápia do congo, *Tilapia rendalli* Boulenger 1912, em viveiros naturais." *Boletim Técnico do DNOCS* 43:151–80.

Silva, J. W. B., F. A. Pinheiro, A. Carneiro Sobrinho, and S. Nobre. 1986. "Resultados dos policultivos do tambaqui *Colossoma macropomum* Cuvier 1818, com machos da *Tilapia rendalli* em viveiros naturais." *Anais do IV Simpósio Brasileiro de Aquicultura, Cuiabá, MT* :123–33.

Silva, M. C. 1991. "Ecologia de subsistência de uma população cabocla na Amazônia brasileira." Master's thesis, INPA/UFAM, Manaus.

Silva, P. C., A. J. Mesquita, C. S. C. Palma, and A. N. Oliveira. 1991. "Aspectos biométricos, bacteriólogicos, e físico-químicos do tambaqui *Colossoma macropomum* criado em consórcio com suinos." *Red Acuicultura Boletin* 5:6–8.

Silva, V. M. F. 1983. "Ecologia alimentar dos golfinhos da Amazônia." Master's thesis, INPA/UFAM, Manaus.

Simon, W. J. 1983. "Scientific Expeditions in the Portuguese Overseas Territories (1783–1808)." *Centro de Estudos de Cartografia Antiga: Série Memórias* 22:1–58.

Sioli, H. 1947. "Possibilidades de criação de peixes em lagos Amazônicos." *Boletim da Secção de Fomento Agrícola do Pará* 6/7:63–72.

——. 1984. "The Amazon and Its Main Affluents: Hydrography, Morphology of the River Courses, and River Types." *The Amazon*. In H. Sioli, ed. Dordrecht, Netherlands: W. Junk Publishers.

Sipaúba-Tavares, L. H. S. 1988. "Utilização do plâncton na alimentação de larvas e alevinos de peixe." Ph.D. dissertation, Universidade Federal de São Carlos, São Carlos, São Paulo.

——. 1993. "Análise da seletividade alimentar em larvas de tambaqui (*Colossoma macropomum*) e tambacu (híbrido, Pacu—*Piaractus mesopotamicus*—e Tambaqui—*Colossoma macropomum*—sobre os organismos zooplanctônicos." *Acta Limnologica Brasiliensia* VI:114–32.

Sippel, S. J., S. K. Hamilton, and J. M. Melack. 1992. "Inundation Area and Morphometry of Lakes on the Amazon River Floodplain, Brazil." *Archive fur Hydrobiologie* 123:385–400.

Smith, N. J. H. 1979a. *A Pesca no Rio Amazonas*. Manaus: INPA.

——. 1979b. "Aquatic Turtles of Amazonia: An Endangered Resource." *Biological Conservation* 16:165–76.

——. 1981. *Man, Fishes, and the Amazon*. New York: Columbia University Press.

Smith, N. J. H., E. A. S. Serrão, P. T. Alvim, and I. C. Falesi. 1995. *Amazonia: Resiliency and Dynamism of the Land and Its People*. Tokyo: United Nations University Press.

Soares, M. G. M., R. G. Almeida, and W. J. Junk. 1986. "The Trophic Status of the Fish Fauna in Lago Camaleão, a Macrophyte Dominated Floodplain Lake in the Middle Amazon." *Amazoniana* 9:511–26.

Spix, J. B., and C. F. P. Martius. 1823. *Reise In Brasilien Auf Befehl Sr. Majestat Maximilian Joseph 1, Konigs Von Baiern In den Jahren 1817 Bis 1820 (3 Volumes)*. Munich: M. Lindauer.

Spruce, R. 1867. "Notes on Some Insect and Other Migrations Observed in Equatorial America." *Journal of the Linnaen Society (Zoology)* 9:346–67.

——. 1908. *Notes of a Botanist on the Amazon and Andes (2 Volumes)*. London: MacMillan and Co.

Stacey, N. E. 1984. "Control of the Timing of Ovulation by Exogenous and Endogenous Factors." *Fish Reproduction*. In J. Potts and R. Wootton, ed. London: Academic Press.

SUDEPE (Superintendência do Desenvolvimento da Pesca). 1981. "Relatório do segundo encontro do grupo de trabalho e treinamento sobre a avaliação dos estoques—peixes da Amazônia ocidental." Brasília: SUDEPE, internal document.

——. 1986. "Controle de desembarque de pescado em nove municípios do Estado do Amazonas." Manuscript.

Tacon, A. G. J., and C. B. Cowey. 1985. "Protein and Amino Acid Requirement." *Fish Energetics: New Perspectives*. In P. Tytler and P. Calow, ed. London: P. Croom Helm.

Taphorn, D. C. 1992. "The Characiform Fishes of the Apure River Drainage, Venezuela." *Biollania (Edición Especial)* 4:1–537.

Thatcher, V. E. 1991. "Amazon Fish Parasites." *Amazoniana* 11:1–571.

Thatcher, V. E., and D. C. Kritsky. 1983. "Neotropical Monogenoidea. 4. *Linguadactyloides brinkmanni* gen. et sp. n. (Dactylogyridae: Linguadactyloidinae subfam. n.) with observations on its pathology in a Brazilian freshwater fish *Colossoma macropomum*." *Proceeding of the Helmintology Society Washington* 50:305–11.

Thatcher, V. E., and V. Paredes. 1985. "A Parasitic Copepod, *Perulernaea gamitanae* gen. et sp. nov. (Cyclopoidea: Lernaeidae), from Nasal Fossae of a Peruvian Amazon Food Fish." *Amazoniana* 9:169–75.

Thoney, D. A. 1993. "Community Ecology of the Parasites of Adult Spot, *Leiostomus xanturus*, and Atlantic Croaker, *Micropogonias undulatus* (Scianidae), in the Cape Hatteras Region." *Journal of Fish Biology* 43:661–810.

Torrealba, L. A. 1982. "Estudio histológico del tracto gastrointestinal de la cachama (*Colossoma macropomum* Cuvier, 1818)." Master's thesis, Universidad Central de Venezuela, Caracas.

Trujillo, C. J., and R. O. Valencia. 1982. "Crescimiento y producción de cultivo intensivo de cachama (*Colossoma macropomum*) con alimentación suplementária." *Revista Latinoamericana de Acuicultura* 11:10–12.

Tundisi, J. G., B. R. Forsberg, A. H. Devol, T. M. Zaret, T. M. Tundisi, A. Santos, J. S. Ribeiro, and E. R. Hardy. 1984. "Mixing Patterns in Amazon Lakes." *Hydrobiologia* 108(3):3–15.

Twombly, S., and W. M. Lewis Jr. 1987. "Zooplankton Abundance and Species Composition in Laguna la Orsinera, a Venezuelan Floodplain Lake." *Archives Fur Hydrobiologie* 79:87–107.

Ungson, R. J., Y. Matsuda, H. Hirata, and H. Shiihara. 1993. "An Economic Assessment of the Production and Release of Marine Fish Fingerlings for Sea Ranching." *Aquaculture* 118:169–81.

Val, A. L., and V. M. F. Almeida-Val. 1995. *Fishes of the Amazon and Their Environment: Physiological and Biochemical Aspects*. Berlin: Springer Verlag.

Valencia, O. 1985. "Ensayo preliminar sobre el cultivo intensivo de la cachama negra (*Colossoma macropomum*) alimentada com um concentrado isocalorico y 3% de su peso corporal." Venezuela: INDERENA, Estación Piscicola de Repelón, internal document.

——. 1988a. "Cultivo intensivo de la cachama negra (*Colossoma macropomum*) alimentada con una dieta semi-humeda, elaborada a partir de pescado fresco molido y harina de arroz." *Red Acuicultura Boletin* 2:25–27.

——. 1988b. "Estandardización de técnicas para la produción massiva de larvas y determinación de los níveles de proteina óptimas en la alimentación para el levante de alevinos de cachama." Venezuela: INDERENA, Estación Piscicola de Repelón, internal document.

Valencia, O., N. Chaparro, and E. M. Fadul. 1986. "Aplicaciónes hormonales para la reproducción artificial de la cachama negra (*Colossoma macropomum*) Cuvier 1818 y la cachama branca (*Colossoma bidens*) Spix, 1829." *Revista Latinoamericana de Acuicultura* 28:20–28.

Valencia, O., and R. Puentes. 1989. "El cultivo de cachama en Colombia." *Cultivo de Colossoma*. In R. Hernández, ed. Bogotá: Editora Guadalupe.

Vanzolini, P. E., and N. Papavero. 1968. *Índice dos Topônimos Contidos na Carta do Brasil* 1:1000000. São Paulo: FAPESP.

Vari, R. P., and S. H. Weitzman. 1990. "A Review of the Phylogenetic Biogeography of the Freshwater Fishes of South America." *Vertebrates in the Tropics*. In G. Peters and R. Hutterer, ed. Bonn: Museum Alexander Koenig.

Vasquez, E. 1989. "Características morfométricas de algunas lagunas de la planécie aluvial del bajo Rio Orinoco, Venezuela." *Memoria Sociedad de Ciencias Naturales, La Salle* L:309–27.

——. 1992. "Temperature and Dissolved Oxygen in Lakes of the Lower Orinoco River Floodplain (Venezuela)." *Revue de Hydrobiologie Tropical* 25:3–22.

Vazzoler, A. E. A. M., and N. A. Menezes. 1992. "Síntese de conhecimentos sobre o comportamento reprodutivo dos Characiformes da América do Sul (Teleostei, Ostariophysi)." *Revista Brasileira de Biologia* 52(4):627–40.

Veríssimo, J. 1895. *A Pesca na Amazônia*. Rio de Janeiro: Livraria Classica Francisco Alves & Cia.

——. 1970. *A Pesca na Amazônia*. Belém: Universidade Federal do Pará.

Vidal Jr, M. V., J. Donzele, D. R. Andrade, L. C. Santos, and A. C. C. Camargo. 1994. "Níveis de proteína para tambaqui (*Colossoma macropomum*, Cuvier, 1818)." *Resumos do Simpósio Brasileiro de Aquicultura, Piracicaba* 8:68.

Villacorta-Correa, M. A. 1987. "Crescimento do matrinxã, *Brycon cephalus* (Gunter, 1869) (Teleostei, Characidae) no baixo rio Negro, seus afluentes e no baixo Rio Solimões." Master's thesis, INPA/UFAM, Manaus.

Waedoff, D. 1991. "Morphologie, Nährwert, und Braelementgehalte hidroch und zoochen Verbreiteter Früchte und Samen aus Amazonichen überschwemmungswäldein bei Manaus." Master's thesis, Universitat Kiel.

Wallace, A. 1853. *Narrative of Travels on the Amazon and Rio Negro, With an Account of the Native Tribes, and Observations on the Climate, Geology, and Natural History of the Amazon Valley.* London: Reeve and Co.

Walliker, D. 1969. "Myxosporidea of Some Brazilian Freshwater Fishes." *Journal of Parasitology* 55:942–48.

Weitzman, S. H., and M. Weitzman. 1982. "Biogeography and Evolutionary Diversification in Neotropical Freshwater Fishes, with Comments on the Refuge Theory." *Biological Diversification in the Tropics.* In G. T. Prance, ed. New York: Columbia University Press.

Welcomme, R. L. 1994. "Editorial." *FAO Aquaculture Newsletter* 6:1.

Welcomme, R. L. 1979. *Fisheries Ecology in Floodplain Rivers.* London: Longman.

———. 1985. "River Fisheries." *FAO Fisheries Technical Paper* 262:1–330.

Werder, U., and U. Saint-Paul. 1979. "Experiências de alimentação com tambaqui (*Colossoma macropomum*), pacu (*Mylossoma* sp.), jaraqui (*Semaprochilodus theraponura*), e matrinchã (*Brycon melanopterus*)." *Acta Amazonica* 9:617–19.

Wheaton, F. W. 1977. *Aquacultural Engineering.* New York: John Wiley & Sons.

Wilson, R. P. 1989. "Amino Acids and Proteins." *Fish Nutrition.* In J. E. Halver, ed. New York: Academic Press.

Winemiller, K. O. 1990. "Spatial and Temporal Variation in Tropical Fish Trophic Network." *Ecological Monographs* 60:331–67.

Wootton, R. J. 1985. "Energetics of Reproduction." *Fish Energetics.* In P. Tytler and P. Calow, ed. London: Croom Holm.

———. 1990. *Ecology of Teleost Fishes.* London: Chapman and Hall.

———. 1992. "Constraints in the Evolution of Life Histories." *Netherlands Journal of Zoology* 42:291–303.

Worbes, M., H. Klinge, and J. D. Revilla. 1992. "On the Dynamics, Floristic Subdivision, and Geographical Distribution of Várzea Forests in Central Amazonia." *Journal of Vegetation Science* 3:553–64.

Worthmann, H. O. 1983. "A Comparative Study of the Growth of the Postlarval and Juvenile Pescadas *Plagioscion squamosissimus* (Heckel) and *Plagioscion monti* (Soares) in a White Water Lake of the Central Amazon." *Amazoniana* VII:465–77.

Woynarovich, E. 1988. *Tambaqui e Pirapitinga. Propagação Artificial e Criação de Alevinos.* Brasília: CODEVASF.

Zaniboni Filho, E. 1992. "Incubação, larvicultura, e alevinagem do tambaqui (*Colossoma macropomum* Cuvier, 1818)." Ph.D. dissertation, Universidade Federal, São Carlos, SP.

Zarnecki, S. 1968. "Algae and Fish Relationships." *Algae, Man, and the Environment.* In D. F. Jackson, ed. New York: Syracuse University Press.

Ziburski, A. 1991. "Dissemination, Keimung, und Etablierung einiger Baumarten der Überschwemmungswälder Amazoniens." *Tropische und Subtropische Pflanzenwelt* 77:1–96.

Page numbers in *italics* refer to illustrations, tables, and charts.

Acanthocephalan worms. *See* Parasites
Adults (tambaqui)
  decline in numbers of, 107
  diet of, 60–79
  fisheries of, 155
  growth rates of, 88–89
  length-weight relationships of, *90*
  market price of, 6, *101*
AFC. *See* Apparent feed conversion efficiency
Africa, 13
Agassiz, L., 97
Air bladder, 17, *18*
Air temperature. *See* Temperature
Ajuda Natural History Museum (Lisbon), 11
Algae production. *See* Ponds
Amazon River, *26*, 28, 38
  current speed of, 35
  oxygen levels of, 34–35
Anacanthorus spatulatus, *126*, *127*
Animal protein. *See* Protein, animal
Anoxia. *See* Deoxygenation
Apparent feed conversion efficiency (AFC), *133*, *134*, 139
Aquaculture
  alternative food sources for, 131–33
  early experiments with, 113
  legal issues in extensive, 150
  mortality rates in, 139
  potential for, 5, 146
  production costs in, 132, *132*, 142–44, 149, *150*
  success of private sector vs. government in, 145
  survival rates in, *139*, 140
  traditional food sources for, 131–33
  see also Hybrids; Monoculture; Polyculture
Aquaculture Station of the Lisandro Alvarado Central–West University (Venezuela), 114
Aquatic surface respiration mode, 92–93
Archaeological evidence, of tambaqui, 97
Argulus multicolor, 127–28
Auchenipteridae, 59

Babaçu palm, 136
Bacteria. *See* Parasites
Bait, *78*, 105; *see also* Fish orchards
Barthem, Ronaldo, 23, 108
Bayley, P. B., 87, 88, 91, 96, 146
Beach seines. *See* Fisheries, technology of
Betendorf, João Filippe, 7, 97
Bignoniaceae, 74
Biomass data, 96, 146–47
Black pacu, 9
Black-water rivers, 15, 27
Bocó. *See* Tambaqui (*Colossoma macropomum*)

Boischio, A. M. P., 109

Bolivia, 25, 31

Braga sp., 129

Branchurian crustaceans. *See* Parasites

Brazilian Institute of the Environment
(IBAMA), 154

Brazilian Shield, 26, 27

Brine shrimp (*Artemia* sp.), 121

Brood stocks, 113–17
induction of spawning in, 114–17, *116*
management of, 116–17
rations for, 116–17, *117*

Brycon (*Brycon*), 60, 139

Cachama. *See* Tambaqui (*Colossoma macro-pomum*)

Cachama blanca (*Piractus brachypomus*), 8

Cachama negra. *See* Tambaqui (*Colossoma macropomum*)

Cages. *See* Monoculture

Cajurana (*Simaba* sp.), 76

Calama study site, 52–53

Calanoida, *55*

Campsiandra comosa, 74

Capybara farming, 3

Carbon-isotope ratios, 83, 85

Carp (*Cyprinus carpio*), 139

Carvajal, Gaspar de, 7

Catch yield estimates, 103, 105–9

Catoré (*Crataeva benthami*), 78

Cattle ranching. *See* Livestock ranching

Ceccarelli, P. S., 125

Cecropia sp., 75

Ceriodaphnia cornuta, 54, 57

Ceriodaphnia reticulata, 54, *55*

Characidae, 12

Characiformes, 13

Characins, 15

Chaubadinema americana, 127, 128

Chironomids, 51

Chronicles of the Mission of the Jesuit Fathers in the State of Maranhão (Betendorf), 7

Chydoridae, *55*

Cladocerans, 50–51, 54, *54*; *see also*
Zooplankton

Classification. *See* Tambaqui (*Colossoma macropomum*), taxonomic classification of

Clear-water rivers, 26–27

CODEVASF (Brazil), 116, 146, 147

Cold fronts (*friagem*), 32

Colônia de Pescadores Z-1, 109

Color patterns, 15

Colossoma macropomum. *See* Tambaqui
(*Colossoma macropomum*)

Competition, 60, 139

Concrete tanks, 118, 120; *see also* Ponds

Copepods, 50, 54, 127, 129

Cost-benefit analysis for tambaqui, *143*,
143–44

Ctenolouciidae, 15

Cucullanus colossomi, 127

Curimatá (*Prochildus* spp.), 114, 139

Curupeté. *See* Tambaqui (*Colossoma macro-pomum*)

Cuvier, George von, Baron, *10*, 11–12, 97

Dams, 149

Daphnia gessneri, 54, *55*, 57

Deforestation, 1–4, 31–32
effect on tambaqui diet, 54, 60
and loss of habitat, 38, 39

Dentition
Cuvier on, 12
description of, 15, 17
fossil evidence of, 21, 22
function of, 64, 153

Deoxygenation, 34–35, 92–94

Diaphanosoma sp., 57

Diccionário Geográphico do Brazil (Pinto), 23

Diet, 6, 49–58, *52*, 92
adults, 60–79
artificial, 121, 132, 132–33
brood stock, 116–17, *117*
composition of, 50–51, 54, *54*, 121,
127–29, 131–33
diversity of, 67–68
hybrids, 141
juveniles, 51–54, 79, 133
larvae, 49–51, 121
nutritional value of, *80, 81*
trees in, *60, 61*
see also Fish orchards; Nutrition; Protein

Disease control, 123–29

Dissolved oxygen, *33*, 34, 39–40, 92, 120

Distribution, 21–35, 38
    and current speed, 34–35
    effect of dissolved oxygen on, 34–35
    effect of flooding on, 28–32
    effect of temperature on, 32–34
    and river types, 25–27
Dolops carvalhoi, 128, 129
Doradidae, 59
Dourada (*Brachyplatystoma filamentosum*),
    109
Dragonfly (Odonata), 120
Drupes, 76; *see also* Fruits

Economics of aquaculture. *See* Aquaculture,
    production costs in; Income; Market
    price
Ectoparasites, 127–29
Eggs, 43
    incubation of, 117–18
    nutrient composition of, 43, 44, 49–50, 95
    size of, 44, 152
Eigenmann, C. H., 12
El Pao reservoir, 138
Energy needs
    annual, 95
    changes in, 79, 81
    of eggs, 44
    and metabolic costs, 94–96
    in spawning, 45, 152
    and stored fat, 83, 152–53
Erosion, 26
Erythrinidae, 15
Estuaries, 29, 30; *see also* Orinoco
Euphorbiaceae, 71, 72
Experimental fishing, 37
Export market. *See* Markets, export
Extensive fish farming. *See* Fish farms,
    extensive

Fat content—filet, 18–19
Fecundity. *See* Tambaqui (*Colossoma macro-
    pomum*), fecundity
Ferraz de Lima, J. A., 120
Ferreira, Alexandre Rodrigues, 7, 9–11, 97
Fertilization ("dry" procedure), 115; *see also*
    Reproduction; Spawning
Fertilizers, commercial, 116

Fig (*Ficus* sp.), 75
Filter-feeding, 57
Finkers, J., 23
Fisheries, 98–102
    as cash generator, 3–4
    seasonal peaks of, 109
    technology of, 102–5
Fish farms, 114, 115, 138
    extensive, 145–50
    intensive, 131–44
    see also Aquaculture; Monoculture;
    Polyculture
Fish-orchards, 54, 71, 72, 78, 135–36, 153–54
Flatworms. *See* Parasites, trematodes
Flexibacter columnaris, 124–25
Floating meadows, 13, 31, 31
Flooding, 27–32, 41
Floodplains, 30–31
    floating meadows, 13, 31, 31–32
    lakes, 32, 37–38, 40, 49, 51–52
    rainforest, 2, 52, 53
    tidal, 29
FNO (Fundo para o Desenvolvimento do
    Norte), 144
Food fish, 18–19, 153
Food-to-fish conversion rates, 144
Foraging strategies, 57; *see also* Tambaqui
    (*Colossoma macropomum*), feeding behav-
    ior of
Forests
    flooded, 30, 31, 60
    seed production in, 63
Fossil evidence, for tambaqui, 21–23, 22
Freezer plants, 109
Fritz, Samuel, 7
Frugivores, 59, 60
Fruits, 53, 59–78, 61
    characteristics of, 68, 75
    nutritional value of, 82
    production of, 63, 64
Fry culture, 117–21, 145–46; *see also* Larvae
    (tambaqui)
Fungi. *See* Parasites

Gamitana. *See* Pacu
Genetic considerations. *See* Hybrids
Genetic diversity, need for, 6

Gill nets, technology of, 4–5, 102–5, *103, 104*
Gill rakers
    in hybrids, 141
    in tambaqui, 17, *17*, 57, 92, 126, 153
Goeldi Museum, 23
Gonadorelin, 115
Gonadotropins, 114–15
Government. *See* Investments, government
    subsidies for
Growth rates, 40, 87–92, *89*, 121
    absolute, 87
    in aquaculture, 133, *134*, 135, 137–38
    effect of food availability on, 91–92
    environmental influences on, 89, 91–92
    in feeding experiments, 114
    relative, 87–88, *91*
    sex differences in, 40
    and stocking densities, 137–38
    and weight gain, *137*, 137–38
Gulping. *See* Tambaqui (*Colossoma macropo-*
    mum), feeding behavior of

Habitats
    characteristics of, *33*
    deforestation and loss of, 38, 39
    nursery, 13, 31–32, 39, 49–58
    protection of, 154
    spawning, 37, 41, 43, 47
Harpoon fishing, 105
Hatcheries, 145–46
HCG (human chorionic gonadotropin), 115
Headstanders (Anostomidae), 59
Henneguya sp., 126, *126*
Hernández, R., 144
Hormones, 114–15, *116*
Human chorionic gonadotropin. *See* HCG
Hunting, 3
Hybrids, *141*, 141–42, 155
Hydrogen-sulfide poisoning, 32
Hypoxia. *See* Deoxygenation

Ice-to-fish ratio, 100–102
Ichythyophthirius multifilis, 125
Ihering, Rodolpho von, 113
Ilha da Machantaria, 59
Income, 2, 144, 149–50; *see also* Market price
Incubation

duration of, 119
    egg densities in, 117–18, *118*
Inga sp., *74*
Insecticides, 120, 154
Intensive fish farming. *See* Fish farms,
    intensive
Investments
    in aquaculture, 143, 150
    government subsidies for, 2–3, 144–46,
    150
    and payback period, 144
Irish, F. J., 15
Iruriz tribe, 97
Isopods, 129
Issac, V. U., 91

Japan, 147
Jaraqui (*Semaprochilodus* spp.), 108
Jatuarana (*Brycon cephalus*), 87
Jauari palm (*Astrocaryum jauari*), 64, 77, 83
Juveniles (tambaqui), 13
    abundance of, *50*
    diet of, 51–54, 79, 133
    exploitation of, *111*
    growth rates of, 90, 91, 133
    length-weight relationships of, *90*
    market price of, *101*
    mortality rates of, 139
    shape of, 13

Kapok tree (*Ceiba pentandra*), 60, 62
Kohla, U., 133

Lago do Rei, 38, 49
Lago Grande de Manacapuru, 49
Lago Manaquiri study site, 51–52
Lampara seines. *See* Fisheries, technology
    of
Larvae (tambaqui), 42, 45–46
    diet of, 49–51, 121
    growth rates of, 88
    predators of, 45, 120
    production of, 117
    rearing of, 118–20
    survival rates of, 119, 141
La Teraza (Colombia), 116
Learnaea sp., 129

Lechythidaceae, 73
Legumes, 64
Leguminosae, 74
Length-frequency distribution data, 38
Length-weight relationships, 90
LH-RH (gonadorelin), 114–15
Linguadactyloides brinkmanni, 126, *126*
Lipids, 79, 83
Livestock ranching, 1, 2–3, *3*
Logging. *See* Timber exports
Louro (Lauraceceae), 76

Machado-Allison, A., 12, 47–48
Macrolobium acaciifolium, 74
Macrothricidae, *55*
Macucu (*Aldina latifolia*), 64
Magdelena River Valley, 21
Mammals, in polyculture, 139, 144
Manaus
    fishing fleet, 4, 100–4
    fish market, 37–38, 106–8, *107, 108*
    prices of fish in, 109–10, *110*
Manure, 116
Market price, 108–11, *110*
    of adult fish, 5, *101*
    of juveniles, *101*
Markets
    databases of, 106
    data from, 37–38, 100, 103, 106–8, *107,
    108*
    export, 1, 4, 18, 153
    location of, *106*
    preferences of, 137
Martius, Carl Friedrich Philipp von, 97
Melo, F. R., 144
Melon family (Cucurbitaceae), 75
Mercury, 109
Merola, N., 138
Metabolism, 82–83, 93–96
    active, 94
    feeding, 94
    routine, 93–94
Micro-crustaceans. *See* Zooplankton
Migration, 35
    age at, 38
    downstream, 39, 44–47
    as issue in extensive fish farming, 148

and reproduction, 37–40, 44–48, *46, 47*
    upstream, 39, 44–45, 104
Mining sector, 1
Moenkhausia. See Tetras
Moina reticulata, 54, 57
Monoculture, 133, *134*
    average production in, 139–40
    in cages, 138, *142, 144*
    efficiency of, 144
    in ponds, 136–38, *142*
Morocotó (*Piaractus brachypomus*), 139,
    141
Mortality rates
    effect of temperature on, 32
    in extensive fish farming, 147, 149
    in ponds, 120, 139
    and stocking densities, 119
Mouth anatomy, 15, 92–93
Muddy-water rivers, 13, 25–27, 31, 37, 104
Mujica, M. E., 126
Munguba tree (*Pseudobombax munguba*), 62,
    63, *63*, 82
Museé d'Histoire Naturelle (Paris), 11
Myleinae, 12
Myletes brachypomus, 12
Myxobolus colossomatis, 125

Names, for tambaqui. *See* Tambaqui
    (*Colossoma macropomum*), names for
Nares, 65–66, *66*
National Department of Works Against
    Droughts (DNOCS), 113
National Institute of Amazonian Research
    (INPA), 100, 106, 123
Nematodes. *See* Parasites
Neoechinoryhnchus buttnerae, 127
Notodiaptomus amazonicus, 57
Novo Dicionário da Lingua Portuguesa, 8
Nursery habitats, 49–58
    effect of deforestation on, 31–32, 39
    floating meadows as, 13
    protection of, 154
Nutrition, 79–85, *80*; *see also* Diet
    and body composition, 82–85, *84*
    and metabolism, 82–83
    and stomach content studies, 79–82
Nuts, 79, 136; *see also* Seeds

Ocellus, 13
Olfaction, 65–67, 66
Operational costs. See Aquaculture, production costs in
Orinoco, 23–24, 27, 30, 31, 47–48
Oscar cichlids (Astronotus ocellatus), 113
Ostracods, 54, 127
Overexploitation, of young fish populations, 5, 6, 37, 38, 155
Oxygen. See Dissolved oxygen

Pacu
    (Mylossoma spp.), 9, 12, 13, 60, 141
    (Piaractus mesopotamicus), 8, 12, 135, 141–42
Pacu-caranha. See Pacu, (Piaractus mesopotamicus)
Palm nuts. See Jauari palm (Astrocaryum jauari)
Parasites, 123–29
    acanthocephalan worms, 127
    bacteria, 124–25
    branchurian crustaceans, 127–29
    fungi, 125
    nematodes, 127
    protozoans, 125–26
    trematodes, 126
Paredes, V., 125
Particulate-feeding, 57
Passion fruit (Passiflora sp.), 75
Pellets. See Diet, artificial
Peru, 24
Perulernaea gamitanae, 128–29, 129
A Pesca na Amazônia (Veríssimo), 98
Pesticides, 120, 154
Petrere Jr, M., 37–38, 100, 106
PH. See Rivers, pH of
Philosophical Voyage through the Captaincies of Grao Pará, Rio Negro, Mato Grosso and Cuiabá (Ferreira), 7
Pig sewage, 139
Pimelodidae, 15, 59
Pinheiro, A. R. C., 109, 115, 117
Pinto, Alfredo Moreira, 23
Piracuí, 99
Piranhas, 4, 13, 17, 59, 102, 148

Piranha-tree (Piranha trifoliata), 71, 72
Pirapitinga
    (Piaractus brachypomus), 23, 35, 48
    (Piaractus spp.), 13
Pirapucu (Boungerella sp.), 15
Pirarucu (Arapaima gigas), 4, 15, 105, 113, 148
Pituitary gland extracts, 114–15, 116
Pole and line fishing, 105
Pollution, 109, 120, 139
Polyculture, 138–39
    apparent feed conversion efficiency in, 133, 134
    average production in, 142
    production costs in, 143, 144
    survival rates in, 140
    see also Aquaculture; Monoculture
Ponds
    algae production in, 116
    zooplankton production in, 116, 120
    see also Monoculture; Polyculture
Porto Velho market, 102, 109
Predators, 45, 120
Prices. See Market price
Prochilodus cearensis, 114
Production costs. See Aquaculture, production costs in
Protein, 79
    animal, 82, 134–35
    costs of, 132
    effect on growth rate, 91, 91, 132–33
    recommendations for, 133
    see also Diet; Nutrition
Protozoans. See Parasites
Pyloric caeca, 17–18, 19

Quinaldine, 115

Rainfall, 28
Rainforest, development of. See Deforestation
Rates
    food-to-fish conversion, 144
    mortality, 119, 120, 139, 149
    survival, 119, 140, 141, 141, 152
Red-finned pacu, 9

Red sea bream, 147
Reproduction, 40–48, 94
    in captivity, 114–17, *116*
    effect of temperature on, 34
    energy investments in, 44, *45*, 152
    and gonadal development, 44, 95
    and gonadotropins, 114–15
    and migration, 37–40, 44–48, *46*, *47*
    see also Spawning
Respiration, 92–93
Restocking. *See* Stock enhancement
Rio Amazonas. *See* Amazon River
Rio Apure, 48
Rio Araguari, 24
Rio Beni, 25
Rio Branco, 27
Rio Cuiuni, 27
Rio Curuá-Una, 24
Rio Guaporé, 25
Rio Juruá, 26
Rio Machado, 38
Rio Madeira, 25, 27, 31, 35, 37, 45, 102
Rio Mamoré, 25, 40
Rio Marañon, 24
Rio Marié, 27
Rio Meta, 48
Rio Negro, 25, 27, 35
Rio Portugueza, 48
Rio Purus, 26, 45–46
Rio Solimões, 25
Rio Tapajós, 26, *26*
Rio Tocantins, 24, 26
Rio Trombetas, 24, 38
Rio Ucayali, 24
Rio Urubaxi, 27
Rio Xingu, 24, 26
River-level fluctuation, 27–32, *29*, 52
    as control on fish production, 149
    effect on diet, 60, 62
    effect on distribution, 28–32
Rivers
    current speed of, *33*, 35
    nutrient levels of, 27, 31, 48
    oxygen levels of, *33*, 34–35
    pH of, 26, 27, *33*
    sediment loads in, 27, 31, 48, 51

types of, 25–27
    see also names of individual rivers under
        Rio
Rolim, P. P., 141
Roman, B., 23
Roosevelt, Ana, 97
Rotifers, 50
Rubber tree. *See* Spruce's rubber tree
Ruelo. *See* Tambaqui (*Colossoma macropomum*)

Saint-Hillaire, Auguste, 11
Saint-Paul, U., 92, 94
Santarém (Brazil), 109
Saplogenia spp., 125
Sapotaceae, 76
Sapucaia nuts, 136
Sardinhas (*Triportheus* spp.), 60, 94
Seasonality
    and dissolved oxygen, 34–35
    and spawning, 41, *41*, 43
Sediment loads. *See* Rivers, sediment loads
    in
Seeds, 53, 57–78
    nutritional value of, 80–82
    production of, 63
Seines. *See* Fisheries, technology of
Selective-feeding strategy, 57
Serrasalminae, 12
Sex ratio, 40
Sexual maturation. *See* Tambaqui, sexually
    mature
Silva, A. B., 114
Sioli, Harald, 149
Size classes, 15, 38, 39, *39*
Snails, 116, 134
Sound, in feeding behavior, 66
Spawning
    energy costs of, 95
    habitats for, 37, 41, 43, 47
    induction of in captivity, 114–17, *116*
    management of, 146
    seasonality of, 41, *41*, 43
Spix, Johann Baptist von, 97
Spruce, Richard, 25, 58
    Spruce's rubber tree (*Hevea spruceana*),

Spruce, Richard (*continued*)
69, 70, 82, 136
Stewart, Donald, 25
Stock enhancement, 146, 147, 149
Stocking densities, 119, 136, 138, 144
Stomach contents, 79–82
and digestion rates, 57
and growth rate studies, 91–92
in high-water period, 53
relationship to flooded forests, 67
and zooplankton size, *54*
Supplemental foods, 133
Surface-water temperature. *See*
Temperature, surface-water
Survival rates
in extensive fish farming, 152
in ponds and cages, 119, 139, *140*, 141

Tababuia barbata, 74
Tambacu. *See* Hybrids
Tambaqui (*Colossoma macropomum*)
anatomy of, 17–18, *18, 19*, 57, 65–66, *66*,
92–93
appearance of, *8*, 13–21, *16*
aquaculture potential of, 5, 146
color patterns of, 15
culinary uses of, 18, 98–100
dentition of, 12, 15, 17, 21, 22, 64, 153
digestive system of, 17–18, *18, 19*, 67, 83
distribution of, 21–35, *24*
fecundity, *42, 43*, 152
feeding behavior of, *5*, 57, 65–67, *66*
as food fish, 18–19, 153
human consumption of, 100
names for, 7–9, *9*, 102
nutritional value of, 18–19
ontogeny of, 13–15, *14*
as place name, 23
sexually mature, 40, *40*, 87
size of, 15, 38, 39, *39*
taxonomic classification of, 9–13
type specimen of, 9–12, *11*
weight and length averages of, *88*
see also Adults (tambaqui); Diet;
Juveniles (tambaqui); Larvae (tambaqui)

Taxonomy, of tambaqui. *See* Tambaqui
(*Colossoma macropomum*), taxonomic
classification of
Tefé (Brazil), 108–9
Temperature, 32–34, *33*
air temperature, 32
effect on growth rate, 91
effect on metabolism, 93
effect on mortality rates, 32, 139
effect on reproduction, 34
for incubation, 118
for larvae, 120
surface-water, 32
Tetras, 13, 59
Thatcher, Vernon, 123, 126
Thermoclines, 32
Tilapia (*Tilapia* spp.), 139
Timber exports, 1–2
Torrential waters, 35
Traíras (*Hoplias* spp.), 15
Travels on the Amazon and Rio Negro
(Wallace), 25
Trees
densities of, 62–63
fruit-producing, 60–65, *61, 63*, 135–36
Trematodes (flatworms). *See* Parasites
Trotline fishing, 105
Tucunarés (*Cichla* spp.), 113
Turtles, 3, 64
Type specimen, of tambaqui, 9–12, *11*

UCLA (Venezuela), 116
Unit of Intensive Aquaculture Station
(UEPI), 113–14
Uxi (*Licania* sp.), 76

"Valdemar C. de França" Aquaculture
Station, 113
Veríssimo, José, 39, *98*, 98–100
Vision, in feeding behavior, 66

Wallace, Alfred Russel, 25, 58, 98
Walliker, D., 125
Water-level fluctuation. *See* River-level
fluctuation
White water. *See* Muddy water rivers

Wild guava (Myrtaceae), 75, 82
Wild rice
  (*Oryza glumaepatula*), 57–58
  (*Oryza grandiglumes*), 57–58
  (*Oryza* spp.), 52, 82
Wild soursop (*Annona* spp.), 75

Zaniboni Filho, E., 120
Zooplankton, 50, 52–57, *55, 56*
  carbon-isotope ratios of, 85
  as food source in aquaculture, 131–32
  nutritional value of, 82
  production of, 116, 120